PUNCH LINES

PUNCH

BERGER ON BOXING

LINES

BY PHIL BERGER

FOUR WALLS EIGHT WINDOWS
New York/London

Published by:
FOUR WALLS EIGHT WINDOWS
PO Box 548, Village Station
New York, New York 10014

U.K. offices:
FOUR WALLS EIGHT WINDOWS/TURNAROUND
27 Horsell Road, London, N51XL, England

Second Printing September, 1995

Library of Congress Cataloging-in-Publication Data:
Berger, Phil—
Punch lines: Berger on boxing/Phil Berger.
P. cm.
Includes index.
ISBN: 0-941423-93-X (cloth)
ISBN: 0-941423-95-6 (paper)
1. Boxing—United States. 2. Newspapers—Sections, columns, etc.—Sports.
I. Title.
GV1125.B48 1993
796.8'3'0973—dc20   92-38537
                    CIP

Designed by Cindy LaBreacht.
Printed in the United States.

DEDICATION

To my father, Jack Berger,
who shared my early enthusiasm for boxing....and to
L.B.D., who made the circle
complete.

ACKNOWLEDGEMENTS

The author wishes to thank *The New York Times* for permission to reprint articles on Kid Akeem Anifowoshe, Trevor Berbick, Riddick Bowe, Leon Calvin, Hector Camacho, Gerry Cooney, Bobby Czyz, Buster Douglas, Lou and Dan Duva, Joe and Marvis Frazier, Eddie Futch, Paul Gonzales, Larry Holmes, Evander Holyfield, Dave Jaco, Don King, Sugar Ray Leonard, John Mugabi, Vinny Pazienza, Felix Rodriguez, Michael Spinks, Mike Tyson, and Rickey Womack.

Certain pieces in this collection appeared first in magazine form. The author thanks the following publications for permission to reprint these articles:

The Daily News Magazine—"Gerry Cooney's Burden" (August 3, 1980); "Ray Arcel and Freddie Brown: The Sushine Boys of Boxing" (June 1980).

Esquire—James Scott (1980).

Los Angeles Herald Examiner—"Tony Ayala Tragedy: A Family Affair" (July 3, 1983).

M Inc.—"Mike Tyson: Tales From The Dark Side" (January 1992).

The National Observer—"Nino Benvenuti" (September 25, 1967).

The New York Times Sunday Magazine—"Sugar Ray Leonard: Boxing's His Business" (June 24, 1979); "Dundee: Champ of Corner Men" (November 29, 1981); "Marvelous Marvin Hagler: Boxing's Angry Man" (March 22, 1987); "George Foreman: Body and Soul" (March 24, 1991).

Playboy—Leon Spinks (October 1978).

Sports Magazine—"George Benton: The Ex-middleweight Who Won Ali's Title" (July 1978).

Sports Travel—"Travels with Tyson" (February 1990; "Lords of the Ring" (September 1989).

TABLE OF CONTENTS

PART THREE: THE BIG GUYS

PART FOUR: THE SMALLER MEN

FOREWORD by Bert Randolph Sugar

Going back to the time right after Father Adam first heard the rush of the apple salesman, we have been treated to the likes of such writers as Pierce Egan, Tad Dorgan, Jack London, A.J. Liebling, Budd Schulberg and others writing about the so-called "Sweet Science."

Now we have Phil Berger. And he's a nice addition to a nice tradition, one who could take his place in the company of the above-mentioned greats and not have to stand in the back row for the group photo.

In PUNCH LINES we are treated to vintage Berger. And those with an eye for fistic delicacies will appreciate what I'm talking about. It's not merely a who-did-what-to-who (or is that whom?) that we all can see on our TV sets or read in our morning papers. It's pulling back the curtain to reveal the doubts, the fears, the trials and the tribulations of some of the ring's greatest heroes.

Mr. Berger is less a glutton than an explorer as he gives us the foibles and fallibilities of some of the greatest names in the last twenty years—names like Muhammad Ali, Sugar Ray Leonard, Marvelous Marvin Hagler, Roberto Duran and even some of those lighter weights who labor in the anonymity of boxing's vineyards and backyards but who are featured in this juicy group of boxing pieces.

Included in this heady boxing bouillabaisse are a long laundry list of fighters and fighter-toids, including promoters who have long been viewed as lineal descendants of Jack the Ripper, fighters who once were light as cucumbers in their salad days and now are old age's credentialed couriers and others more dangerous in warfare than the most terrible Turks and are now suddenly human.

ix

In fact, they're all made by Berger whose writing is at one and the same time keen and hard like the tip of a wedge and soft and caring like a warm glove.

And although I've attended thousands of fights at ringside, probably going all the way back to Cain and Abel, it is this different view from a different pew that most appeals to me about PUNCH LINES.

If I were Siskel & Ebert, I would give this book a two thumbs up. But, then again, with thumbless gloves now in vogue, I'm reduced to telling you that you're in for a "good read" worthy of Pierce Egan, Tad Dorgan, Jack London, A.J. Liebling, Budd Schulberg—and Phil Berger.

Bert Randolph Sugar
February 14, 1993
Chappaqua, New York

INTRODUCTION

Here's the equation: boxing is to real life what Fellini is to the movies—a little bigger, a little gaudier than the strict facts. All the great literary themes—money, power, sex—get played out in the careers of marquee fighters and, because a boxer's skills erode a lot quicker than, say, the Grand Tetons do, there's an urgency to get one's money's worth while it can be had. So the best fighters live accelerated lives, and it's a rare instance when they emerge untouched by events.

But we are speaking here of the elite fighters, a minority in the pugilistic arena. For other guys—from the routine contender to that species of misfit that boxing men call, derisively, "tomato cans"—their lives are not usually as brimming with possibilities. Contenders sometimes have a shot at the big rewards. A few attain their moment; most fall short and, in time, become the designated obstacle to the next wave of contenders. Tomato cans? Their lot is to absorb the blows of men far superior to them and in that way to advance others' careers.

That's the hierarchy of the sport and, on whatever level fighters exist, they co-exist with boxing's adjuncts, men who make their living from the fights without ever having to throw a punch. These are the trainers, managers, promoters, booking agents. Theirs is another brand of cunning and resourcefulness, exercised in a business whose politics are so labyrinthine that any and all plans are subject to the whims, the exigencies of other schemers.

For me, what makes the fight world so intriguing is that multitude of levels on which it's played and the relative fluidity of commerce. It's a sport where a penny-ante manager whose fighter is seen strictly as an opponent can rub shoulders with a big-time counterpart. But with one well-delivered punch that fighter and his

xi

obscure attendant can know the pleasures of topsy-turvy. It's the crazy roulette that boxing, like no other sport, offers. Ibid: Buster Douglas: here today, gone tomorrow...but $20 million richer.

It's chic among many, I know, to regard boxing as the sewer of the sports page and in that way to dismiss it as inconsequential. But as I see it, that's just looking down the wrong end of the telescope. Boxing is a user's game, no question. It's a pitiless greedhead enterprise that I daresay is pretty much what other so-called legitimate businesses are. The excesses of an Ivan Boesky, the connivances of international corporations, the misappropriation of an Art Buchwald story line by a movie studio—these are all, in the word of Don King, "trickerations"—scamming on the grand scale by suit-and-tie smoothies on whom we mistakenly confer credibility and respect.

Whatever. For me boxing is as complex a business as any, and has the added pleasure of great characters, men and women diverse in their backgrounds and filled with their own dreams. Off and on for more than twenty years, as a freelancer first and, since 1985, as the boxing reporter of *The New York Times*, I've been writing about these people. Their stories often have had a complexity and raw emotion that made me want to know more. Good stories are good stories, irrespective of who tells them. But I'm glad I had the opportunity to try my hand on these.

—New York, 1992

PART ONE: THE CYCLE

Most fighters' careers have beginnings, middles and ends. Between the new guy's soaring hope and the veteran's long goodbye is the jagged line of the journey.

Mostly it's poor boys like Felix Rodriguez and John Mugabi who become fighters. Then sometimes there's a kid like Marvis Frazier who climbs through the ring ropes because of a father's past attachment.

FELIX RODRIGUEZ: There's Always Next Time (1987)

At rush hour Thursday night, in his neighborhood in the South Bronx, Felix Rodriguez boarded the Number 6 train on the Lexington Avenue line and rode to work.

The twenty-year-old Rodriguez, a junior welterweight, was making his professional debut as a fighter in a four-round bout at the Felt Forum.

By 5:55 P.M., Rodriguez and Luis Camacho, his manager-trainer, were in Dressing Room 5, a small, roughly square-built space. On a folding chair, Rodriguez laid out his red satin trunks and protective cup, and over the back of the chair he folded a clothing bag and a white towel with a hole cut through that he would wear over his shoulders later like a serape. His white high-top boxing shoes, with red laces, were placed beside the chair on the floor.

Those who try boxing for a living are usually poor men, and by that measure Rodriguez surely qualified. The distance from his home on Cypress Avenue, off East 138th Street, to the Felt Forum, was measured not in subway stops but rather in one man's hopes for bolting a dead-end barrio.

The Rodriguez household—the father Rafael (unemployed since an industrial accident years ago), the mother, Iris, a sister, a nephew and Felix—lives on welfare payments of $260 every two weeks. From that comes the $198 monthly rent for their three-bedroom apartment in a building with a billboard for Beefeater's Gin

3

("Smooth, with style") nailed to its front exterior, and a gutted dwelling to its rear.

A window facing the street affords the Rodriguezes a view of what the fighter said was perpetual drug traffic. From that window he had seen men beaten and sometimes knifed in drug-related incidents. On one occasion he witnessed a shooting on the sidewalk across the street from his building, in front of the graffiti-covered corrugated shutters of a supermarket.

"The guy walked around the corner, onto 138th Street, and dropped dead in front of St. Luke's Church," said Rodriguez.

On another night, he said, a car went out of control and careened through a vacant lot up the block when its driver and passenger were shot.

"When you walk on the street," said Rodriguez, "you have to watch with four eyes, two in the front and two in the back, 'cause you don't know what can happen. If I can make it in boxing, to the point where I leave the neighborhood, I would buy my mother a house in Puerto Rico. Away from all this trouble."

By 7 P.M. Thursday, Camacho was taping the fighter's hands in Room 5. A forty-nine-year-old postal worker, Camacho had run the Bronxchester Boxing Club during evenings, developing a constituency of mostly young amateurs. The best boxer to emerge from his program had been Alex Ramos, a middleweight who enjoyed limited success as a professional.

Ramos turned pro in 1980, the year Rodriguez began training at Bronxchester. Under Camacho, Rodriguez had had enough success in the amateurs to fill two shelves in his living room with trophies. For his pro debut, he would receive a $350 purse and a percentage of the proceeds from fifty $10-tickets he had sold to family and friends.

To get ready for this fight, Rodriguez, a high school graduate, took a week's leave of absence from the Manhattan trade school where he is studying to become an electronics technician. On the day before his first professional fight, his primary text— "Electronics: Principles and Applications"—lay on a bedroom shelf while Rodriguez watched "The Joe Louis Story" on his VCR.

Before Thursday's card began, Rodriguez would be told that his match was a "swing" bout, a fight to be patched into the evening's program as suited the promotion. From 7:45 P.M., when Rodriguez was ordered to "glove up"—don his boxing mitts—he was obliged, then, to be in a state of readiness.

As the night passed, rumors filtered in to Room 5 that his bout was next, then the rumors would be invalidated. He warmed up by shadowboxing or hitting Camacho's hand pads; then he sat and awaited the next rumor.

From inside the room could be heard the ringside bell and the swell of crowd noise from the arena. Hours passed. Sometimes the fighter paced up and back, loosening his arms and legs. Sometimes he sucked an ice cube for his dry mouth. Sometimes he just sat. At one point, his right hand became numb from wearing the gloves for so long, and Camacho had to get official permission to remove the glove briefly so Rodriguez could restore feeling to the hand. At 11:16 P.M., the last fight of the night, Rodriguez versus Luis Castillo, was called.

For the first minute of Round 1, Rodriguez outboxed Castillo, who was born in the Dominican Republic and now lives in Brooklyn. But by the end of the round Castillo was landing the heavier punches.

In the second round, Castillo knocked Rodriguez down for a count of three. With his nose bleeding, Rodriguez arose, but moments later was knocked down again. By the time he struggled to his feet, blood was streaming from his nose and mouth, and Jim Santa, the referee, was signaling that the fight was over.

On Monday, Felix Rodriguez goes back to his electronics classes downtown, and presumably, to the gym. For, after his loss, he said: "There's always next time. It'll be different. Believe me it will."

Felix Rodriguez never fought again as a professional. Today, at age twenty-five, he works as a dispatcher for a mid-town Manhattan messenger service.

JOHN MUGABI: At Boxing's Front Door (1986)

Earlier this week, camp aides of the middleweight contender John (The Beast) Mugabi were worried about the rattlesnakes of Rio Rico, Arizona, a small settlement tucked away in mountainous territory, sixteen miles from the Mexican border.

It seems that unseasonably high temperatures there, reaching into the 90's, were threatening to wake the creatures from their winter hibernation, making an adventure of Mugabi's early-morning training runs over mountain roads.

Aside from the potential problem with the rattlers, though, Mugabi's advance on the middleweight title—he fights Marvelous Marvin Hagler for the crown on March 10 at Caesars Palace in Las Vegas, Nevada—appeared to be proceeding smoothly.

A sure sign of that was the woebegone condition of Mugabi's sparring partners. Some of them did not last long enough to draw their second paycheck, and had left Rio Rico looking like extras from "Night of the Living Dead."

The heavyhanded treatment is typical of his no-nonsense approach to sparring sessions, and this time around probably owed a little extra to the protracted wait he has had in getting this shot at the title.

The fight, originally scheduled for last November 14, was postponed when Hagler suffered a broken nose. Back then, Mugabi was training in the sunken lobby of the Eden Roc Hotel in Miami Beach, a circular room with a crested overhang supported by eight fluted pillars big enough to do duty on the Acropolis. From Miami Beach to the Sheraton in Rio Rico to Las Vegas—Mugabi arrived there Thursday—the settings have been consistently first-class, and for Mugabi the very lavishness of them has ironic echoes.

6

For in his distant past in Kampala, Uganda, Mugabi used to be chased away from such swank places. He was a schoolboy then, a poor and unlettered child who kept regular hours in boxing gyms, and away from them was often in trouble. When international amateur boxing events were held in Kampala, fight officials would convene at receptions where food and drink could be had. Mixing among them came an uninvited guest.

"Everybody would be in his best clothes," recalls the boxing official Jack Edwards, an Englishman who owned a tea plantation in Uganda at the time. "And John would slip in in his ragged shorts, no shoes. Wolfing food. You'd throw him out. And there he'd be again. I'm not trying to run down his character, you understand, but rather trying to give you a picture of a lad making his way in the world. It was a tough situation for John. And he was not the kind to give in to the tough life."

John Mugabi, who will turn twenty-six this week, no longer slinks through boxing's back door. Twenty-six fights into a professional career that began in December 1980, he will earn $800,000 to fight Hagler.

Twenty-six fights—and twenty-six knockouts: It is a record that beguiles aficionados who try to dope out whether the punch with which Mugabi has leveled opponents like Frank (The Animal) Fletcher, Gary Guiden, Curtis Parker, James (Hard Rock) Green and Wilbert (Vampire) Johnson can prevail against Hagler.

The doubters see Mugabi as an economy-sized George Foreman, a bombs-away puncher who can be had by a fighter clever enough to expose the oaf in him, as Muhammad Ali did Foreman with his rope-a-dope tactic.

Mugabi's style encourages such a view. When he lets fly, he is not as circumspect as most fighters are about protecting themselves from counter-attack, sometimes even leaping off the canvas to launch a punch. Yet Mugabi may turn out to be one of those gifted exceptions who can defy the conventional wisdom about his sport, as Ali did. Like Ali, Mugabi has good reflexes and hand speed that forgive transgressions against orthodoxy and add an unpredictability to his style.

Still, a perfect record like Mugabi's is bound to prompt suspicions that he is a product of a shrewd buildup, and also raises questions as to how he will react to adversity. His toughest fight was against Hard Rock Green, a small tank of a man at 5-feet 5-inches and 154 pounds. He is the only opponent to make it to the tenth round against the African before being stopped on February 19, 1984. In that fight, Mugabi was thumbed when both men continued to battle after the bell ending Round 2. In his corner between rounds, he complained about blurred vision and, according to some fight people, wanted to quit. But his co-manager, Mickey Duff, persuaded him his vision would clear up in Round 3 and pushed him off his stool when the bell rang.

Mugabi absorbed heavy damage from Green in Round 3 and showed an inability to tie up his opponent. But his vision did clear and he survived.

"At the end of the third," says Duff, "John was sitting there furious. The doctor puts the torch in his eyes and says, 'Where are you?' John can hear and he can understand. But he's in one of his arrogant moods and stares straight ahead. I could see he was not going to answer. So I lied, 'Doc, he doesn't understand a word of English.' And he took my word and let him go. As far as John was concerned, it was like: 'Leave me alone. Don't ask silly questions.'"

From Round 4 on, the fight swung to Mugabi, who recalled thinking of Green: "I say it in my heart, 'Short man, no way.' I went there, and he knew now I was powerful. He start to run away."

The reactions of Mugabi, in the ring and in his corner, showed nuances of personality that his nickname denies. The use of The Beast is a promotional tool. As The Beast, Mugabi has posed against zebra-skin rugs for glossy photos, and for the Hagler bout he did a commercial in which he materializes in a mock wilderness clearing to warn the champion, in accented English, "I'll knock you out," before disappearing to the roar of a wild beast.

As just plain Mugabi, though, he is not so horrific a figure. When not in training, he resides in Tampa, Florida, where he lives with his fiancee Eva Namazii and a Ugandan boxer and boyhood friend, John Munduga.

At rest, Mugabi is an easygoing, not overly talkative sort, who likes his glass of beer, music videos, kung fu movies and just hanging out with friends.

"Right now," says Ferdie Pacheco, the fight analyst for NBC-TV, which has telecast many of Mugabi's fights, "he is unspoiled, unfettered. Like the bushman in that film, 'The Gods Must Be Crazy.' Walking somewhat bewildered through this world. Getting a lot of money to do what he does naturally. He's not complex. *Right now.* If he wins the title...it might be another story. He eats and sleeps boxing. And the only measure of sophistication is the credit card. And that's gonna be his undoing.

Mugabi spends. Duff says, "He has a black belt in shopping." Shirts, hats, video cassettes, musical instruments, jewelry—in civilian cloths, Mugabi wears enough gold chains to qualify as a lounge act in Vegas—are regular items on his frequent shopping trips. "No, he hasn't saved the way he should," says Duff. "He tells me, 'I'm young. A lotta things I haven't got yet. I know I've got to start saving soon.'"

Early in Mugabi's career, when he lived in London, George Francis, the fighter's trainer, saw Mugabi spend his money on Ugandan friends who came around. Concerned that Mugabi was being too liberal with the buck, the trainer inquired about it. "He told me," says Francis, "'In our country if you have food, you share it. If you have a roof and someone does not have a roof, you let him come in. It happens to be I'm the one with the money.' I thought it rather nice the way he explained."

In Tampa, Brad Jacobs, matchmaker for Alessi Promotions, handles Mugabi's money, but he has no veto power over deposits and withdrawals. "Early on, when John came to Tampa," says Jacobs, "I got calls from the telephone and electricity people: 'Hey, your boxer is not paying his bills.' I sent one of our people over. He found all the bills in the garbage. John wasn't aware what the bills were, and the only letters he'd take in were those with handwriting he recognized. So now all the bills come to me." Mugabi cannot read, and writes only his signature.

When in training, Mugabi becomes withdrawn, a man whose mood swings are not easy to fathom. "Of all the boxers I have had," says Francis, "and I've had four hundred, possibly more, he is the one I never understood. He changes from day to day. By the hour. He could be smiling, joking. In an hour's time, he's a different guy. He don't like you yapping and playing...except when he's ready for it."

Early-morning training runs make Mugabi most testy, and many times he has told Francis he would rather pass on roadwork. But Francis, a former porter in London's Convent Gardens who trained amateurs for seventeen years, takes his wake-up calls seriously, and this has led to bickering between the two men. At times Mugabi has even dismissed his trainer, invariably reinstating him later.

Once, when Francis knocked on Mugabi's door at the fighter's Tampa home to wake him for roadwork, and then rapped at his bedroom window to rouse him, Mugabi came to the door with an angry expression. "And he said to me," recalls Francis, "'This house is private. You don't knock on my window. If you don't go away, I will shake you.'"

Says Duff of Francis and Mugabi: "They fight regularly. And after every bout, John tells the trainer he's the best in the world."

Mugabi began boxing in Kampala at the age of six, often training twice a day and not bothering to go to school.

He had the big punch early. "At nine, ten years," says Munduga, "he used to knock boys out. He was the only one that age who could."

Away from the gym, he carried his aggressive style to the streets. Recalling it, Mugabi spoke in sometimes faltering English, delivered with an earnestness underscored by his gentle expression. "Trouble," he says. "We used to make trouble. Just fight people, beat people. Fight in the street. We used to go to jail when they catch us. They lock me up."

Mugabi advanced through the amateur boxing ranks and, as a teenager, fought for the Ugandan national team. At the time, Idi Amin was head of government and, with his regard for boxing—

Amin had once been the country's amateur heavyweight champion—Mugabi and teammates made out well. "Trophy," says Mugabi. "Big party. A lot of money. Four hundred dollars. Amin would hand you an envelope and say, 'Good boy, good boy. Keep doing that.'"

Mugabi kept doing it, and eventually made his way to the 1980 Olympics in Moscow, where he won a silver medal in the welterweight division. Soon after, he turned pro under Duff—an ex-boxer (given name: Morris Prager) who was the son of a Hasidic rabbi—and a German industrialist, Wilfred Sauerland. For the fighter it meant relocating in London.

"It was cold," says Mugabi. "I didn't like it cold. I left the family. I miss my mom."

Charles Agaba, a Ugandan businessman and a friend, was with Mugabi then. "Charles say, 'Don't mind it, You'll go back after your first fight,'" Mugabi recalled. "I say, 'When? It's too long.'"

"He was crying," says Agaba, "when I went to the airport to go back home. He felt homesick. I said, 'Keep it up, boy. That's the only way of making your future. Once you build a foundation, the future will be good.'"

Struggling with a new language—Mugabi, a Mutoro tribesman, speaks Swahili—he did not adjust easily to being away from home. He cried on occasion, and fought the loneliness by phoning home more often than a boxing beginner's finances can bear. "Tired," he says. "Everybody in this world get tired. Tired in head. Tired in place. I don't like it in London. I don't enjoy."

But as he began disposing of the available competition ("I start knocking them out straightaway. Knockout, knockout. All Europe—no fighter can fight me") in West Germany, London and Zambia, life turned more pleasant. "Start to find friends to move with," Mugabi says. "Talk to people. Go out with people. It makes me big heart."

By 1983, Mugabi had landed in America and was scoring quick knockouts over legitimate opponents. After one victory, a Los Angeles fight manager, Jackie McCoy, told Duff: "Man I got sixteen good prospects. I'd swap you the whole lot for him. He's a beast." The nickname followed.

The nickname will be scrapped, Mugabi has said, after this fight. Instead he will use John Paul Mugabi, the name he took when he was baptized last month at the Sacred Heart Church in Nogales, Arizona.

Settled in Tampa, Mugabi has become a local hero, recognition he welcomes. "They start to love me more than Uganda," he says. "Everybody knows me. I go out: 'Beast. Beast. John. Hello, Beast.' They are my people there. I love Tampa. When I fight, I fight first for Uganda and Tampa second."

For Mugabi, though, the trips back to Uganda—which had been torn by fighting between rebel factions—have become fraught with danger. As Cornelius Boza-Edwards, a ranking junior lightweight contender and former world champion from Uganda, says: "On his last time back in Kampala, John got pushed in a nightclub by a young army private. And when he resisted, the army people told him, 'You wait. You'll see. We'll get you.' There they don't care. John knows the situation. Life is worth a penny there. They don't care if you're a pauper or Ronald Reagan."

Says Mugabi: "You go to Uganda now, people want to shoot you. People there are jealous. People have locks on house. Is too much shooting in Uganda. You die, you die forever. You won't show up in this world again. So I don't like to die now. Stay for many years...if God still likes me."

John Mugabi lost twice in his attempt to win a world title, to Hagler and Duane Thomas in 1986. On his third try he won the W.B.C. super welterweight title when he scored a first round TKO over Rene Jacquot in July 1989. He lost the title when he was knocked out in one round by Terry Norris in March 1990.

MARVIS FRAZIER: Does Father Know Best? (1986)

From the nearby railroad bridge, it must look to the passing Amtrak commuter like just another old, creaking building in this rundown North Philadelphia neighborhood. The upper floors of the three-story building at 2917 North Broad Street have gray-white stucco patches where windows used to be, and the rest is brown brickface.

But the designation on the exterior—"Joe Frazier's Gym"—is a good clue that this place is no candidate for the wrecker's ball. It is instead a kind of boxing landmark, a gym where fighters have been training since 1968, when Cloverlay Inc., the syndicate sponsor of the heavyweight contender, Joe Frazier, bought the gym for him to use. Smokin' Joe used it well. He became world champion and, on retiring in 1976 (there was a one-fight comeback, a draw against Jumbo Cummings, in 1981), he bought the gym from Cloverlay for $75,000.

These days Frazier has offices up a flight of stairs at the back of the gym. From that elevated spot, through a wide window, he can gaze down onto the gym floor and watch a second generation of Fraziers have a go at the manly art. Since 1980, when Smokin' Joe's oldest son, Marvis, a 6-foot-1-inch, 210-pound heavyweight, turned pro, he has presided over a corps of fighting Fraziers. Besides Marvis, they are Rodney (13-3, 10 knockouts), a heavyweight who is the son of Frazier's sister Rebecca; Mark (10-3-3, 9 knockouts), a super-middleweight who is the son of Frazier's brother Tom; and Hector (15-4-3, 12 knockouts), a junior-welterweight who is another of the former champion's sons and fights as Joe Frazier Jr.

Of them all, only Marvis (16-1, 7 knockouts), currently ranked ninth by the World Boxing Council, is regarded as a world-class fighter. The fortunes of the other Fraziers have lately declined.

13

This year alone, Rodney was knocked out by James Broad and Elijah Tillery; Mark by Ralph Smilie, and Hector by Vinny Pazienza and James Sudberry. That leaves twenty-five-year-old Marvis—who fights Mike Tyson on Saturday in Glens Falls, New York—as the only Frazier with any chance to bring glory again to the family name in the fight arena.

If he can beat Tyson (and the consensus is that Marvis is over-matched), it would, in no small way, redound to Smoking Joe's credit, too. For in guiding Marvis and his other boxing kin, Frazier frequently has been the subject of second-guessing. Many fight people say that the fullbore aggression Joe brought to his own bouts, and his complete assurance in his talents, may have suited the fighter he once was, but they are not necessarily an advantage for a boxing manager—in whom discretion is often the better part of valor.

"He's a stubborn, opinionated guy," said Lou Duva, a manager and trainer. "But a good guy. I love Joe."

"But the question is does he book his fighters' matches from here," said Duva, touching his heart, "or here," tapping his head. "Who's fighting the fight: Joe Frazier or his fighter? He'd like them to fight as good as Joe Frazier could. But there's only one Joe Frazier."

Yet another manager, David Wolf, who took Ray (Boom Boom) Mancini to the World Boxing Association lightweight title, credits Frazier with doing the job a manager is supposed to: making a handsome living for his charges. "People underestimate Joe as a manager," Wolf said. "I say Marvis exceeded his potential in the purse Joe got him to fight Holmes when Holmes was the champion."

In November 1983, Marvis received $750,000 to fight Holmes, who knocked him out in one round. Afterward Joe was criticized for rushing his son into a title fight for which he was not ready. Wolf disputes that assessment. "Anytime you're offered the amount of money he got to go after Holmes in what was a no-lose situation, you take it," Wolf said. "Marvis was not a whole lot less marketable afterward, because nobody expected him to win. And beyond that, he hasn't matched Marvis poorly in any other fight. He successfully resurrected his career by picking good opponents."

For fighting Tyson, Marvis will earn $250,000 and, though Smokin' Joe has again been criticized for overmatching him, Wolf disagrees. He says that for Marvis to earn $250,000 he would have had to fight five bouts against quality opponents. Besides, said Wolf, there are not so many network fights these days that Marvis could say to himself, "I'll fight every other month because I'm Marvis Frazier."

Just who Marvis Frazier is these days as a fighter (and who he might have been) is a question that gets entangled in a role that Joe did not originally have in his son's development—that of his trainer. When Marvis first came to the North Broad Street gym as a sixteen-year-old, it was George Benton, a former world-ranked middleweight, who shaped the aspiring fighter.

"I had him a boxer—a fighter who didn't get hit with a lot of punches," said Benton, who now trains Evander Holyfield, Tyrell Biggs, Pernell Whitaker and Meldrick Taylor. "Then somewhere down the line he became more a brawler type fighter."

Toward the end of Marvis's amateur career (he had a 56-2 record, losing to Tony Tubbs and James Broad), Benton said that Smokin' Joe gradually assumed control of his son's training. "The air got a little thin," Benton said. "It was hard for me to breathe in that relationship. One day, Joe just said: 'I'll train the fighter when I'm here. I'll handle the boxing.'"

The version Marvis and Joe tell is that Benton was often on the road in those days with his other fighters, and that because he couldn't give his full attention to Marvis, it behooved Son of Smokin' to have the old man—or Pop, as Marvis calls him—take over. "Besides," Joe said, "there was the basis of the bloodline."

Whatever. The fact is that the fighter Marvis was as an amateur and the fighter he became once his father mobilized him were different creatures. Under Benton he was an agile, quick-handed boxer-puncher, a defense-minded amateur good enough to beat Tubbs, Mitch Green, David Bey, Tim Witherspoon and James (Bonecrusher) Smith. "The word about the kid as an amateur was extravagant," said Mort Sharnik, boxing consultant to CBS-TV. "From the most critical sorts, I'd hear that he was the best-looking amateur in the world."

Under Smokin' Joe, the style changed. As Marvis tells it: "The only thing Pop added was my standing my ground a little firmer. Rather than my being so defensive, a little more offense was added." That "little more offense," which in Marvis's account sounds rather like a quarter-turn of the wrench in a subtle mechanical refinement, has struck others as radical retooling—a change of psyche, and outlook.

"Joe's only fault," Duva said, "was trying to make a replica of himself rather than letting the talent come out of the fighter's own style. George had Marvis cuter, more defensive. See, a guy like Marvis Frazier shouldn't be going in to a fighter and trading. He should box and be cute. It'd make him a better fighter."

Gary Hegyi, a Philadelphia manager who used to work out of Frazier's gym early in Marvis's career, was surprised to see the trouble the fighter had later in extricating himself from jams that opponents like Holmes and James (Quick) Tillis put him in. "The Marvis Frazier I knew wouldn't be in them kinds of predicaments," Hegyi said. "The kid was clever. Flat-footed was not his style."

Talk to Joe Frazier about how he has influenced his son's style and he will deny molding him in his own image. "You can't make guys like yourself," he said. But in the next breath he will say, "Sure, you have to move around the ring, but when you jump in a guy's face, you got to get the job done."

When Marvis spars, his father is wont to bark commands like "Breathe on him," which means he wants Marvis to fight his man at close quarters. Or he will shout "Fall down," shorthand for Marvis to throw the left hook. Smokin' Joe's jargon underscores the attack-minded approach he had as a fighter and seems to have retained as a trainer. Why wouldn't he? When Joe Frazier threw the left hook, "fall down" was an appropriate tagline. Opponents went horizontal when struck by that blow.

In contrast, Marvis's biggest victories as a professional—against Broad, Joe Bugner, Tillis and Bonecrusher Smith—all have been in fights that went the distance. Marvis, with a longer, leaner physique than his father, has never shown the brute force as a puncher that his father had. Instead, he has been a boxing version of Pete Rose, a scrappy performer relying on drive and superior conditioning. A recurring phrase heard when boxing men discuss Marvis is: "The kid has heart."

The kid is also uncommonly close to his father. "Dutiful son," are words by which others frequently describe the relationship, and Marvis captures the underlying spirit of it when he says: "When we come in the gym I'll holler to pop, 'HEYYYY,' and he'll holler back 'HEYYYY!' We say it real loud. I don't know what it means. But it feels real good."

Though Marvis grew up in a sixteen-room stone split-level house in the predominantly white Philadelphia suburb, he was not, as Hegyi puts it, a spoiled brat. "This kid," Hegyi said, "was one of the nicest, most decent young men you'll want to meet."

Sharnik concurs. "Boxing is so remote from his character and instincts," he said. "He is such a gentle man, such a godly man." (Marvis is a deacon and a member of the choir in the Faith Temple Church of Christ in North Philadelphia.)

After Frazier beat Bonecrusher Smith in February, he stopped by to see the promoter of the fight, Sam Glass. "He thanked me," Glass said, "for having him on the card and said he hoped I was satisfied with how he performed. He was uncommonly gracious. Fighters just don't do that sort of thing."

Marvis's upbringing apparently instilled that instinct for doing the right thing. And when necessary, Smokin' Joe, as his son relates it, would guide him in that direction.

"We called the cellar of our house 'The Zoo,'" Marvis recalled. "When I was ten, I got into a fight with my sister Jackie. My mom said, 'Up to your room, wait til your father gets home.'"

"Pop came home," Frazier said. "I heard mom say, 'I want you to talk to Marv.' *Poom poom poom*—he bangs on the door of my bedroom. 'Get up, boy. You ain't asleep.' I was trying to act asleep. 'What's this I hear about you hitting girls? We're going to The Zoo. Get the gloves.' There were two pairs of boxing gloves in his room. I'm going: 'I'm sorry.' Crying and all. And Pop: 'Put them gloves on.' He started jabbing me. I covered up. 'You want to hit girls, huh?' Jab jab. 'You know how much strength you've got?' 'Sorry, daddy.' 'I'll teach you what to be sorry for, you sissy.' He got mad. I haven't hit a girl since."

Marvis was not disposed toward boxing until his parents, hoping to remedy their son's bad grades, sent him as a tenth grader to a private school that had no varsity sports. Marvis, who had wrestled and played basketball, baseball and football previously as a schoolboy, asked whether he could work out in Frazier's gym to keep active. "I knew after three months in the gym that it was boxing for me," he said.

It took his father longer. "When Pop realized I wanted to fight, he said no," Marvis said. "Gave me a lecture: 'This is nothing to play with. You've got to be serious. Guys are in there to tear your head off. No one gets in there unless he's serious.'

"Then one day after that, me and my cousin Russell came in, Russell boxed, too. Pop liked him. Russell had a style like Pop's. Russell and I worked out together. But Russell had been slacking....while I'd been working.

"Anyway, one Saturday we come in. And Pop says to me, 'I want to see what you got.' Got in the ring. I started tagging Russell, and then getting out of the way of his left hook. Pop hadn't expected it of me. So Pop said to Russell, 'Don't want to do your roadwork?' Then he said to me: 'Hit him to the body.'"

"HEYYYY."

Marvis Frazier was knocked out in one round by Tyson and retired not long after. Today he helps his father in the operation of Frazier's Gym and is active in amateur boxing in Philadelphia.

The thing about boxing is that the happy days are rarely for long, and the struggle to endure can turn hellish, as Vinny Pazienza and Paul Gonzales have discovered. With both these men, I was there when things were good and then not so good, and I wrote about the changes.

VINNY PAZIENZA
A Comeback in More Ways Than One (1992)

The car that cut in front of Kurt Reader's Camaro last November on U.S. 1 in Warwick, Rhode Island, forced Reader to jam on the brakes. In the passenger seat, Vinny Pazienza watched in horror as the Camaro skidded across the highway and into oncoming traffic. In that instant, Pazienza, a world champion boxer, grabbed the door handle to brace for the collision he knew was inevitable.

At first, Pazienza believed that it was Reader who had gotten the worst of the crash.

"Kurt's head banged against the door window," said Pazienza. "He was cut all over and bleeding. He was trembling and in shock. I grabbed him and said, 'Are you all right?' He was moaning. The next thing I knew, they were prying the car open. When they touched me, the pain shot through my whole body. I screamed: 'No, no, no, don't touch me! My neck is killing me!'"

Reader would get his cuts stitched and proved to be fine. Pazienza was not so fortunate. As a chiropractic neurologist, Richard Cervone, recalled: "The emergency medical people put Vinny on a backboard with straps and placed him a in stiff-neck collar, with Velcro pillows stuck to the side of his head. All of that was to stabilize his neck, to keep it from moving."

At Kent County Hospital, Pazienza was examined by Dr. Walter Cotter, a neurosurgeon, then X-rayed.

"Dr. Cotter told me that the third and fourth vertebra was cracked and the fourth vertebra had popped out," said Pazienza. "He was going through all of that medical talk when I said: 'Hey, let's cut through all the baloney, doc. What's the deal? Can I fight again?'

"That's when he hit me with the classic line: 'Sorry, son. You'll never fight again.'"

Cervone, a friend of the fighter, knew that Cotter's prognosis was based on the danger that the dislocated fourth vertebra represented.

"If that fourth vertebra touched the spine, there was the real chance of paralysis," said Cervone.

Yet lying flat on his back, Pazienza was more intent on his career than on medical forebodings.

"There was a teardrop in his eye and an expression of disbelief after Cotter told him he wouldn't box again," said Cervone. "Vinny actually had a tantrum, striking his arms and legs against the examining table. We had to hold him down and tell him not to move because he'd do further damage. But see, with Vinny boxing is his whole life."

As a lightweight and junior welterweight, Vinny Paz, as he is known, bled for his money.

In the ring, he was a dervish presence, fighting with a passion that sometimes seemed to surpass his talent. Pazienza got hit, and hit plenty, but always came back for more.

Still, he was more than occasionally referred to as a glorified club fighter, a designation that had prompted his father, Angelo, to take a swing at one ink-stained wretch who had deigned to use that description.

Pazienza had been world champion back in June 1987, when he won the International Boxing Federation lightweight title by a decision over Greg Haugen. But eight months later, Haugen would take back the title on a decision, and after that Pazienza (now 31-5, 24 knockouts) would lose his next three shots at world junior welterweight championships: to Roger Mayweather (World Boxing

Council, November 1988), Hector Camacho (World Boxing Organization, February 1990) and Loreto Garza (World Boxing Association, December 1990).

Against Garza, he was at his worst. By the eleventh round, he was battered and bleeding and so frustrated by the pounding he was taking that he threw Garza to the canvas. That got the Cranston, Rhode Island fighter disqualified and led critics to say Vinny Paz should retire.

Easier said than done. Just one month after Pazienza lost to Garza, on January 1, 1991, Governor Bruce Sundlun of Rhode Island announced that forty-five banks and credit unions would be closed indefinitely because of the collapse of the private fund that insured them. More than 150,000 depositors discovered that their personal savings had been frozen; among them was Pazienza and $300,000 of his funds—or, as he said, "about four-fifths of my money."

At that point, Pazienza had lost four of his last ten fights. But as fighters do, he came up with a rationale to explain the losses. Making the junior welterweight limit of 140 pounds, he was convinced, depleted him, inhibiting his talent. So Pazienza fixed on an unorthodox move. Rather than step up one weight class, to the welterweight division (147-pound limit) he would fight at 154 pounds—a junior middleweight—even though it required a fourteen pound jump.

Typically, a fighter making that great a leap in weight loses quickness and power. But Pazienza was not typical. As a junior middleweight, he won the United States Boxing Association title from Ron Amundsen last July and then won the W.B.A. title from Gilbert Dele in October.

In becoming a world champion again, he would earn only $20,000. But in beating Dele, Pazienza was now in position to stabilize his finances. He signed for $250,000 to defend his title against Pat Lawler on January 10 for Home Box Office and was counting on even bigger purses to cover the mortgage on his new three-bedroom home in Warwick and insure his future.

Then came the accident.

Vinny Paz is driving the blue Bronco 11 on U.S. 1, pointing to the accident site. He shows a sheepish grin when it is pointed out that he hasn't put his seat belt on. How come?

"'Cause I'm crazy," he said. "I'm a fighter. I take punches. I don't think about accidents."

That hell-bent attitude—he wore no seatbelt when he broke his neck—is typical of the twenty-nine-year-old Pazienza and infuses his objective to fight again. There are no guarantees that he will. Although Pazienza's promoter, Dan Duva, said he had received a letter from Cotter last week saying that the prognosis was good for a return to the ring this year, final clearance is due around July. Pazienza, who has maintained faith in his full recovery since November, regards this as mere medical caution that is bound to fade.

From the moment he landed in Kent County Hospital, Vinny Paz has been acting as though his return to the ring was a fait accompli. That's when he told Angelo to phone Duva.

"Tell him not to let 'em take my title," said Pazienza. "I'll be back."

A month after the accident, with a four-and-one-half-pound metal halo screwed into his head, Pazienza began doing aerobic and weight workouts, hefting barbells and shadow boxing while looking like a refugee from a "Star Wars" set. When the halo was removed on February 14 ("the most excruciating pain in my life—like a 747 flying through my head"), Pazienza was ordered into a hard plastic neck brace that he discarded well before the prescribed period ended. He said: "I told the doctor, 'I'm through with this.' And you know what? He told me, 'Whatever you're doing, you're doing it great.'"

On a day not long ago, Pazienza continued to work his way back into condition, aiming for a year-end defense of his title against Julio Cesar Vasquez, the W.B.A.'s mandatory challenger. The stove and refrigerator had yet to be installed upstairs in the Warwick home, but Pazienza's basement gym was stocked: weight racks and pulley contraptions, a treadmill, stair climber and exercise bike. For nearly two hours, Pazienza lifted weights, jumped steps and shadow boxed.

"That Vasquez figures he's got a gimme with Vinny Paz," he said, as he did nine repetitions of an eighty-pound dumbbell press. "He probably thinks I'm dwindling away on a couch. He's gonna be in for a surprise."

On this day, in that basement gym, Pazienza's is a tunnel vision that brooks no barriers to the moment in which he will do what few figure he could: fight again.

"I'm a warrior in every sense of the word," he said, as he halted a moment in his shadow boxing. "I love to meet a challenge. Which this definitely is. Another challenge in the Vinny Pazienza saga. And I'm going to meet the challenge. You watch. Vasquez, I beat him in dramatic fashion. I can see it now. On HBO and all. I beat him and I'll be the biggest thing that lives."

In September 1992, Pazienza became a victim of boxing politics when the WBA stripped him of his title for failing to defend it in what that organization deemed a timely manner.
That December, against all adds, Pazienza returned to the ring, winning a unanimous decision over Luis Santana. His declared objectice? Regain his title.

PAUL GONZALES: Yesterday Is a Cancelled Check (1992)

He was adroit and swift. Punches flowed with a measured assurance, as though the message of victory was imprinted on his nerve ends. Jab, bap-bap. Jab bap-bap. Nice. Elegant.

His name was Paul Gonzales and in the summer of 1985 he was the-little-pug-who-could, a fighter who appeared skilled enough and charismatic enough to do what no flyweight before him ever had—make America care about diminutive boxers.

CBS-TV gave him $40,000 for his first professional fight—a decision victory over Jose (Pulga) Torres in August 1985. Forty grand—the precise sum that another prince of the ring, Ray Charles Leonard, had made for his professional debut. Forty grand for a fighter who weighed a mere 112 pounds. It wasn't as large a miracle as, say, the parting of the Red Sea. But in its way, the greening of Gonzales, a kid from the barrio of East Los Angeles, was pretty radical stuff.

That's because to fight promoters any boxer beneath 126 pounds is, typically, not worth the bother. The conventional wisdom is that there is no real money to be made with the little guys and therefore no little guys worth remembering since Doc, Sleepy, and Grumpy.

But CBS saw Gonzales as different.

"You couldn't find a more stylish fighter than Gonzales," said Mort Sharnik, who ran the network's boxing programming at the time. "Besides that, he was handsome, had a great smile, was well-spoken. And of course there was that good story with the cop."

The cop was Al Stankie (real name Stankiewicz), a brash lean police officer who'd taken East Los Angeles as his territory and redeeming its youth as his mission. Stankie, who had quit the force at one time to box professionally, had dragooned a nine-year-old

Gonzales off the streets and into the gym, challenging him to make his way up from poverty through boxing.

It was an engaging tale and, in the summer of 1984, it transformed Gonzales into a three-dimensional hero as he won a gold medal at the Olympics in Los Angeles. The cop and the kid provided a story line that had more than narrative value. It put Gonzales in a context that made the public curious about what-happens-next?

It was on that accrued interest that CBS banked on its little big man commanding a TV audience. And for eleven months—from his debut to his successful North American Boxing Federation flyweight title defense against Orlando Canizales in July 1986—Gonzales was a fighter who mattered.

Not only did he earn around $150,000 for his first five bouts, but after the victory over Canizales, on CBS, he appeared to be on course for a world title fight. For Gonzales and manager-trainer Stankie the future was a roseate picture.

Then suddenly it was not.

Paul Gonzales, now twenty-eight, fought three times last year, in boxing outposts like Albuquerque, New Mexico, Jacksonville, Florida, and San Bernardino, California.

His total boxing earnings, he said, came to $10,500.

The fighter he beat in 1986 to position himself for a title shot, Orlando Canizales, is a world champion today. Gonzales, who lives with his mother Ana, in the three-bedroom home he bought her in Montebello, California, in 1985, is not ranked and no longer taken very seriously. When he phoned his original promoter, Don Chargin, earlier this year and asked Chargin if he'd be interested in resuscitating his career, Chargin said no.

"The last time I saw him was on TV, from the Great Western Forum," said Chargin. "Paul wasn't fifty percent of the fighter he used to be. He had lost speed and he was getting hit with punches that he'd never get hit with before. From a pretty little fighter, he'd become very very ordinary...

"1984's been a long time now."

What happened? What went wrong to turn a fighter Chargin said "had everything" into an also-ran?

Well, there are no shortage of explanations to account for the fall of Gonzales. Chargin and Sharnik say that the kid's Los Angeles-based attorneys, Jim Blancarte and Ron DiNicola, had unrealistic expectations of what their fighter was worth and that, in imbuing Gonzales with that perspective, they created a monster.

"At times he was a real nice kid," said Chargin. "Very charming. But he got caught up in all the hype. He got to believe what his attorneys were saying. For a short time he was listening to me. I told him, 'You've got to get experience and not every fight is going to be on national TV for that kind of money.' For a while he understood. That was short-lived. It reached a point where, when you'd come up with a suggestion, he'd give you this look. Like: 'Let's get this conversation over.' We were constantly in meetings. A huge board room. Paul would be at the head of the table. The whole thing became a pain in the neck."

Sharnik said that what Gonzales was to the network was a noble experiment.

"It's never easy to sell little guys," said Sharnik. "But we were willing to work at it. Trouble was nothing was simple. There was never any organization. You didn't know who you were dealing with. Was it the lawyers? Stankie? Chargin? Rather than a plan, everything was difficult. It led to confusion. The kid became too absorbed in himself. He bought a Corvette. He was not concentrating on the fight life. He was too absorbed by play things. The ratings for him were not that great and eventually the network tired of him."

The attorney's version differs. Blancarte said that Chargin and Sharnik were too typical of boxing men: "Like everybody else, they wanted something for nothing. It was never the right price."

DiNicola said that Gonzales was resolute without his lawyer's prompting in wanting to get his money's worth, particularly for matches off television. Gonzales does not dispute that, saying he was willing to fight for small purses and gain experience, but not against, as he put it, "the rock-em sock-em robots" promoters offered him as opponents.

"Don't put me in there hard and offer me three-, four-, five-thousand dollars," he said.

But that considered economic outlook was not, he insists, what derailed his career. Plain and simple, it was injuries, injuries that sidelined him and blew the continuity a beginner pro needs. Gonzales's record shows gaps of inactivity, from six to twelve month's duration, that the injuries caused.

And how bizarre were the circumstances by which he incurred the injuries: he broke a knuckle on his left hand (1986) in a street brawl with a fighter who'd beaten up a younger brother of his. He broke his ankle and sustained knee damage (1987) when he stepped into his red Corvette—the one he drove with a black motoring glove on—and jarred the gear shift, causing it to run over his trail leg. He fractured his hip (1988) while out riding a ten-speed bicycle when a horse forced him into a boulder.

"I did a lot a crying 'cause I felt I was jinxed," said Gonzales. "I felt there were a lot of people out there who disliked me and wished bad luck on me. 'Cause I was ready to fight and injuries just kept happening. It freaked me out so bad my fiancee said I should get myself cleansed. Like a spiritual cleaning. But I'm Catholic, and you can't do that. It's like devil worship.

"I cried, I punched walls. I was seeing all my Olympic friends—Pernell Whitaker, Meldrick Taylor, Mark Breland—fighting for world titles, and I wasn't. And it hurt. I'd ask myself, 'Why's this happening to me?'"

But as bad as it was for Gonzales, things would prove to be worse for Stankie.

Even during Gonzales' early success, Al Stankie was a hyper character, moving on foot or by car as though there was an emergency straight ahead.

He had the cocksure manner and an easy charm then, greeting friends and near strangers with, "Hey, handsome," or "Hi, darling."

With Gonzales he showed the soothsayer's alluring manner, conjuring up a future of glory and just desserts in that raspy voice of his that favored the melodramatic intonation.

Stankie filled Gonzales with his conviction and reinforced it with pet sayings like, "Patience attains all you strive for: and this more elaborate one: "Yesterday is a cancelled check. Forget it. It's over. Past. Done. Tomorrow is a promissory note. It may or may not happen. But today...today is cash in hand. Live today as best you can."

Best-you-can for the forty-nine-year-old Stankie is no longer what it used to be. Stankie hit hard times after he retired from the LAPD in late 1986. His objective back then was to guide Gonzales—the most skilled, most successful of his barrio fighters—to a world title. He had invested heart-and-soul into Gonzales, who had lived in Stankie's five-bedroom home in Cerritos after graduating from high school, along with the policeman's two sons and daughter.

But by '86 Stankie was experiencing recurring problems, induced by his dependence on alcohol, a bent for violence and a draining and complicated love life. There were fist fights, drunk driving arrests and domestic turbulence that saw him forced to sell his home in Cerritos while his marriage was breaking up. In November 1989, Stankie received this note from the LAPD:

"...You have conducted yourself in a manner contrary to the provisions of the Retired Officers Declaration you signed upon retiring. Therefore, according to police commission policy, the firearms privileges granted upon retirement have been revoked."

The letter referred, among other things, to an incident at the Hollenbeck Area Police station, where Stankie had appeared "in an intoxicated condition and at one point challenged a sworn member of the department to fight."

At the very time the LAPD was renouncing Stankie, Gonzales let him go. In boxing circles, Stankie was well-liked, and his devotion to youth was regarded as authentic, with Stankie going to extremes to get money to move his fighters out of the barrio. Stankie's departure from Gonzales's corner was seen by many as another example of Gonzales's uppity attitude. But Gonzales insists that there was more to his dismissal of Stankie than folks would ever have suspected.

Gonzales said that from amateur days Stankie had a drinking problem that repeatedly led to his misbehaving, sometimes on the very day of important competitions, an unnerving experience. By the time he turned pro, Gonzales said, Stankie was out of control.

"Cussing at everybody," said Gonzales. "Fights with people at the gym. Yelling at kids. Yelling at trainers."

On November 13, 1989, Gonzales fought Antonio Lozada at the Forum in Inglewood, California. Stankie, Gonzales said, showed up drunk again and wrapped his fighter's hands so badly that it cut off circulation and forced Gonzales to ask Tony Curtis, the Forum matchmaker, to re-tape them.

"Al," said Gonzales, "was high as a kite. It was a tough fight and I won. Afterward, Al came in the dressing room and said, 'I'm sorry. Forgive me.' By then I was crying in the shower because I almost lost the fight. He was hurting me mentally. I knew I just couldn't go on with him any more."

Stankie's twenty-four-year-old daughter, Andrea, does not fault Gonzales for walking away. While her memories of her upbringing are warm ones ("My dad was always an encouraging father, making you feel loved"), she said that after Stankie resigned from the force his behavior turned erratic.

"He became very aggressive," she said. "Like a whirlwind. Talking a mile a minute one day. And in the next instant out the door. Sometimes he'd go into the depressed mode. Then he'd become crazed again. There was so much anger, and he took it out the only way he knew. By being aggressive and fighting. My mom finally couldn't put up with it and left. When you'd try to approach him about his problem he'd turn mean and nasty, and very defensive. You couldn't reason with him. Everything was so aggressive— the stories he related to you—about fights and barrooms and old police tales. The tone was almost like a crazed man."

Seven months after he severed his ties to Stankie, in June 1990, Gonzales finally fought for a world title against Canizales, by then the International Boxing Federation bantamweight champion. Without Stankie in his corner, Gonzales was stopped on cuts in two rounds.

In April of 1991, Stankie was arrested for drunk driving. When a computer check turned up two outstanding drunk-driving warrants, he was tried, found guilty and sent to Los Angeles County Prison. There he received a letter from his son, Andy Stankiewicz, who plays second base for the New York Yankees.

"Andrew wrote, saying, 'Pops, maybe you got to get on your knees before you can stand on your feet,'" recalled Stankie. "In other words, talk to God before you can stand up and be counted. When I read the letter I cried, I wasn't proud of how far I'd fallen."

There was a soft cast on Al Stankie's right forearm and hand. The pinkie and ring fingers stood upright and apart from the rest of the hand.

Stankie had on a Yankee cap worn backward, a Gold's Gym t-shirt, black training pants, rubber sandals and there was an unlighted cigarette in the side of his mouth. He had been talking incessantly, at a lickety-split pace—a plaintive recitation of the facts of his life, his orchestrating emotions—sadness, anger, optimism—all cranked up beyond normal dimensions.

And now, on a sidewalk not far from the Cache Gym in Vernon, California, where Stankie trains fighters for Joe Hernandez, a friend of his who owns the place and manages boxers, he was telling how that hand was injured in a barroom fight."

"I told the guy, 'I'm twenty years older than you, son,'" Stankie recalled. 'He says, 'Who you calling son?' I tried to reason with him. Avoid a fight. But he kept pushing it. So I told him, 'Look, son. I'm the very best in the west and those who mess with the best may end up with the rest.' He laughs and says, 'Listen to this guy.'"

Abruptly Stankie stepped forward.

"WHAP!," he said, throwing his right hand toward a reporter, a gleam in his eye. "Three-quarters of a second. Could you have blocked that? I broke two bones in my right hand. But that's the ghetto cop in me."

Whatever. On this day not long ago, Stankie was soon back in the gym, pacing as he waited for Gonzales to appear. Yes, the two men had reunited and, though Gonzales had not fought since July

1991—under another trainer then—Stankie was convinced it would be like old times again for the two of them.

"I was the rudder that kept him straight," he said. "We're gonna prove it's not over. 'Cause the wind is back." Hernandez, who has known Stankie since the mid-1970's and has provided him with a place to live and meals these past few years, was not impressed. When Stankie asked why a fighter of Hernandez's, who was to spar with Gonzales, had disappeared, Hernandez shook his hand in mock nervousness and said, "He was scared of your guy."

"No doubt in my mind, he'd have gotten a spanking if he came in the ring," said Stankie. "You're talking about a kid who won the gold. Not some kid from Tia-juana."

That day the kid who had won gold would spar with a sixteen-year-old East Los Angeles amateur of Stankie's, Salvador Jasso. Jasso, a 132-pounder, would outbox Gonzales, making him repeatedly lunge like a novice. Three rounds of sparring that exposed Gonzales's ring rust and obscured the glory that once was gold.

Yet for both Stankie and Gonzales 1984 was not so long ago that the vision of it could not invigorate their picture of the future.

"In the gym, I always looked terrible," said Gonzales after sparring. "I'm not a gym fighter. Put me in the ring, I'll win, now that I'm healthy and have the right trainer. Wait til people can see what I can do. I'm destined to be world champion."

"I felt it with my heart then," said Stankie, "and I feel it with my heart now. 'Yesterday is a cancelled check...'"

"'Forget it. Past. Done,'" said Gonzales.

And the two of them recited the rest together.

Gonzales was scheduled to fight in the summer of 1992, but withdrew from that Atlantic City bout after a niece of his was the victim of a barrio shooting. "I couldn't concentrate on boxing," he said at the time. By the end of the year, he still had not returned to the ring.

*Good fighters and bad fighters hold on to the illusion that
things are never so bad as they appear. Dave Jaco didn't start
out with the notion that he'd end up as merely an opponent.
And Kid Akeem didn't figure one brutal fight would make him
a civilian before his time.*

DAVE JACO: A Body for Better Men to Beat On (1990)

Dave Jaco sometimes works on short notice.

That's not unusual for that species of fighter used for building
the records of rising young attractions. In the boxing business, they
are known simply as opponents.

Jaco, a heavyweight who lives in Sarasota, Florida, is an opponent.

At the age of thirty-four, he has no illusions of competing for a
world title.

In January 1986, when Jaco fought a hot young contender
named Mike Tyson, it was, as it so often is, a last-minute call that
summoned him to the ring. At the time, Jaco was in Atlanta,
earning $50 a day, plus meal money, as a sparring partner for Tim
Witherspoon, who was training for a World Boxing Association
heavyweight title fight against Tony Tubbs.

"Tyson had just made the cover of *Sports Illustrated*," Jaco
recalled. "Kid Dynamite, they called him. And because of the reputation he was getting as a vicious puncher, the promoter was
having a hard time finding a guy to fight him. Nobody wanted to
get in the same ring with Tyson. They offered me $5,000 to fight
Tyson. Five grand sounded like a lot. Back then I was always
behind on child support for my twin boys, Adam and Aaron. I took
the fight. I didn't care. I'd been in tough fights a lot of times
before."

The bout, fought in Albany, ended quickly.

"I got decked three times in the first round," Jaco said. "The third time I went down, the bell ending the round rang. I went back to my corner, talking to myself: 'What are you doing? The guy is knocking the stuffing out of you.'

"That's when the referee told me the fight was over. Three knockdowns ends a fight. At that point, I thought I'd been down only twice. 'No,' my corner man said. 'You were down three times.' That tells you about Mike Tyson's punch."

Since Tyson knocked him out, Jaco has been stopped often. Tony Tucker, Johnny Du Plooy, Mike Evans, Gary Mason, George Foreman, Alex Stewart and, most recently, Tommy Morrison, all beat Jaco by knockout.

For the fight against Morrison, Jaco was contacted forty-eight hours before the match after Morrison's original opponent, Danny Sutton, canceled. For a $2,000 purse, Jaco trekked from Sarasota by car, and, when the car broke down, by plane, to Jacksonville, Florida, a trip that quickly seemed not worth the bother.

Jaco lasted thirty-seven seconds of the first round against Morrison, who knocked him out with a powerful left hook. After the 6-foot-6-inch, 201-pound Jaco was counted out, he crawled two paces to his corner on his knees before his second could get to him and help him to his stool.

Jaco holds a 1985 victory over Tyson's next opponent, Donovan (Razor) Ruddock: it is Ruddock's only defeat. But even Jaco, whose record is 21-17 (18 knockouts), acknowledges that lately he has been merely a body for better men to beat on.

"But even though I'm a common opponent," Jaco said, "I don't go in there thinking I'm a loser. Promoters know I don't go down with a phantom punch. Every time Tyson knocked me down, I got up."

Jaco's boxing odyssey began relatively late. He was twenty-four years old when he was laid off from his $300-a-week job as a pipe-fitter at Interlake Steel in Toledo, Ohio, in 1979.

"It came at a bad time," Jaco said. "I felt kind of, like, lost. I was hurt from a divorce and the fact that my wife got custody of the boys. I had no job, just $180 a week unemployment."

When a friend who was an amateur fighter suggested Jaco join him for a workout, Jaco discovered he had a knack for the sport. It led to his competing in Tough Man contests in Pontiac, Michigan, and Toledo (he won the Ohio event), and that in turn nudged him to a pro boxing career in 1981. Although he had no amateur fights, Jaco won his first twelve bouts as a pro.

"I was twenty-five years old and still unemployed," Jaco said. "At that time, boxing was a kind of dare. As I won my first twelve fights, I developed a bit of a following, thirty or forty fans who'd travel to where I fought."

Jaco's first loss, a first-round knockout in June 1983, was to Carl (The Truth) Williams for a purse of $3,000. Other losses followed, too regularly to suit Jaco. But when he got custody of the twins, he kept fighting for money he could add to the weekly $350 paycheck he draws as a delivery driver for a Sarasota appliance company. The $10,000 he earned for fighting Foreman, and getting knocked out in one round in December, was his best payday as a professional.

"When I started out, I figured maybe one day I'd become a contender," Jaco said. "These days, I give it my best. But I'm always rusty. My timing is off. I have a full-time job. I just can't devote myself like you have to."

Through boxing, Jaco has traveled the world: Dusseldorf, Germany; Budapest, Hungary; Windsor, England. And he's also been to the emergency room of more than a few hospitals.

"I've had sixty-five stitches, a broken cheek bone, a fractured nose, a fractured bone in my eye and fractured ribs," Jaco said.

The toll of hard times has him talking lately of ending his fight career.

"It's too easy to get hurt," Jaco said. "With my boys to raise—they're twelve years old now—I'm figuring to fight one more time this year, on the live card to the Leonard-Durán closed-circuit show here in Sarasota, and then retire so I can concentrate on them.

"I want to make sure they grow up right. The world is so corrupt. And things happen. Like their friends know I'm a fighter, so the boys are expected to be that way. I have to tell them: 'You don't make friends being mean.' Just because your dad is on TV, and gets beat up, doesn't make you any meaner."

Dave Jaco, thirty-six, continues to fight. In the past few years, he has been a fulltime boxer, no longer working a civilian job. "I'm just getting by," he says. "But it feels good to be in shape and be physically and mentally prepared. I'm looking for a couple of big paydays before I quit."

AKEEM AND THE DREAM (1991)

One morning this week, a world-class Nigerian boxer named Akeem Anifowoshe looked into his bathroom mirror, and then cried.

What he saw were legs that had lost muscle tone and turned stick-like, and a once-sinewy body that had become attenuated, like a figure from an El Greco painting.

"I cry so many times," said the twenty-two-year-old Anifowoshe (pronounced anna-fee-OH-shee). "Whenever I look in the mirror and see myself, I say, 'Oh, no.'"

But worse was what his eyes could not see and his mind refused to register: the head injuries he suffered during his last fight, a bloody twelve-round world title match against a junior-bantamweight champion named Robert Quiroga.

Those injuries put the fighter up against the edge of his own mortality and began a harrowing few weeks that took him from the brink of a world boxing championship to a critical-list coma and finally to consciousness and a wheelchair. And the brutal quality of Quiroga's match would provide critics of the sport with still another reason to call for its being banned.

In the view of virtually everyone but Anifowoshe himself, the injuries have all but ended a promising future for a young Nigerian immigrant and former Olympic hopeful who saw a chance to make a life for himself as a boxer in Las Vegas. Only the fighter does not see his career as being over. In spite of damage he suffered a month ago, he insists, incredibly, that he will fight again.

The International Boxing Federation fight that brought him to this point took place on June 15 in Quiroga's hometown, San Antonio. Soon after Quiroga was declared the winner by unanimous decision. Kid Akeem—Anifowoshe uses that as a nom de

36

guerre—sank to one knee and began vomiting blood before he abruptly collapsed to the canvas.

"By the time I got into the ring, Akeem was having convulsions," said Dr. Gerardo Zavala, a neurosurgeon who was one of two attending ringside physicians that night. "He was unconscious, having difficulty breathing and the pupil in the right eye was dilated. A dilated pupil means that the brain is trying to push through the hole that is between the head and the spine in the neck. And that the pressure inside the head was very high. It was like toothpaste being squeezed."

What was one man's calamity and burden soon became fodder for the continuing debate over boxing. In the weeks that followed, Kid Akeem's injuries raised questions about the wisdom of the use by smaller men of six-ounce gloves in title matches, as he and Quiroga had done, rather than the more heavily padded eight-ounce gloves Anifowoshe wore in his twenty-three previous fights, all victories, eighteen by knockout.

Contending that the heavier gloves offered more protection against injuries, boxing authorities in Texas blamed the International Boxing Federation, which mandates the use of the lighter gloves in championship bouts in lighter weight classes.

Bob Lee, president of the boxing organization, defended the rule, saying heavier gloves could cause smaller fighters to tire as a bout goes on. Lee said that the six-ounce gloves had been used in other title fights, with no problems arising, but that the federation would consider recommendations to change the rule.

The damage that night was not one-sided. Spindly though he is at 115 pounds, Anifowoshe has always been a heavy puncher, and he showed that against Quiroga. By the end of the fight, Quiroga's face was bloody and swollen, and more than a few people at ringside later said that had the bout not occurred on Quiroga's home turf it might well have been stopped and Anifowoshe awarded the victory. At the final bell, Quiroga looked far worse than the loser, who was virtually unmarked and had finished strong in the twelfth round.

Even as a comatose Anifowoshe was being treated in the intensive care unit of the Baptist Medical Center in San Antonio,

Quiroga was in the emergency room getting stitches for cuts on his chin, left brow and eyelid.

Hardly was he out of the hospital when Quiroga was saying the I.B.F. should outlaw the use of six-ounce gloves, a clear enough admission that his victory had not been easy.

Post-fight reports said Anifowoshe had absorbed more than 400 blows to the head. By contrast, in last month's twelve round heavyweight rematch between Mike Tyson and Donovan (Razor) Ruddock, the total number of punches both fighters landed to the body and head was fewer than the number of blows that bounced off Anifowoshe's head in the Quiroga fight.

Anifowoshe's manager, Billy Baxter, said it was the intensity of the bout and not the gloves that had caused his fighter's injuries. "The fighters more than the gloves did the damage," he said. "You'll see a fight like this every ten years. Neither fighter clinched. Every round was three minutes of bombardment."

After doctors cut a hole in his skull to relieve the pressure on his brain, Anifowoshe remained in the hospital until July 4. That was the day when, against Zavala's advice, the fighter's wife, Sharon, took her husband back to Las Vegas, where he was reunited with his two sons, Akeem Jr., three years old, and Kazeem, one-and-a-half. The family lives in a modest two-bedroom apartment on Steelhead Lane.

The day before Anifowoshe left the hospital, a magnetic resonance imaging test showed evidence of small damage on both sides of the brain, Zavala said, adding that the full extent of the fighter's problems would not be known for another two to three months.

The day Anifowoshe left the hospital, he was able to move his left leg for the first time since being admitted there. While Zavala took that as a sign that Anifowoshe would be able to walk in three to six months, he was not entirely sanguine about the overall medical outlook.

"If I had to speculate," Zavala said, "I would say that there is only a thirty percent chance of Akeem's full recovery." And even if Anifowoshe fully regains his physical powers, Zavala said, he would be such a high-risk candidate for serious reinjury that it would be folly for him to think of fighting again.

But Anifowoshe sees his injuries as simply a temporary setback in reaching his objective, a world title. "Believe me, I will fight again," Anifowoshe said as he lay in bed days ago. "Everything is on me."

When it was suggested that the damage wrought by Quiroga hardly recommended a future in boxing, Anifowoshe replied: "I tell you what. I pray every day and have people pray. Quiroga did not harm me, or anything. The decision—that's what make me to collapse."

But wasn't the coma as clear a sign of brain damage as a man could get?

Anifowoshe took a moment to consider that, then said: "Believe me, when I am in a coma, I know what is going on. I know what is going on. Listen. What happened to me messed my mind up. It just make me mad, everyday. Even when I see Quiroga at the hospital: 'Robert, you know I won the fight. We must do it again.' He looks at me and says 'You're crazy.'

"I am still thinking of winning a world championship—it is very important to me. I want to get myself back as soon as possible. Believe me, I will do anything to fight again. Slow by slow. Take your time. The dream is not over yet."

For Anifowoshe, the odyssey that brought him to the brink of that dreamed-of title began in Lagos, Nigeria.

He grew up there in a family of nine children. His father, Ashru, was a truck driver; his mother, Nimota, ran a bar.

Anifowoshe's introduction to boxing had a comic undercurrent. It was only after his sister beat him up that an older brother, Dada, took him to the gym so he could learn to defend himself. But Anifowoshe, who was nine then, was more interested in street life and it wasn't long before he stopped going to the gym. By twelve, he said, he was smoking "weed" and loitering at a bus station, where he became deft at picking pockets.

He was fourteen when he snatched a purse from the wrong woman. She pummeled him so badly that he returned to the gym and began boxing again. This time, he stuck with the sport and began to win local and national competitions.

In 1984, he was a member of the Nigerian Olympic team. In Los Angeles, site of the Games, he filled out a form, and where he was asked to list his age, he wrote, truthfully, that he was fifteen, too young for competition. He was declared ineligible.

But rather than return to Nigeria, he decided to stay on in the States and shoot for the 1988 Games. He settled in with Doc Broadus, a coach who had met him in a pre-Olympic training camp for fighters from African nations.

Broadus, who discovered George Foreman in the Job Corps in the mid-1960's, lived in Las Vegas. When Anifowoshe arrived here, it was nighttime, and the city was lighted with neon.

By daylight, he discovered that life in the desert was not so glamorous. He had no car and was constantly short of money. Even so, he routinely lent money to others, particularly fellow Africans, and while living with Broadus and, later on his own, he allowed those without shelter to stay with him, rent-free.

In May 1986 he fought in the world amateur championships in Reno, and felt so victimized by the judges' decision in a quarterfinals bout against a Soviet boxer, Yuri Alexandrov, that he sobbed uncontrollably afterward. "My life, my life," he said, through tears. "I've been training every day. I haven't missed. My God."

The disappointment led him to abandon his Olympic ambitions and instead turn professional in January 1987.

Anifowoshe fought nearly every other month, earning purses ranging from $350 to $600 in bouts arranged to accommodate his senior-year curriculum at Ranche High School. "I was a straight-A student," he said. "Nobody likes school, but anything I do I like to do best."

That dedication extended to boxing.

"He was always asking for more sparring," said Miguel Diaz, his trainer. "'Let me go one more round,' he'd say. He wasn't afraid of work. And he was very respectful. Never talk back to nobody. Always, 'Thank you.' He was a kid from another generation."

In May 1988, Sharon and Akeem were married at a time when his purses were rarely better than $1,000 a fight, hardly enough for him to support a family. But Baxter figured he had a potential champion in Anifowoshe and was helping to support the fighter, paying his rent and providing him with spending money.

His objective was identical to his fighter's: a world title that would be an open-sesame to the serious money that boxers can make. In fighting Quiroga, Anifowoshe would earn a modest world championship purse of $15,000, still more than double his previous best pay day of $7,000.

A glimpse of what might lie ahead if he won was provided by a delegate from the Nigerian President, who in the pre-fight dressing room envisioned Anifowoshe making his first title defense in his native land in an outdoor stadium filled with 50,000 to 80,000 of his countrymen.

Then Nnamdi Moweta, a friend and fight manager who, like Anifowoshe, was from Lagos, began rousing him by telling him in tribal tongue, "You are the lion."

A little more than three weeks later, he lay in bed, a wounded man trying not to let go of a dream.

The promoter's insurance covered each fighter for only $10,000. His medical bills would be far more than that.

Last Sunday, Baxter flew to Las Vegas, trying to simplify the future. The manager arranged for free physical therapy for Anifowoshe while seeking to put together a benefit fight card as well as a foundation to help support him. So many things to worry over in a life grown very fuzzy.

Two days later, Baxter visited his fighter at his apartment.

"I was walking today," Anifowoshe said from his bed. "Outside. Fifteen minutes."

Baxter appeared skeptical: "Did you have help?"

"Sharon walked behind me. Just in case."

Two hours later, when he was helped to his feet so he could be moved to the living room, Anifowoshe tried to move his left foot forward but was frozen in place. He tried and tried again, without success. Finally, his father-in-law, Willie Scott, cradled him in his arms and walked him to a wheelchair in the living room.

Soon after, Sharon returned home with her husband's medicine and was asked if he had really walked outside that morning.

She said he had not.

Anifowoshe would regain full use of his legs and return to the gym, still vowing to fight again. But more than a year after the Quiroga bout, his life took a troubling turn. On July 21, 1992, Anifowoshe and another man were arrested for selling cocaine to an undercover officer in Las Vegas. Anifowoshe was scheduled to stand trial in May 1993.

Fighters are often angry and/or troubled men. Sometimes the anger cannot be contained by sport, and then lives go out of whack. Badly out of whack in the cases of Tony Ayala, Rickey Womack and James Scott.

TONY AYALA: The Baby Bull (1983)

It was last November when Antonio Ayala Jr. awoke in his hotel room in Atlantic City and saw his father, Antonio Sr., known as "Big Tony", pacing the floor, a look of concern on his face about that night's bout against Carlos Hererra, the W.B.A.'s number-one junior middleweight contender.

Through half-shut eyes, the son watched the old man, who is 5-feet 7 1/2 inches, 250 pounds, move restlessly about the room a while before letting him know he was awake. "Don't worry, Fat Man," he said. "This guy (Hererra) is all mine."

That night, Tony Jr., whose ring nickname is "Torito," (Spanish for "baby bull") knocked out Hererra at 2:43 of round three to become the mandatory challenger for the W.B.A. junior middleweight championship at the time held by Davey Moore, who lost his title June 16, to Robert Duran. It was Ayala—not Duran—who was originally signed to fight Moore this spring in a bout that could have been the shining hour in the Ayala family's long quest for title glory in the fight arena.

For of the three sons that Big Tony trained from their childhood and saw become professional fighters—Mike, Sammy and Tony (a fourth, Paulie, is an amateur)—Torito was considered the best of the bunch. At 5-feet 7 1/2 inches, 154 pounds, Ayala was short-armed and thick-waisted, broad through the chest and shoulders. It was a brawler's torso and, in a pro career that started at age

43

seventeen in 1980, Ayala used it with a fury that saw him occasionally snarl and curse at opponents, and hit them after the bell.

In one fight, he spat on a foe, Jose Luis Baltazar, after knocking him down, because Baltazar had the temerity to insult him before and during the bout. With a left hook as textbook perfect as Ted Williams' swing or Oscar Robertson's jump shot, Ayala won twenty-two consecutive fights, nineteen of them by knockout. His future in the prize ring looked bright.

Today, that future is bleak. On New Year's Day, Ayala was arrested after a West Patterson, New Jersey woman told police that he had broken into her apartment and sexually assaulted her. In court proceedings, Ayala claimed he had been invited into the woman's apartment, that she had asked him to tie her up and have sexual relations with her.

Ayala's account, according to his attorney, William DeMarco, was undermined by evidence introduced in court, over the lawyer's objections, of the fighter's arrest last August in his native San Antonio. In that incident, Ayala was found in a stranger's house not far from the $90,000 residence into which he had moved only weeks before.

At the time, Ayala's Texas attorney contended that his client had wandered into the wrong house while drunk—a regrettable mistake, but no crime. Though the authorities saw it differently, the point became moot when the complainant chose not to press charges against Ayala.

But the fact that at the time of his arrest Ayala was carrying an I.D. tag belonging to and bearing the name of a young woman who lived at the trespassed address and the fact that he had entered the house through a window damaged his credibility in New Jersey.

Then on April 13, Ayala was convicted of burglary and rape by a jury in Paterson, New Jersey and two months later was sentenced to thirty-five years in prison and was ordered to serve at least fifteen years before becoming eligible for parole. That means Ayala—barring a successful appeal or permission to box inside prison walls—is unlikely ever to be a contender again.

How Ayala, on the verge of his life's objective—the championship bout against Moore—could blunder so badly is a puzzle without an easy solution. The temptation to mark him as just-plain-rotten is not lacking for substantiation. For Ayala's current dilemma stems from a scene—the abuse of a woman—that has occurred before.

When he was fifteen, Ayala assaulted a young woman—a stranger to him—in the ladies' room of a drive-in movie theater in San Antonio. The woman suffered vaginal bleeding and a ruptured bladder. Ayala was tried as an adult and received a ten-year prison sentence, but was saved from doing time by a plea from the victim that he be granted probation for what was a first offense. He ended up on ten years probation, and it was later revealed that the victim of Ayala's assault had reached a $40,000 financial settlement with the Ayalas to drop the civil suit she had intended to bring.

The tidy resolution of the matter follows a pattern in Ayala's life. Over the years, his gift as a fighter excused a variety of transgressions, from speeding tickets that somehow got dismissed from as early as age twelve, when, as a precocious motorist, Ayala began driving, to the more troubling incidents later. For Torito, there was always an "out" that went with being a prodigy of the manly art, and the best little boy in Big Tony's household stable of boxers.

Yet to ascribe Ayala's dark side to a permissive court system, or to the "bad seed" theory, is to ignore the Spartan early years the boy spent under Big Tony as a budding fighter. Ayala's fall from grace may be seen as an object lesson in what can happen when a boyhood is fraught with adult-like pressures and expectations. And while that does not excuse his misdeeds, it does alter the one-dimensional perspective with which some viewed him.

But even for those who saw his better side, Ayala's comedown eludes glib analysis and leaves them feeling puzzled (and betrayed) by the fighter.

For Ayala himself, these are long days and nights spent trying to fathom how a million-dollar career abruptly went bust.

Passaic County Jail; a balmy day in June.

In the office of a deputy warden, Tony Ayala, Jr., sits in olive-green prison fatigues and rubber sandals, staring through the cloud of cigarette smoke he blows. Ayala's expression is wistful as he speaks:

"I've cried a lotta nights thinking about what could have been. You know, after the jury's verdict, I felt I didn't want to go on. I lost a lotta weight. I told Bill Demarco to forget about the appeals. But that passed. 'Cause I decided I'm not a bad person, man. I don't give a damn what they say about me. I know I'm not like a lot of these other guys (inmates) I see in here. They joke about the crime they've done.

'They're proud to be here. They can't wait to be out on the street so they can boast: 'yeah, man, I did time.' Me, I made mistakes. And I'm man enough and intelligent enough to correct them myself. Meantime, I spend a lot of hours writing. About my life. Not to sell, just to resolve what went wrong. From days going way back..."

From grade school on, boxing was an Ayala family obsession, with Big Tony intending the sport to be his sons' ticket out of the San Antonio barrio where the Ayalas and many other poor Mexican-Americans lived. "Browntown," it was derisively called. And it was no place for the meek. "In our neighborhood," Ayala Sr. said, "either you roared like a tiger or you'd be a pet. Some kids were abused. I don't believe in turn-the-other-cheek, and I made damn sure my sons didn't either."

Like the American pit bull terriers the Ayalas bred, Big Tony's boys were raised for battle. "Dad," said Ayala last winter before his most recent arrest, "might squeeze my thigh or Sammy's or Mike's and say, 'Willpower.' And see how much pain we could take.

"Once he lined us up and gave us each a bit of raw jalapeño pepper to see if we were man enough to stand the burning it caused our mouths. Mike ran to the bathroom, but me and Sam stayed the course. The thing about my father, though, is he wouldn't ask us to do anything he wouldn't do first. He'd eat jalapeño pepper before making us try it. And same with the pinching. He'd have us pinch him hard as we could. 'See that,' he'd say. 'Now, it's your turn. Men don't cry. Willpower. Willpower.'"

For Tony, the discipline was part of a relentlessly thorough boxing regimen. The Ayala boys were educated in the art of slipping punches at an age when most youngsters are learning hickorydickory-dock. By the time they were in grade school, Mike and Sammy were in pee-wee competition throughout Texas, and their father had built a backyard gym, paying quarters to neighborhood youngsters to spar with his boys so he could gauge their progress.

At five, the younger Torito—who until then had declined to matriculate in Big Tony's fight nursery—had a change of heart. Tagging along to Robstown, Texas, where Mike and Sammy were to compete, he demanded a chance to box.

"I told him," recalled Ayala Sr., "'But you haven't trained, Torito.' He wasn't impressed. Tells me, like kids do, 'I wanna box. I wanna box.' What could I say? I let him box. He fought barefooted that night—all he had were cowboy boots—and got his ass whipped. Cried afterward too because he'd lost.

"Next night, I come home from work and Torito wasn't waiting in the driveway for me, like he usually did. He'd always be there to look in my lunch box for the apple I'd buy him on the way home. 'Where's Torito?' I asked my wife. 'In his room.' I go to his room. He's sad. 'What's wrong, Torito?' He says to me, 'You don't love me any more.' I told him that wasn't so—of course I loved him. But I said that if he wanted to box, he had to have the discipline to train—nobody could win without training."

"Here at Passaic County, I'm confined to the receiving area. It's where guys who just come in are brought. There's a TV I watch. I read some. I'm thinking of getting my high-school equivalency diploma. Some days I play cards with a couple of guys I've gotten to know—loser does pushups. As often as I can, I talk to my wife. There's a phone in the cell. You can make collect calls out.

"Three days a week, I see the psychiatrist here. Monday, Wednesday and Friday—an hour at a time. It's helped me understand myself—the fears I have, and had. See, I was always scared shitless that I was not good enough. Not good enough as a person, or a fighter."

The Ayala War Wagon—as their vehicles through the years were known—transported the boys to boxing venues throughout Texas, Mexico and beyond. At some sites, fans would throw coins and bills into the ring after the bout to express their pleasure—as much as $20 and $30 for the pee-wee fighters to split.

When not in competition, Torito and his brothers trained regularly under Big Tony, whose moods fluctuated according to how his boys performed in the gym. As Ceasar Cano, a San Antonio fight trainer, recalled: 'I saw the father as a man who loved those kids. His love was so great that he wanted them to be perfect. One day he'd be so hard, the next he'd kiss them on the forehead and neck. He was like a lion with his cubs."

On days when his sonsdid poorly, the father might shake them vigorously by the shoulders and upbraid them loudly. Sometimes, his displeasure flared to rage. Cano saw him smash a wristwatch of Sammy's against the floor, and slap him for training errors. Others, like middleweight Robbie Epps, who as a youth trained under Ayala Sr., says Big Tony was not averse, when dissatisfied with his youngsters' training, "to take a jump rope to their behinds."

But the taskmaster father got results. Torito became too skilled to fight boys his own age, and soon was fighting older opponents.

"I first saw Torito compete in San Antonio's Municipal Auditorium in 1972," said Epps. "I couldn't believe it. Nine years old he was, and he was fighting a guy with a moustache and a tattoo—a fifteen-year-old man. It was the first time I'd ever seen a kid that young whose punches made a thudding sound when they landed. He had that squatty body of his, but he beat the hell out of the moustached guy. Stopped him in the third round. It was amazing."

His ring skills, his attitude were so far beyond his years that when the W.B.A. welterweight champion, Pipino Cuevas, came to San Antonio to train in 1977, a fourteen-year-old Ayala was convinced he could hold his own against Cuevas.

Big Tony, who knew of Pipino's reputation for being heavy-handed with sparring partners, was reluctant. 'Tony," he said, "weighed 147 (the welterweight limit) and was in intense training for the National Junior Olympics that were to be held in Green Bay, Wisconsin. 'Don't worry,' he told me, 'Cuevas can't hurt me.' He talked me into it. Well, word got out. The gym that day was packed with spectators. And for the first two rounds, it was nip and tuck, man against boy. At the end of the second round, I asked him, 'Torito, is he hurting you?' He says to me, 'He (Cuevas) may be world champion, but he ain't shit to me.' And he went out and kicked his butt the next round."

San Antonio fight promoter Tony Padilla, who has had his differences with the Ayalas, was there the afternoon Cuevas and young Tony went at it. He remembers Lupe Sanchez, Pipino's manager, saying to Cuevas afterward, "Aren't you ashamed a fourteen-year-old boy doing that to you?"

"And Pipino," Padilla said, "was muttering, *'Increíble, increíble*—which is 'incredible' in English."

"As a professional, I had a fear of failing. It was scary. Everybody telling you you can't lose. Nights...I'd be up thinking about it. After a while you want to get away from the pressure. I'd pretend everything was hunky dory. 'You OK?' I'm OK.' Lies. Saying I'm OK when I really wasn't. There was nothin' to take away the pressure. The people around me saw something was bothering me. They saw it before the Hererra fight. During training camp I was miserable. Not happy. Not content. But to everybody, I'd say: 'I'm okay.' Lies so as not to hurt other people's feelings."

Though Torito went on to win two Junior Olympic titles and later a National Golden Gloves title, he did not emerge from his combatant's life without psychological scars. Ayala's was a lost boyhood.

At age twelve, he had fixed up the Chevelle Malibu that Mike and Sammy in turn had wrecked and was soon driving it to school and all over San Antonio, and hanging out with older hot rodders. By thirteen, Ayala was drinking, smoking pot and having relations with women of consenting age. In this fast life, he was emulating his older brothers, who, Epps recalled, used to tease him when he was younger about being sexually underdeveloped: "They'd say how small it was. And: 'What you gonna do when you get a girl friend?'"

Removed from the mean streets of San Antonio, or its gyms, Ayala was less sure of himself. "I always wanted people to like me," he said, "but I lacked self-confidence in the way I carried myself, or in the way I spoke." Even conversing with his mother, Pauline, or later with his common-law wife, Lisa, he often cut short his thoughts, as if what he had to say was not worth pursuing.

Only through boxing could he express himself and keep the approval of Big Tony. In the Ayala household, the father was boss, a strong figure whose imminent arrival would set his wife and sons scrambling to tidy up, and whose word had the force of law. His sons knew that the father's ever-present need for manly action existed hard by his deeply-felt familial concern. To this day, Big Tony is a man who hugs and kisses his sons in public and shows no uneasiness in relating how Paulie, the youngest, slept in the same bed with father and mother until he was fourteen. Paulie's arrival was the blessing that followed the untimely loss of another Ayala son, who died only twenty-seven days after his birth.

The father's authority extended beyond boxing, into his sons' lives, and in time was resented by Mike, leading to a rift between father and oldest son. (In June 1979, Mike Ayala fought for the featherweight title against champion Danny Lopez and was knocked out in the 15th round in what *Ring Magazine* rated as "the most exciting fight of the year." Mike is currently also on ten-year's probation for an incident in San Antonio in which he shot a man.)

When Mike switched managers, leaving his father for Dennis Rappaport, co-manager of heavyweight Gerry Cooney, it was viewed by the old man as a betrayal, and the ensuing events—a reconciliation and another falling out—are spoken of in charged language, with Ayala Sr., swearing he'd "sell my soul to the devil" before commencing a civilized dialogue with his ingrate son.

For his part, Mike—now fighting out of New York after a year's layoff for a 'liver disorder'—insists that he only needed some slack in the relationship. His father's love, well-meaning though it was, left him no room for Mike. Says Rappaport: "The only thing this kid wants is a pat on the back from his father."

By contrast, Torito always marched in step with his father. His youthful errors, unlike Mike's, were never viewed as being directed against Big Tony. Only weeks before his last arrest, he added this postscript during his final civilian interview: "Make sure to put in, 'I love you, dad,' in your story," and then watched as the words were scribbled across a notebook page, nodding with a smile as he read them before he got up to go.

Dutiful son—and world-caliber fighter—he never did manage to flesh out the rest of Tony Ayala, and occupy that part of the world beyond the ring, where thought and feeling proceed from more complex perspectives. It was that chance to contact emotions beyond the warrior's code that Big Tony had instilled that prompted Mike Ayala to stay with Rappaport. Under Rappaport, Mike was able to vent fears, tears, anguish and frustrations that in San Antonio he was expected to keep to himself. Living in New York, he would write poetry to deal with feelings that back home had been so hard to manage—hard enough to drive him to heroin.

...Hey, Crazy Sam. Pass me a beer.
To ram down this fear
I've got inside of me!
They're planning their escape of these badlands
Where the password is survival
Some will make it while others will fall to their own secret rival...

By contrast, Tony never surmounted the limits of the macho response to life. One afternoon in a West Paterson, New Jersey gym, he bumbled through a training session and became so annoyed with himself that he finally stood in the ring with his hands at his sides and let his sparring partner punch him at will. Co-manager Lou Duva was startled enough to phone Big Tony, who said, "Oh yeah, he does that all the time."

"There was," says Duva's daughter-in-law, Kathy, who is a boxing publicist, "a sense of —'If someone else won't punish me, then I will.'"

"...'cause in my life I was always pushed with the boxing. No questions asked. Don't get me wrong. I'm not pointing a finger. Like, as far as my dad...nobody could ever take the place of my dad. It should have come out of myself to change things. I was the one hurting. I should have spoken up. Because, you know, a lotta times I hated boxing."

Tony Ayala is still serving his sentence. In a later interview, he revealed he had been sexually assaulted as a youngster by someone close to his family. Those experiences, he said, set up terrible conflicts within.

EVANDER HOLYFIELD AND RICKEY WOMACK
Two Paths That Crossed in the Ring (1987)

It was 1983 and, in the dressing room before they fought each other for the first time, Rickey Womack made an impression on Evander Holyfield.

"We both had our gloves on, and were warming up," Holyfield recalled, "and Womack walked all the way across the room and casually stomped on my toe, the big toe. Then he made a face at me. Like, 'So what?' I was so mad, there were tears in my eyes. I remember there was a little kid in the dressing room, and he turned to his father and said, 'Look, daddy, he got that guy crying.'"

That night, an angry Holyfield would beat Womack in the ring. But over the next year—as both men zeroed in on a berth on the 1984 United States Olympic team—Holyfield, a light heavyweight from Atlanta, would not always get the best of Womack.

Womack, who was from Detroit, beat him later in 1983 and, more important, defeated him in June of the next year at the Olympic trials in Fort Worth. By then, Womack—ranked number one in the world among amateur light heavyweights—needed to beat Holyfield only once more to make the team.

But on successive days in the box-offs in July, Holyfield defeated Womack twice and became the United States representative in the 178-pound class. In each fight, four of the five judges awarded Holyfield the decision.

In defeat, Womack, who believed he had been victimized by the judges, retreated to Detroit and sulked. He declined to go to Los Angeles as an alternate and even refused to watch the Olympics on television.

Holyfield got the bronze medal after a controversial disqualification, and turned pro with a four-year, $2.5 million promotional

53

contract. As for Womack, he remained a valuable property, signing a promotional deal with the Kronk boxing team in Detroit that guaranteed him $150,000 over two years.

With advantages like these that most new pros never know, Holyfield and Womack took their first steps in a business where finding success is often a game of roulette. Over time, as they pursued boxing glory, the two men would take widely divergent courses—one to a world title, the other to crime.

But back in the autumn of 1984, Holyfield and Womack must have thought their paths would cross again, somewhere, sometime, as professionals.

It seemed a good bet at the time.

On a brisk day last autumn, inmate B-155461 stepped out of cell 21 and, on his way to meet a reporter, walked down a long narrow corridor at the Reception and Guidance Center of the State Prison of Southern Michigan in Jackson.

Rickey Womack wore dark blue institutional trousers and shirt, a black belt and a pair of Fila athletic shoes. His hair was in symmetrical braided rows. The center, a holding facility for convicted criminals, on this morning held 548 such inmates who were being processed before they would be sent to more permanent quarters.

Womack had arrived in Jackson, following plea bargaining, by being sentenced to concurrent terms of twelve and twenty-five years for armed robberies he had committed in Redford Township, Michigan, near Detroit, on December 30, 1985, and January 9, 1986. He drew an additional two-year term for possession of a firearm while committing those felonies.

In both crimes, Womack had used a nine-millimeter pistol. He had beaten a female clerk with it during the first robbery after she gave him the money and videotaped films he had demanded; during the other robbery, he shot and wounded a man who had walked in while it was in progress. In each robbery, a charge of assault with intent to murder was dropped as part of the plea bargaining. According to the holding center's warden, Dr. John Prelesnik, the earliest Womack could be considered for parole, with maximum good-behavior credits, would be eleven years after he began the sentence.

At the time he broke the law, Womack was undefeated as a professional boxer, having won all nine of his matches. He lived rent-free in Detroit in a condominium that Emanuel Steward, his manager and trainer at Kronk, had provided since his amateur days. The place came with a twenty-six-inch color television, video-cassette recorder, microwave oven, dishwasher and washer-dryer. Steward had also given him a gold Renault Alliance. After it was wrecked, the manager replaced it with a beige Volvo.

Money was no problem for Womack: Steward and his wife, Marie, were close to him and would lend him spending cash practically on request. And there was still the contract that guaranteed Womack $100,000 for 1986.

To risk those material comforts—and the likely chance of eventually fighting for a world title—for the few hundred dollars and the cache of videotapes he got in the robberies resisted a rational explanation.

Even to Womack, seated in a prison office, it did not add up. "You know," he said, "I'm still wondering why it happened. Because, you see, it didn't have to happen. It wasn't supposed to happen. And if I could change time, it'd never have happened."

Late last October, Womack was sent to Ionia (Michigan) Reformatory, an adult prison. Several days later, Holyfield, in a black business suit and striped tie, strode into his neat, woodpaneled office at Ken Sanders Buick in Morrow, Georgia.

On the wall of the office were photos of Holyfield posing with celebrities, and the usual civic proclamations that celebrate a boxing champion. A sign said: "Friendship is a matter of time... the time that it takes to be kind."

Although he did not win a gold medal, Holyfield, now twenty-four, progressed more quickly than any of the Olympic class of '84. By early 1986, after overcoming stamina problems, he had established himself as a world-ranked contender. In the process he developed a style that reminded his trainer, George Benton, of another great boxer-puncher, Ezzard Charles. Last July, he won the

World Boxing Association junior-heavyweight championship—in only his twelfth pro fight—when he beat Dwight Muhammad Qawi, the champion, in a fiercely contested match.

As important as his ability was the dedication that Holyfield brought to his profession, and the maturity he acquired out of the ring. For instance, after the fighter went on an early spending binge as a pro, learning about expanding credit lines, he heeded the advice of his manager, Sanders, to be more circumspect with his money. "I was buying stuff I didn't need," Holyfield said, "just because I had a credit card. Ken sat me down and explained so I'd understand. He spoke to me nicely and respectful and in a manly way. Told me, 'You're in a high-risk business.' You don't know these things unless someone sits and talks to you. I'm grateful he did."

The way Rickey Renardo Womack begins to tell it, he and his twin brother, Mickey, were the only children of Alfred and Marlene Womack.

But later during an interview a couple of sisters materialize in his account, and Womack tries to assure a listener there were only four children in the Womack family.

It doesn't take long to see that the facts of Womack's early life are troubling enough to him to make evasion an autobiographical technique.

The facts are not pretty. As Mrs. Womack attests, there were nine children, pawns in a pattern of domestic violence. When the twins were very young—seven years old, according to documents in Womack's prison file—the mother was shot by her husband in Jackson, Tennessee.

She survived the shooting, and soon after took the children with her to Detroit. But Alfred Womack followed, bringing with him more violence and familial complications. "My mother and father could not get along," Mickey said. "He was always jumping on her. The state came out and put us in foster homes. Nine of us."

By 1970, the "extremely erratic" home life that social workers described had resulted in the Womack children's being declared wards of the court. From age seven to fourteen, Mickey said, he and his twin were in and out of boys homes. "They'd be switching us around," he said. "Back and forth, back and forth."

Such events are brushed over by Rickey. Even with Steward, who became a kind of father figure to the fighter (Alfred Womack was shot dead in a robbery while Rickey was a teenager), Womack was not inclined to talk about his early years. "As I pieced it together," Steward said of Rickey Womack, "he was stealing to survive. He'd sleep in cars and in empty, abandoned houses."

Boxing is a poor man's sport; its history is filled with athletes who transcended their terrible origins. In many cases, the individual gains self-awareness and he changes, learning to redirect his anger.

Holyfield, for instance, was one of eight children in a single-parent family that was forced to move to government housing when the mother, Annie, was unable to work after suffering a heart attack. Holyfield took a job at an Atlanta airport from 6 A.M. to 2 P.M., fueling planes. It was work he remembers approaching with a slacker's instincts. "I was immature for my age," he said. "The manager there stayed on me."

The attitude that Womack had at age seventeen was characterized as "angry and immature" by prison psychiatrists who examined him the first time Womack was delivered to the Michigan penal system, for an armed robbery he committed in 1978. He served almost three years in various institutions, and the reports on him as an inmate showed him to be insolent before authority and abusive with other prisoners.

Yet on being paroled, he showed a talent for boxing that quickly won him recognition—and the attention of Steward, to whom he seemed "quiet and real nice."

Womack could be charming when he wanted. But as he rose in international competition, there were signs that his worst instincts—the anger and immaturity found in psychiatric evaluations—had not been altered much by success.

He was, as Holyfield remembered him, a young man who seemed in need of constant attention, going to extremes to get it. According to Holyfield, Womack might slap a smaller teammate on a dare, snatch food off another fighter's plate or ignore team protocol while challenging coaches to straighten him out.

According to Steward and Farris Purify, then the amateur boxing coordinator for the Kronk team, teammates' possessions would disappear on trips to boxing venues. Inquiries on the items would end with Womack's turning up at either man's door with his head bowed and a contrite expression on his face as he handed over the stolen goods.

While in Tokyo, Womack and two other amateurs, Mark Breland and Steve McCrory, were in a store when a merchant showed them a wristwatch. Womack picked up the watch off the counter and walked out of the store with it, leading to Breland's and McCrory's being detained by police until, as Steward recalled, the manager-trainer could straighten out the matter.

In the gym, Womack's cassette player invariably was the loudest, and he would take it as an affront when asked to lower the volume. He wanted what he wanted when he wanted it. He complained when a fight of his in the Soviet Union was not scheduled to be televised back to the United States. "You're seeing a ghost," he told amateur boxing officials, "if you think I'm hanging around." When he did not get his way, he bolted the Soviet tour, returning to Detroit.

"If you could do something for Womack, he tolerated you," Purify said. "But he was a totally rude person."

In 1983, Womack began dating Michelle Lawdins, the fifteen-year-old daughter of a Detroit clergyman. Steward said that with Womack's attachment to Lawdins, whom he would marry two years later, came a withdrawal from the Kronk team.

"He was losing contact with everybody," Steward said. "It was just him and her and the stereo music in his ear. I'd tell him, 'Take that damn music out of your ear when I'm talking to you." He'd always be polite when I spoke to him, and give a childish smile."

Womack became a big spender as a pro, impulsively buying leather jackets, lizard-skin shoes and $200 sweat suits that he would discard after a few wearings or pass on to Mickey. But as much as he spent on himself, he spent more on his family and particularly on Lawdins.

He could be especially generous to children, with whom he apparently identified. "There was a gas station near our place," Lawdins said, "and kids would hang out there and ask for dimes. Once, on a cold day, he gave a little girl $5 and told her to go home and get out of the snow. Her face lit up. Another time, a little boy was selling mirrors. He bought all six of them for $12. He loved seeing kids doing something honestly."

By 1985, when the money had run low, Womack would become depressed, sometimes not bothering to go to the gym to train. By then, another phenomenon was occurring that disturbed Stewart. Womack, according to Steward, had taken to watching violent films, like "Scarface" and "The Terminator," again and again on his video-cassette recorder, often replaying the bloodiest scenes and laughing at them as if they were cartoons.

"He was programming himself with his own movies," Steward said.

In November 1985, a fight of Womack's was canceled. After Christmas he began brooding again over his diminishing funds. On December 30, he told his wife he was taking the Volvo to the gas station. She watched from the window of their apartment and wondered when he turned in the direction opposite that of the gas station.

In December, Womack was separated from the rest of the Ionia prison population for twelve days for assaulting another inmate. Reports of Womack's trouble came as no great surprise to one who had visited him almost two months before, back at the holding center in Jackson, Michigan. Then, Womack seemed unable to face the reality of doing time. He conjured up first a millionaire and then a deity who would miraculously deliver him from his sentence, so he could once again pursue a boxing career. Later on still, seeing a pair of pigeons settle on a ledge outside the barred windows of the office, Womack tried to angle his hand round a bar to touch the birds. But they were beyond reach.

As he stood staring at them, he said: "I bet it's nice out there. Your own freedom. Nobody telling you when to go bed, what to eat. I bet it's beautiful."

Rickey Womack continues to serve time in Michigan.

JAMES SCOTT (1980)

The state prison at Rahway, New Jersey is constructed like a cartoon sun, its four wings of mustard brick radiating from a round copper-domed building. Each wing houses inmates—1,150 men in all. In Number One Wing, the cells are stacked four tiers high along a steep, narrow passage, and are connected by a white metal stairwell. On the topmost tier, one of the cells belongs to inmate #57735, James O. Scott.

On this gray drizzly fall morning, the six-foot-one, 175-pound Scott awakens as the World Boxing Association's second-ranked light-heavyweight boxer, a rating that qualifies him as one of the fight game's most remarkable stories. Only a year earlier, he was unranked and virtually unheard of in sports circles. But with a relentless bore-in style and a shave-headed Muscle Beach physique, Scott fought his way through an unprecedented series of bouts behind the walls of Rahway that lifted him from anonymity. His celebrity, though, does not guarantee that Scott will ever fight for the championship crown he covets. Between the jailhouse boxer and his shot at the title lie a tangle of institutional red tape and the machinations of fight promoters scuffling to protect their turf.

Still, Scott has taken a sweet leap forward from earlier hard times at Rahway. In a previous stint there—he is a three-time loser at armed robbery—he was assigned to the prison's laundry. His life as a laundry man ended when he feigned a fainting spell and was thrown into the hole, penal jargon for isolation.

From the hole to a standard Rahway cell is an improvement only by the skewed standards of penal life. To an outsider, a first glimpse at the roughly five-foot-wide, nine-foot deep space that Scott occupies is numbing. Expectations based on TV and movies do not prepare the uninitiated for the gnome's slot that a cell is.

Scott is no stranger to such confined spaces. As a teenaged incorrigible from Newark and later an adult repeat offender, he has spent the better part of his thirty-two years in New Jersey's reformatories and prisons. He has a three-inch scar on his chest, suffered while trying to ward off a makeshift weapon—a razor blade inserted in a matchbook—in one of several youth institutions where he spent time. Other, less visible scars are part of the con's makeup. Scott, who has an assertive and sometimes blustery manner, can turn to sullen retreat when his version of things is poked at too persistently.

On this September day, though, James O. Scott is thinking like a civilian. Hours from now, in a courtroom in downtown Newark, a hearing is to be held to determine whether the fighter can be released on bail while his case is on appeal. The possibility of freedom has Scott thinking ahead, plotting which possessions to take with him and which to have forwarded. There are books, clothes, and letters sent from all over the world, including the one from an inmate at another institution challenging him ("Chump, can you thump?") and another from a Hawaiian wondering whether he wants to go in on a partnership selling women's pubic hairs to inmates.

Scott is anticipating the phone call from Newark that will send him out into the world again. He is mulling over what to do on his first night out. There are dinner invitations from a television producer and a woman who is doing a book based on his life story. Probably, though, he will go to Trenton to be with his common-law wife and her three children. A weekend to rest, then back to training. Win the W.B.A. title, then the W.B.C., beat Larry Holmes' butt for the heavyweight crown and retire. Scott has it all worked out. "They say the word," he declares, "and I'm gone."

Somehow, though, running through Scott's mind, there must be a trace of *déjà vu* in all this.

On January 8, 1974, James Scott was paroled from Rahway to a group of Miami Beach businessmen who managed prize fighters in an enterprise called The Mendoza Group. The Mendoza Group was headed by a graphic designer and former boxer named Murray

Gaby. Scott had never fought as a professional when he turned up at the 5th Street Gym in Miami Beach for his first workout.

"It was right out of Warner Brothers," says Dr. Ferdie Pacheco, who was Muhammad Ali's physician and is a friend and corner man of Scott's. "Scotty had no money. He was in basketball shoes and cut-off denims. From odds and ends, we put him together. Willie Pastrano's protective cup. Head gear from another guy. And then James got into the ring with the resident heavyweight, a well-regarded fighter named Oliver Wright."

"When Scott started throwing punches," says manager Gaby, "there was dead silence in the gym. Other fighters stopped and watched. He went two rounds, had the guy out on his feet. Everybody gave him an ovation. Very dramatic."

It got better. In his pro debut two weeks later, Scott was matched against 210-pound John L. Johnson at the Miami Beach Convention Center. Out of fear that light heavyweights didn't have sufficient box office appeal, Scott had sold himself to Gaby as a heavyweight whose 175-pound frame was susceptible to fattening once he left behind prison life.

Johnson knocked Scott down in the first round, but James fought back. "He got off the canvas," says sportswriter Jack Wilkinson, then working for the Miami News, "and beat the stuffing out of Johnson. Really pounded him. The people went nuts. Scott won in a fourth round knockout. But that wasn't the end of it. I remember they brought James back out to the ring. I don't know if it was just boxing bullshit. But his father was there and they said it was the first time Scott has seen him in twelve years. Scott was in old black boxing shoes and black trunks. His people got word the crowd was still going crazy for him, they wanted him back out for a curtain call. His first fight and the ring announcer's saying 'Ladies and gentlemen, let's bring back out James Scott.'"

Over the next five months, Scott fought regularly in Miami Beach, winning his first seven bouts, and dispatching five of those opponents by knockout. From his fourth match on, he was a main event fighter. In white trunks and white shoes now, calling himself Great Scott, he was a real crowd pleaser. "Everybody," says Gaby, "knew his story—about coming out of Rahway to box—and they had tremendous empathy for him."

Out of the ring, though, Scott was still adjusting to his new life. "Different things," says Scott. "Like in prison, you get one spoon that you keep with you in your cell and you take it to and from meals. Lots of times in Miami Beach, I'd automatically pick up a spoon in a restaurant and put it in my pocket. And then I'd see the look on the waitress' face. In her mind—'They're all the same, all thieves.'"

Scott did not lose the con's reflex defenses easily. "He gave the impression of being surly, truculent, aggressive," says Pacheco. "People were mildly scared. Scotty was on guard all the time because he didn't know how to relate to the people on The Beach, who were mostly whites. The boxing crowd liked him because of his bang-bang style. But when they'd try to talk to him he had the kind of candor that catches a lot of guys by surprise...people who are used to filling the silence with bullshit. Fans of his would say, 'Jesus, the guy's mean. Like Sonny Liston or Hurricane Carter.'"

Though off to a good start, Scott was twenty-six-years-old and impatient. He wanted to accelerate his progress in the boxing world and was wary of being waylaid. "He was concerned and paranoid," says Gaby, "about being cheated, about getting a raw deal. He was making, oh, $1,300 or so for his sixth, seventh fight, which, for Miami Beach, was terrific. But he was convinced of being cheated. There were tirades. Later he'd calm down."

Scott groused about other things as well. There were, he'd say, never enough sparring partners, a shortage caused by his inability to lighten up in workouts. Few people were willing to put on the gloves with him because, as Pacheco puts it, "James was tough. He looked like he'd eat the ring ropes."

In thirteen months as a pro he was 11-0-1. He was a Miami Beach media favorite, often going out of his way to promote Great Scott in the press and on radio and TV. With Gaby passing up the usual one-third manager's cut of the purses, Scott had earned roughly $15,000 from his fights. He had his own apartment, a blue four-door Chevrolet, a girlfriend. It was natural, though, for him to celebrate his career in a way he could not behind the walls at

Rahway. So the money went—and Scott persisted in believing things were moving too slowly.

Against the advice of Gaby and Pacheco, he'd begun journeying up to New Jersey. Scott thought that on his home grounds he might be able to draw the kinds of crowds that would result in big paydays. He stayed in Jersey, where he had plans for hyping Great Scott into a title bout against John Conteh, a match that he claimed was on the verge of being made. Not quite, says Gaby: "I was attempting to get an over-the-weight match with Conteh. Scott, as usual, was doing things to promote himself. So he'd gone to Newark to put together a press conference about a Conteh-Scott fight.

"He was trying to create news, what Archie Moore did to get a fight with Rocky Marciano. James Scott had an incredible talent for self-promotion, which I didn't mind at all."

On May 8, Scott heard that police in Newark wanted to talk to him—something about his car. He drove up from Trenton and presented himself at Newark police headquarters. He was without an attorney. "I thought," he said, "that I was a celebrity and there'd be no problem. I hadn't did anything wrong. What I need a lawyer for? I figured to take my car down there. Answer some questions and come on back home."

The Essex County prosecutor's version goes like this:

Toward midnight on May 7, 1975, Everitt Russ was standing out front of a bar on Howard Street in Newark with a friend when he was approached by James O. Scott. Russ climbed into a blue four-door sedan with Scott and others. The car proceeded to the Lincoln projects in Newark, where Russ led them to the apartment of Leo Skinner. The way Russ told it, Skinner would be able to buy drugs for them in a building next door.

In that adjoining building, the men held the elevator for Yvonne Barrett, who lived up on the tenth floor with her sister Antoinette. The Barrett apartment, as it happened, was where the group was headed. Reluctant to take so many people there, Leo Skinner stopped the elevator on the eighth floor. At that point, one of Scott's companions, William Spinks, pulled out a pistol and ordered the project residents, Skinner and Barrett, out. Scott exited too. Everitt Russ rode to the lobby and waited in the sedan with the other man in Scott's party. Back on the eighth floor, Spinks handed the weapon to Scott, who pistol-whipped Skinner and ordered him to disrobe. Later, Spinks, holding the gun on Yvonne Barrett, robbed her sister's tenth floor apartment of $283 and glassine bags with white powder in them. At about 1:30 that morning, the body of Everitt Russ was pushed from a blue four-door sedan, dead from gunshot wounds.

A passing motorist wrote down the license plate number. The car was traced to Scott.

Scott's story is that he lent his car to Spinks and that he himself had nothing to do with the crimes. He contends that Newark police coerced others into identifying him and that Spinks's accomplice was actually a Newark character known as "Black Jack," who bore a striking resemblance to James Scott.

Spinks himself was never able to settle the confusion surrounding the differing accounts. Before he could be apprehended, he was killed in another stick-up in June 1975.

In the July issue of *The Ring* magazine, James Scott is listed as the sixth-ranked American light heavyweight. By that time he was charged with armed robbery and murder. The trial began in November.

Questioned in court by the Essex County prosecutor, Skinner conceded that Black Jack and Scott, in his phrase, "could go for brothers"—they looked that much alike. But Skinner claimed there were differences, that Black Jack was smaller, his hair style slightly different. Then:

Q: Did Black Jack beat you up on the night of May 8, 1975?

A: (Skinner): No sir.

Q: Did Black Jack stick a gun in your mouth on May 8, 1975?

A: No sir.

Q: Did Black Jack make you strip off all your clothes on May 8, 1975?

A: No sir.

Q: Did Black Jack threaten to throw you off the roof on May 8, 1975?

A: No sir.

Q: Who did all those things to you on May 8, 1975?

A: Scott.

A jury was unable to reach a verdict on the murder charge, but found Scott guilty of armed robbery. Judge Ralph L. Fusco sentenced him as a multiple offender to a thirty to forty-year prison term.

On March 22, 1976, Scott was returned to the New Jersey penal system—and Trenton State Prison. A day later, he was sent to the Vroom Building on the grounds of Trenton State Psychiatric Hospital, where extreme cases and inmates in protective custody are kept. At the time, there had been bloody violence between Muslim factions at Trenton State Prison. So Scott, like other Muslims, was placed in the Vroom for his own security.

On May 27, 1977, inmate #57735 was transferred to Rahway and was assigned to run the new boxing association there. The warden at Rahway was Robert S. Hatrak, a former high school and college basketball coach who was amenable to new ideas, unorthodox programs. Some Rahway guards considered him too eager to placate the inmates. But under Hatrak the "Scared Straight" program—confrontation sessions between inmates and hard-core juvenile offenders—went ahead. And under Hatrak, so did Scott. Hatrak told him that if he could persuade a promoter to get involved with the boxing program at Rahway, the warden would do what he could to see that his boxing career was resurrected.

Scott phoned boxing's two major promoters, Bob Arum and Don King, who turned him down flat. "They told me," says Scott, "'You're not going anywhere.' Only one promoter came. A guy like me. A guy trying to get ahead. And that was Murad."

Murad R. Muhammad, a thirty-year-old Newark man, had gone from operating several fast-food restaurants to the world of prize fights, first as part of the Ali entourage and then into promotions. Muhammad served his apprenticeship working for King and Arum, and then set out on his own. After talking to Scott, he agreed to promote bouts at Rahway.

At the time, Scott was training in the prison's gym, which had no boxing ring. Gloves were sent in from the street. "But I worked and worked," says Scott. "Ran an hour every morning in the prison yard. Did push-ups and sit-ups by the thousands. And I sparred and got myself ready."

The first fight, on May 24, 1978, was against Diego Roberson. Scott knocked Roberson out in the second round. In September, Fred Brown went four rounds. But these victories were virtually unnoticed. The bout that brought him national recognition matched Scott against the W.B.A.'s number-one-ranked light heavyweight, Eddie (The Flame) Gregory.

For the rights to show Gregory vs. Scott on a delayed telecast, Home Box Office put up $25,000. Gregory's share was $15,000, Scott's $2,500—an improvement on what he'd received for beating up Roberson (a steak dinner) and Brown ($600). But the October 12 bout was more than a payday for Scott. It was rapid transit to the big time. At Rahway, the odds against his beating Gregory were four to one, with cartons of cigarettes as currency. The boxing crowd on the streets considered those odds overly optimistic. No way, they said, James Scott would douse The Flame.

Pacheco, Gaby and trainer came up from Florida on the day of the fight. The twelve-round bout was supposed to be a tune-up for Gregory, but it quickly became apparent that it was more than that for Scott. "When the opening bell sounded," says Pacheco, "Scott roared. Literally roared. It startled Gregory. He looked at him, like—oh, shit. After that, James was relentless. I'd never seen him like that. Those three years away from boxing—all that held-back emotion. He let it ride that night." Working in close to Gregory, Scott pummeled him to the body, then to the head. In a style reminiscent of Smokin' Joe Frazier's fearless aggression—a style Scott has adopted as his own—he did not let Gregory back away, did not give him breathing room. Scott was always on him, throwing punches, forcing the number one-ranked fighter to think and react defensively. With inmates shouting, "Kill the cocksucker," Scott pounded out a unanimous decision. Great Scott was back.

A technical knockout over veteran contender Richie Kates on March 19, 1979, proved that the victory over Gregory was no fluke.

By now, though, Scott realized that if ever he were to fight for the title, the bout would have to take place outside prison walls. No champion—and few legitimate contenders—would come to Rahway. But his dream of a shot at the title was tied to another sort of infighting, which would pit him against the bureaucracy of the penal system and the sharkish world of boxing promoters. James Scott would find that confrontation every bit as tough as going the distance with a top contender.

Scott's parole date was 1989. Though an inmate can earn time off for good behavior, maximum commutation time for Scott narrowed his release date to only 1982, too distant for a man who turned thirty-two last October and is bent on a title shot. That left "full minimum."

Full minimum is the most liberal of prison classifications. It allows an inmate to take part in work and study programs *outside* the institution's walls. Given full minimum status, Scott would have been able to box at major sites—the Meadowlands, Atlantic City—in the state of New Jersey. Scott, however, was a maximum security prisoner, under constant supervision and not allowed beyond the walls. By Department of Corrections standards he did not become eligible for full minimum until June 1980. Even at that point, full minimum would not be automatic. The fighter would have to appear before Rahway's eight-man classification committee, which considers inmates on a case-by-case basis, and more often than not rules against full minimum.

There *were* provisions however, for jumping the June 1980 date—an "exceptional cases" clause that Warden Hatrak alluded to in interviews with the press. The feeling Scott had was that Hatrak would find a way. In April 1979, though, Hatrak was dismissed as superintendent of Rahway and reassigned to a lower-paying administrative job in the Department of Corrections.

With Hatrak gone, Scott had lost an ally. "Mr. Hatrak," he says, "gave me one-hundred-percent support. Like my special steak-and-eggs diet [for which Scott pays the prison $100 extra a month]. For a warden to do that was out of the ordinary. He set up an open-door policy for the press. He deviated from the course."

Hatrak was replaced by Sidney Hicks, who became Acting Superintendent at Rahway. He was a former prison guard who had worked his way up through the ranks. Scott had crossed paths with Hicks before. In his first adult penal facility, Trenton State Prison, Scott was charged with hitting another inmate with a pipe, and put in isolation. The prison guard who brought the charge was Sidney Hicks. As an administrator, Hicks had a reputation as a man who "went by the books"—as opposed to Hatrak's more flexible approach.

As a fighter, Scott is a ward of the state, with no manager of record, though he refers to a long-time confidante and fellow Muslim inmate, Al Dickens, as his manager and spiritual advisor. But it is the Department of Corrections—and not Dickens—who approves Scott's fight contracts. His purses go into a non-interest bearing inmate account and may be drawn on only for reasons sanctioned in the "regs"—work-related expenses, canteen purchases and the like.

A week after he was refused permission to send some of the proceeds of his bouts to his common-law wife, Scott retained attorney G. Richard Malgran of Woodbridge, New Jersey. Malgran immediately shot off a letter to Department of Corrections Commissioner William H. Fauver, asking that Scott, as a special case, be given full minimum. Fauver noted that the fighter was ineligible and declined, writing: "Obviously, such preferential treatment for Mr. Scott would have serious repercussions with our inmate populations who are already questioning some of Mr. Scott's preferential treatment."

Scott himself wrote to Fauver the next day, proclaiming, "I have reached a crucial point in my career as a fighter, destined to win the title." He asked the commissioner to allow him to create the boxing programs in the state's juvenile facilities—an alternate route to full minimum. Fauver did not respond.

Scotteeeeeeeee!
The window in the office of the Rahway Boxing Association flies up. It is early afternoon of the gray drizzly day on which Scott awaits word on making bail. Downstairs, an inmate is hollering up—Scotteeee, any news?

No news.

Scott sits at a desk in a wide-collared brown shirt and matching trousers. The office is a small, white-panelled room with photos of people like Archie Moore, Howard Cosell, Joe Frazier, Jersey Joe Walcott on the wall. There is a collage of news headlines and pictures of Scott. A sign: Dependability always leads up.

Another voice sounds out from one floor below. It is that of Scott's younger brother, Malcolm, who is serving a life sentence at Rahway for murder. (James says there are ten brothers and sisters in the Scott family.) Malcolm wants to know whether the visitor needs photos for his story? James confides that Malcolm acquired the photos when another magazine did a story on Great Scott, and from time to time he tries to sell them as if they were his own.

The drawers of the desk in the boxing office are crammed with copies of letters, memos, news stories on Scott. Most fighters rely on the publicists of various promoters to get them space in the paper. Scott does his own PR. The promotional instinct is part of Scott's assertive, cocksure manner. He is a man full up with opinions and visions, many—but not all—of them revolving around James O. Scott. On this fall afternoon, as he awaits word from the Essex County courthouse, he does a riff that mixes conservative and liberal precepts in Great Scott proportions.

"There are no more Pattons," he begins. "No more Teddy Roosevelts. Take a doctor today. He's somebody who looks like a hippie and smokes grass. His girl friend does his homework. An artist is a guy who rides his bicycle over the canvas. Not like the Old Masters. People who do something worthwhile, who pay their dues, are not appreciated. The same with boxing. They locked me up. I came to prison, I just about punched my way out of prison. But they got me going every which way. This administration says I'm not an exceptional individual and the only way they can grant me full minimum is if I was an exceptional case. If *I'm* not an exceptional case, I don't know who is. If a guy can pick himself up in a place like this—the mud of civilization—if a guy is able to rise above that, then that should be what they're trying to encourage every inmate to do."

At 3:40, the phone call comes.

Scott gets up from the desk and prowls the room with the receiver to his ear. There is a patch of perspiration on the right front of his shirt. "Yeah, yeah," he says. His hand is in his pocket. He continues pacing. Finally, he sits, says, "They denied bail."

The wire service story that appears the next day indicates that Malgran was "caught off guard" by black marks on Scott's recent record at Rahway—use of marijuana and morphine in December 1977. Before the bail hearing, Malgran had asked Scott whether his record showed any indiscretions during his current Rahway term. While James alluded to charges brought, he glossed over them and indicated that no case was made. The record showed otherwise.

In the Rahway Boxing Association office, the calls start coming. Scott is cool and reassuring to his supporters. With news people phoning in, he glances at notes made earlier in the day in the event the decision went against him. "If James Scott can rehabilitate himself," he says, "despite all odds, then institutions and agencies should be supportive. And if they're not, then we have a case against them. If you kill all hope, then rehabilitation is a myth. Don't worry, this is not over yet. This is only round one."

Some hard rounds follow.

On September 28, Murad Muhammad is in Miami Beach for the final day of a W.B.A. convention. Earlier in the week, the organization stripped lightheavyweight champion Victor Galindez of his title for failing to meet a commitment to defend it against Marvin Johnson.

Holding a contract for a December 1, 1979 bout between Yaqui Lopez and Scott, the number-one and number-two ranked contenders, Muhammad formally asks that the bout be elevated to championship status. Discussion ensues over Scott's odd status as a jailhouse fighter. At the end, the W.B.A. votes to strip Scott of his ranking. Poof: like that, he is a non-being in the eyes of the W.B.A.

These are not good times for James O. Scott. Whichever way he turns, it seems, he's in a jam. The appellate court denies his appeal for bail. Taking note of Scott's boxing income, the Newark Public Defender's office, which had represented Scott in his 1975 trial, makes him promise to pay $4,000 for transcripts of his trial record before turning copies of it over to Malgran, who needs them to prepare Scott's appeal.

Amid all the troubles, though, Malgran is still attempting to win Scott's release on bail and overturn his conviction. Outside the courts, he is working up a plan to bypass the Department of Corrections and Murad Muhammad by securing a letter of particulars from Arum, which would spell out the specifics of a title bout and commit a percentage of Scott's purse to the New Jersey Crime Victims Fund. He would take that letter to New Jersey Governor Brendan Byrne and ask him to use his authority to confer full minimum on Scott. As for Muhammad, says Malgran: "I'd leave the burden on him to sue."

But it is a plan fraught with "ifs." In conjunction with the series of recent setbacks, it makes the message inscribed on a caricature of the fighter in Malgran's office more pertinent than ever. Just above Great Scott's signature are these words: Get Me Out!

James Scott never fought for a world title.
He is still incarcerated in New Jersey.

Win a world title: that's the objective of every boxing beginner. When lightning strikes, it makes the struggle upward seem worth it, as James (Bonecrusher) Smith—kayoed in his first pro fight— can attest.

BONECRUSHER SMITH (1990)

The life of James Smith, of Lillington, North Carolina, has had the variegated richness that used to be virtually mandatory for the biographical blurb describing any red-blooded novelist.

You know the kind.

"This is Mr. Doe's third book. Before turning to prose, he was a stevedore, a lifeguard, an orderly in a psychiatric institution and a librarian."

James Smith, age 33, a.k.a. Bonecrusher, has been a farm boy, college graduate, soldier, prison guard, car salesman and...heavyweight champion of the world.

Not the usual dossier of a fighter. But then for Smith, the World Boxing Association champion who fights Mike Tyson, the World Boxing Council champion, Saturday night in Las Vegas, Nevada, the path he has taken to glory in the ring has been anything but typical.

To begin with, he did not throw a punch in anger until he was twenty-three years old and stationed in Wurzburg, West Germany, with the Army. A file clerk for the military, Smith would wander into the base gym to play basketball—a sport he had lettered in at James Kenan High School in Warsaw, North Carolina.

"Before then," said Smith, "I hadn't even been in fist fights. I was a big kid and nobody picked on me. Then one day in Germany, the boxing coach there, Herbert Ruffin, asked me would I be interested in fighting."

Smith was interested. Though he "didn't know anything about boxing," he knocked out his first opponent.

Success provided its own impetus. Smith began to fight in military tournaments and, when he was mustered out at Fort Dix, he went on to Philadelphia and enrolled at Joe Frazier's gym to find out, in the fighter's words, "how good I was."

"It was a chance to spar with Michael Spinks, with Marvis Frazier, with Jimmy Young," said Smith. "I was star-struck. To be there with Joe Frazier—it was a pleasure to be in the same gym, even though guys were beating me up in the ring every day. But I kept learning."

Eventually, fight managers were approaching Smith—who won his share of amateur bouts—with offers to turn professional. But after each offer, the next manager to speak to him would warn him off the fellow before. For a self-described country boy—Smith grew up on a forty-acre tobacco farm in Magnolia, North Carolina—all the whispers and insinuations made him uneasy and eventually got him "all confused."

"Pro—that was all new to me," said Smith. "I decided, 'I'm getting out of here.'"

In 1979, Smith and his wife, Reba, returned to North Carolina, where he began to work as a prison guard for $700 to $800 a month, a job that quickly enough became an inducement to return to boxing.

"It was depressing seeing guys locked up," said Smith. "And for eight hours every day, I was locked up too."

Three nights a week he would drive fifty miles from Magnolia to Fort Bragg in Fayetteville to train at the base gym. It was there, in November 1981, he heard that Teddy Brenner, the matchmaker for Bob Arum's Top Rank organization, was looking for an opponent for James Broad.

"It was a chance to fight on national TV, on ESPN," said Smith. "Live from Atlantic City."

In his debut as a professional, James Smith was knocked out by Broad in four rounds.

"I figured afterward that professional boxing is not for me," Smith said. "I got knocked out on national TV. The heck with pro boxing."

Thinking it over, though, he became convinced he could do better. In 1982, he beat Rickey Parkey (the current International Boxing Federation cruiserweight champion) on a decision, then knocked out Mike Cohen and Lou Alexander.

"After Broad, raw strength got me over," said Smith. "Nobody else believed I could do it. I was an opponent. At least they thought I was."

On September 11, 1982, he was supposed to be just an opponent against Chris McDonald, a promising young heavyweight with a network TV deal. Against McDonald, in his fifth professional bout, Smith scored an upset decision.

Watching the fight on TV that night were two New Yorkers, a real-estate broker named Alan Kornberg and a mortgage banker named Steve Nelson. Both men had spoken of taking a fling at managing a prizefighter together. An unknown like Smith seemed just right for a pair of managerial beginners.

But Kornberg and Nelson were not the only ones who thought Smith had potential. Brenner, for Arum, bid on the fighter, too.

"But I was a little nervous, I'd heard so many things about Arum and Don King," said Smith, indicating his fears about the magnitude of their operations. "I was a little scared to make that commitment." Smith was more comfortable with Kornberg and Nelson, who "seemed like down-home people."

Kornberg and Nelson gave Smith a $5,000 signing bonus and put him on a $100-a-week salary, enough to enable him to quit his job as a prison guard. Then they hired Emile Griffith, the former world champion, to train him.

"Griffith," said Smith, "taught me to get balance. With that I began getting more power."

After beating McDonald, Smith, called "Crusher" by his trainer, scored nine straight knockouts. Late in 1984, he was offered his first main event, against Frank Bruno of Britain. Smith's purse was $60,000, a significant improvement on the $300 to $500 purses he had received the year before.

Griffith's strategy for beating Bruno was to have Smith bang him to the body and soften him for the knockout.

But nine rounds into the fight, Bruno, with a commanding lead, was nailing Smith with every jab he threw and was absorbing Smith's body blows without noticeable effect.

"Between rounds 9 and 10," said Smith, "I told Griff, 'Let me do it my way.' I went out and hit Bruno with a left to the body, a right to the head. He went back to the ropes. He was tired. I kept hitting him. Boom boom boom. Finally he fell and didn't get up."

With his dramatic knockout victory, Smith was suddenly in line for a title shot against Larry Holmes, the I.B.F. champion. But from the high of his triumph over Bruno, there followed more difficult times. Though he would have Holmes in trouble during their title bout, on November 9, 1984, he succumbed to the champion in the twelfth round. After that, he lost three of his next four bouts, to Tony Tubbs (March 15, 1985), Tim Witherspoon (June 15, 1985) and Marvis Frazier (February 23, 1986).

After the Witherspoon defeat, Nelson, the co-manager, suggested that Smith retire and, walking out of the fighter's dressing room, the mortgage banker just disappeared from Smith's career. Smith himself was discouraged enough to quit for a while and sell cars in a dealership in Fayetteville. And then, when he decided to try boxing again and lost to Frazier, he consulted a psychiatrist in Raleigh.

"I was depressed," said Smith. "Four out of five fights I'd lost. I thought I was losing it mentally. The psychiatrist told me, 'If you want to win, you'll win.' That made me madder, paying $70 an hour to hear that."

Smith changed psychiatrists. The new one told him, "The ring is your domain. You've got to protect your turf."

In his next fight, on April 5, 1986, he knocked out Mike Weaver in one round. Soon after, Carl King became co-manager with Kornberg."

The psychiatrist was with him again for his W.B.A. title fight this past December 12 against Witherspoon. Smith knocked out Witherspoon in one round and became the champion.

"Nobody expected me to be here," said Smith. "The champion. It's kind of like I'm unannounced. But I'm here and it's been a struggle to prove I belong here."

The struggle continues, against Tyson.

Smith lost his title to Tyson on a decision. Nearing forty, he was still an active fighter in 1992.

...And sometimes winning a world title can trigger chaos,
as Leon Spinks and Mike Tyson found out.

LEON SPINKS: Champagne Days (1978)

New Orleans, April 8, 1978: Leon Spinks was foot-loose again.

It was not on The Leon Spinks Calendar, the increasingly speculative chart of the new heavyweight champion's day-to-day appearances that his lawyers had plotted for him, but Spinks was gone.

Bulletins followed. Spinks, it was reliably reported, was in the Jacksonville, North Carolina, area, his precise whereabouts unknown. There was a woman involved.

Spinks' flight presented a problem. An agreement had just been reached in the negotiations with a group of New Orleans financiers. The Spinks-Ali rematch was set for September 15 in the Superdome. The problem was that Top Rank chairman Bob Arum did not want rival promoter Don King to steal his thunder.

King had scheduled a press conference in Las Vegas for that Wednesday, April 12, to announce his World Boxing Council title fight between Larry Holmes and Ken Norton. Arum wanted to stage his press conference the day before. That required Leon Spinks, Jr., to be there. The phone lines hummed.

On Monday, April 10, the day before Arum's press conference, there was no change. Nobody had a fix on Spinks. With time running out, Arum made an unusual move. He asked Butch Lewis, Spinks' Svengali during the climb to the championship, who had recently been exiled from the Spinks camp for leaning on the champ a little too heavily, to send for Leon.

78

Dispatched to Jacksonville, Lewis located Spinks and transported him to New Orleans, apparently persuading him en route to
let bygones be bygones.

On April 11, twenty minutes before the scheduled start of
Arum's press conference, a Top Rank official discovered that room
1543 of the New Orleans Hilton was empty.

Since that was Spinks' room and since Spinks' wayfaring was
by then a pattern, there was cause for alarm. But Leon, it turned
out, was only tardy. An hour late, he finally arrived. As Leon
entered, Muhammad Ali ducked under the table at which he was
sitting, in a comic show of fear. Lured back out, he remarked on
Spinks' tardiness.

"I'm important now, brother," Spinks rasped, his bloodshot
eyes twinkling.

Ali inspected the champion's brown suit and the smartly
knotted tie, turned to Lewis and said, "You done fixed his tie and
everything, ain't you?" Then to Spinks, he said, "You used to be
quiet and didn't dress up." Ali's voice took on exaggerated tremolo,
"You...done...chaaanged, man."

"You gave me my gusto, brother," Spinks quipped.

The crowd roared.

"You don't act the same no more," said Ali, pretending to be
perplexed. "You used to be early. Now you late. Making everybody
wait."

"Well, that the way it supposed to be. You got to let the smell
come before you come."

"You crazy," Ali told him. "I ain't going to fight you."

In New Orleans, Ali adapted his wit to Spinks' rough-edged
humor. The mood was cordial. The Ali ego did not rankle Spinks
as it had some of his other opponents. Leon liked him. (After he'd
beaten Muhammad, Spinks went to Ali's dressing room, kissed
him on the cheek and said, "Good fight.") Ali, in turn, was not
bent on unnerving Spinks. His reference to Spinks as crazy was
meant as praise. He had not been able to psych Spinks during their
Las Vegas title fight, a fact that colored the comic material Ali
fashioned from his defeat. At one point during the New Orleans

press conference, he interrupted Leon, saying, "I'll do the talking now"—a smile on his lips.

"Now, wait a minute. Shut up," Spinks said, acting cross.

"You tell me to shut up?" Ali shook his head and looked out at the audience with an aggrieved expression. "I got to take all this?"

"That's right," Spinks told him. "I'm champ now."

"Yassa, boss."

It was perfect timing that had Leon writhing in laughter, his curled tongue poking through his teeth. He reached for the microphone and said, "Ali is a wonderful person. He's a beautiful man. I love him. I love him with all my heart. Plus, he give me respect...can't get that nowhere."

If Spinks was feeling that he couldn't get any respect except from Ali, he was probably just reflecting on some of the events that had taken place in the past few months.

Within six weeks of defeating Muhammad Ali, Spinks had been sued by a motel for unpaid bills; had been sued for back rent by his landlord in Philadelphia; had been arrested and then photographed in handcuffs for driving the wrong way on a one-way street and for operating a motor vehicle without a license in his home town of St. Louis; and had been discarded as heavyweight champion by the World Boxing Council in favor of the number one challenger, Ken Norton. By then, the reeling Spinks could only say, "I haven't done anything for anyone to take my belt. I ain't disrespect no one."

And as if to add insult to injury, a look-alike of the new champion had turned up in Philadelphia. The dead ringer was, in Leon's term, "imposturing" him—signing autographs in public and encouraging local merchants to lavish complimentary goods on him.

For a couple of weeks the man sampled the high times that Spinks calls his gusto. Then he prudently faded away.

The man may have known something. For by then, the pleasure of being the real Leon Spinks Jr. was paling.

Nowhere was the pleasure more diminished than in Spinks' dealings with Butch Lewis of Top Rank, Inc., the champion's exclusive promoter. On the morning of March 2—two weeks after he beat Ali—Spinks arrived at Top Rank's New York office to confer with Lewis, who had told him there was business to discuss at ten sharp.

When Spinks arrived, the Top Rank office was undergoing a paint job, which left its quarters cramped for seating space. Leon settled himself on top of a packing crate and waited for Lewis to appear. He was still waiting by early afternoon, when a Top Rank aide wondered if Spinks were hungry. Leon conceded he was and let the man buy him a ham and cheese on white.

Lewis appeared shortly afterward, saying he'd been trying to track down Spinks' accountant. That Spinks had been waiting half the day did not appear to trouble Butch. It disturbed the champion, though, who was beginning to reassess Lewis' role in his life.

Throughout Spinks' brief but tumultuous pro career, Lewis had been in the midst of the struggle for control over Spinks. The earliest infighting had involved Lewis and Millard "Mitt" Barnes, a white Teamsters organizer from St. Louis who was Spinks' manager of record. Although Barnes would retain his 30 percent managerial cut of Spinks' purses, he quickly lost the influence he'd had when Leon was an amateur and Barnes was his benefactor, investing time and money in Spinks' boxing future.

It was through Lewis that Barnes first learned that his past contributions (according to Mitt, he gave Spinks more spending money than strictly permitted by Olympic regulations) had been devalued. After Spinks' first pro fight, Lewis told Barnes that Leon's wife, Nova, was consulting with attorneys about canceling Mitt's contract as manager—*she* wanted to be the manager.

Barnes began to feel a chill in Leon's attitude toward him.

Spinks' disaffection for Barnes apparently was not so deep-rooted that he had qualms about asking him for more money. On August 8, 1977, shortly after Leon suffered an eye injury in training, he phoned Mitt for $500. According to his Western Union receipt, Barnes wired the money at 4:35 p.m. that day. An hour later, Spinks phoned back and asked for $1,500 more.

"I just wired you the $500," Barnes told him. "I got to come to Philadelphia—we've got a few things to discuss. So I'll just bring the $1,500 with me." When Barnes went to Philadelphia, Spinks had already received the $500 and split.

In Barnes's place, Lewis had taken charge of Spinks, involving himself in every facet of Leon's career, even tracking the fighter down when he went A.W.O.L. from training.

Lewis, a thirty-one-year-old former car salesman who had become a vice-president of Top Rank, had the animated style of his former calling and an inclination for the ornate gesture. In the Manhattan phone directory, he was listed as "Lewis, P.A.," the initials referred to the nickname he'd taken for himself—Park Avenue Butch—an allusion to Top Rank's prestigious address.

It was a flair that Barnes, a slow-moving, plain-talking man, distrusted. He suspected Lewis of promoting himself with Spinks at his expense. After several "incidents" with Lewis, Barnes began to think of consulting an attorney for the problems he anticipated.

Spinks' trainer Sam Solomon had a wary eye on Lewis, too; he did not take to Butch's idea of bringing in another trainer, George Benton, to assist him.

Solomon, a short, rotund man, sixty-three years of age, had fought in tent shows and social clubs as a semipro boxer, and also had been a catcher in Negro baseball. Solomon is usually an affable individual, but on this occasion he became angry at having his authority as trainer undercut. Lewis thought it was a justifiable move.

"Solomon did a good job," Lewis recalled, "of being with Leon and his brother Michael. [Michael Spinks had turned pro with Top Rank in February 1977.] He'd pick 'em up all the time, get them to the gym. I'd tell him they needed this or that—and he'd get it done. Never a problem. And it wasn't until early summer that I started to see that they really weren't progressing. Sam was just great for my overseer, but he wasn't great in training them. In fact, Mike and Leon were complaining that he wasn't teaching 'em anything.

"What happened is that one day in the gym, Leon went over to George Benton, who worked in Joe Frazier's gym. He saw George showing fighters things that he thought he should know. He went to Benton and asked him, 'Man, would you show me how to do that?' Later, Leon called me and asked, 'Can't we get Benton to work with us?'"

Benton was a former middleweight contender who was training Frazier's stable of fighters, which included Frazier's own son Marvis, a promising amateur. As a fighter, Benton had been a clever operator, with a knack for avoiding punches. A classic stylist.

"George himself came to me," said Lewis, "and said, 'Look, man, I don't want to start no trouble. I want you to know your fighter came over to me and asked me to show him a couple of tricks he saw me showing to some other fighters. I don't want to start no problems.' See, Solomon noticed what was going on... and got a little pissed."

To avoid problems, Lewis held back on hiring Benton for the time being.

By September 1977, the in-house politics occupied too much of Leon's attention. There were Barnes's calls to re-establish old ties and the warnings from others to ignore him. There was Solomon's resentment to balance against the advanced techniques that Benton probably could provide. There was hard-sell Lewis, pulling and tugging and telling Spinks so many things that it was hard to keep them all straight. In the ghetto of St. Louis, Spinks hadn't had to worry about receipts for documenting expenses or about being on time.

The worst of it was Spinks' gnawing concern that he was being manipulated against his better interests. Two other Olympic boxing gold medalists, Howard Davis and Sugar Ray Leonard, had landed exorbitant guaranteed-income deals with the TV networks. By contrast, Top Rank's guarantee to Spinks of only $30,000 for eight bouts was a pittance.

If those elements were not sufficient to cloud Spinks' thoughts, Arum provided another twist. Although Spinks had fought only five professional fights (all won by knockouts), Arum signed him to box Ali for the heavyweight championship.

The original plan called for Spinks to qualify for the title fight—he was required to defeat at least one ranking boxer—

against Alfio Righetti of Italy, on September 13. Spinks' eye injury caused the fight to be rescheduled for November 18. As a tune-up for that bout, Top Rank matched Spinks against a journeyman heavyweight named Scott LeDoux in October.

The LeDoux bout was what prompted me to begin looking into the Spinks story. It was not the fight telecast from Las Vegas or the news accounts that piqued my interest. It was what a deep-throat source I'll name Whisper reported. Whisper is a nondescript individual, given to the sort of tinted glasses Spinks himself wears. On Leon, it is for effect, a kind of flair. For Whisper, it deepens his seedy anonymity, his gray slouch of a figure. He is a boxing aficionado, though, with a computerlike memory for names, dates and the curious facts of the sweet science. He is also privy to all the intrigues and bent turns of the game.

"The thing about the LeDoux fight," Whisper said, *"was what occurred outside the ring, not inside it. There was a craziness at ringside in the Spinks camp, particularly with this Butch Lewis fellow.*

"Lewis sat down in the press row...maybe twenty feet from LeDoux's corner...middle of the ring. Into the ring comes Michael Spinks to fight in a prelim. And Butch stands up in the press row...on the floor...Michael is in completely the opposite corner...and Butch hollers, 'Hey Sliiiiim'—Slim—that's his nickname for him. The kid turns around. Butch hollers, 'Give me fiii- iive.' The kid dutifully walks across the ring and...you know that give-me-five thing. Two gloves, palms down. And Butch gets his jollies. Same thing with Leon when he comes into the ring. 'Give me fiiiiive, big man.'

"Then the LeDoux fight starts. And LeDoux, of course, pulled every trick in the book—the elbows, the thumb in the eye, the head butts. Meantime, though, he's managing to bang home some legitimate punches, too."

"OK. Leon was under a little pressure. And here's where Lewis began shouting instructions from the press row. I couldn't believe my eyes: Leon would turn toward this guy for advice instead of to his corner!

"Butch's screaming and ranting led a couple of people to start heckling him. And he's done this before... at other fights, I've been told. 'You got faith in that white man up there? Bet $500!'

"The morning of the fight, I'd run into Joe Daszkiewicz, the trainer of LeDoux. He tells me, 'Whisper, you should have heard what went on yesterday. LeDoux is staying on the same floor as Leon. We're going past the door to his room, we hear Butch Lewis inside, carrying on. Trying to psych Leon, "If you don't win the fight, you're going back to the ghetto. You've got to win or you're through!" Really laid it on!'

"Toward the end of the fight, Leon is dragging. It's his first ten-rounder. The word was that he'd been partying pretty good a few weeks before. At this point, it's a close fight. The shot at Ali is on the line. All of Spinks' people are going crazy. And here comes Lewis, running up to the ring ropes and yelling at Leon: 'Remember the ghetto? Remember the ghetto?' Really weird stuff, but I'll give him this: Maybe it helped. Because Leon sparked up at the end.

"The fight ended in a draw. Afterward, Johnny Mag, of the Nevada Athletic Commission, wrote Top Rank a letter of reprimand...that this will not be countenanced anymore...that Butch Lewis is to be kept out of press row. All that sort of stuff. A very stiff letter."

The unsettling atmosphere continued for the Righetti fight. Benton was in camp. Sensing Solomon's antagonism, though, he bowed out after Spinks beat the Italian, telling Lewis he wanted to avoid further hard feelings. Lewis, though, felt that George's expertise could help against Ali. He kept after Benton and eventually persuaded him to work with Spinks. It produced a triangular training approach that involved Benton, Spinks and Lewis' brother, Nelson Brison, who was an assistant trainer of Spinks.

"George," said Lewis, "would phone Nelson and tell him things that he should be showing Leon. And Nelson would then repeat to Spinks what George had told him. This is how it was done! OK? This is how fucked up it was. And then, as the championship fight approached, I said, 'Look, George, we coming down to the wire. I need you down here...if nothing else, to work the last week or so. To do whatever you can do. And if you have to do it, continue doing it through Nelson. 'Cause we can't afford to have any confrontations at this point.'"

In Las Vegas for the title fight, Benton had to continue to funnel his ideas through Brison. He showed him tactics for defensing Ali and explained a strategy he had. The key to the Benton strategy was for Spinks to pound away at Ali's left shoulder during the fight and tire the muscles that controlled Muhammad's jab, a weapon that had been crucial to Ali late in past fights. Benton also found a way to exploit Ali's energy saving rope-a-dope tactic: When Muhammad covered up, bang away at the shoulder. When he opened up, throw the uppercut through his gloves to the chin.

"Then," said Benton, "the few times I'd see Leon alone, I never talked loud to him. Always talked soft to him. You can take a person who's excitable and talk him down by your tone of voice. I'd tell him, 'You're going to be champ. All you got to do is do the right things. Small things. Goddamn it, you'll be riding around in a Rolls-Royce. I can see you with the pretty clothes on.' And right behind that, I'd say something that would pertain to boxing."

But the dominant figure in training camp for the Ali fight was, of course, Lewis. He used his position like a gong: He was loud and insistent and sometimes got on people's nerves.

A sparring partner of Spinks quit camp after telling Lewis that he ought to learn to respect people. Eventually, Solomon, whom Lewis berated in public on more than one occasion, got to feeling similarly. One night, he told Lewis, "You acting like you want to fight, nigger. Treating people like they're nothing. I'm not afraid of you. I may be an old man. But I'll punch you right in the mouth." A similar threat was made by Top Rank PR man Chet Cummings when Lewis kicked at his hotel door to get his attention.

After Spinks won the heavyweight crown, Lewis was not overly modest about his role in the title coup. "What you all taking Bob Arum's picture for?" he'd ask photographers. "What you all doing that for? *I'm* the guy that brought Leon Spinks in." In Top Rank's office, Lewis continued to berate aides, sometimes in front of Spinks. And he could be just as pushy with the champion himself.

On the evening of March 2, Lewis told Spinks he wanted him to attend the Mike Rossman vs. Alvaro "Yaqui" Lopez light-heavyweight fight at Madison Square Garden. This followed Leon's nearly daylong wait for Lewis in Top Rank's office. When Spinks declined to see the fight, Lewis insisted. He said that as champion, Leon owed his public such appearances. Later, Spinks would complain about being badgered yet one more time. On that night, however, what made it more galling was that, with Nova back home, Leon had been looking forward to spending the evening with a lady he'd flown up from North Carolina. That was *personal* turf. And it made it one push too many.

By then, he'd suffered Lewis' dervish style too long. One sticky situation after another. Never a moment's peace. Now, as heavyweight king, he thought he'd earned the right to an orderly reign. And if his old mahatma, Lewis, was not built for that, then Spinks was prepared to go elsewhere.

The morning after the Rossman-Lopez match, Leon met with a forty-nine-year-old former Wayne County, Michigan, circuit-court judge named Edward F. Bell. Bell, a tall, thin man of dignified mien, was now a practicing attorney in Detroit. Spinks told Bell that his affairs were chaotic and needed changing.

Bell impressed Spinks. The attorney had a cool, understated manner that contrasted sharply with the klaxon style of Lewis.

Indeed, later on the same day that Spinks met with Bell, Lewis again showed the champ surprising contempt—and disrespect. Fearing he'd miss an airplane flight, Butch hurried into a limousine on Park Avenue that had been hired for Leon's use. "Grab yourself a cab," Lewis told Spinks, as he commandeered the limousine and sped to the airport.

A few days later, in Detroit, Spinks announced that Bell now represented him. With Bell, he hoped, would come a semblance of order.

March 30, 1978: In suite 840 of Detroit's Buhl Building, where the law firm of Bell and Hudson maintains its office, the Spinks watch was on its third day.

Spinks' attorneys, Bell and Bell's colleague Lester Hudson, had sent a former Detroit police officer, who also tracked down bail jumpers, out to St. Louis to find the heavyweight champion.

The ex-cop, who had just been hired as a Spinks bodyguard, had left Detroit, saying, "If the motherfucker is there, I'll find him."

Bell and Hudson hoped so. They had Arum on the phone daily, talking to him about a deal with a group of Africans (who were later replaced by the New Orleans people) on the Spinks-Ali rematch. The negotiations soon would require their flying to New York in the company of Spinks.

Bell and Hudson were not the only people who wanted Spinks in Detroit. Richard J. Smit did, too. Smit was a car salesman who had driven up three days before from the Johnny Kool Oldsmobile agency in Indianapolis, Indiana, in a 1977 custom-built white Lincoln Continental limousine that he meant to sell to Spinks for $35,000—$5,000 down, a ten-month lease and a final "balloon" pay-out.

The vehicle went with the new image that Bell and Hudson were insisting soon would fit their client Spinks as snugly as the three size-42 tailor-made suits that had been hand-delivered three days earlier by a clothier from across the border in Windsor, Ontario.

For those three days, Bell and Hudson had been talking persuasively into my tape recorder of the mechanisms that they had set up to ensure that Spinks' career would run smoothly and that he would rise up as a Palookaville do-gooder, a shining example to the youth of America. It was the image Leon talked up, too: "He'p the kids, gotta he'p the kids," he'd say—an ambition that somehow always was being waylaid.

The mechanisms were supposed to change that. Like G.M. and Howard Hughes, Leon was now incorporated in Delaware, so he could enjoy that state's liberal corporate advantages. Spinks Jr. Organization Inc.: At that date, Spinks was its only officer. The setup provided him tax relief, as well as a sense of his own future. He had, it turned out, taken to carrying an attache case, prompting a gag:

Q.: What's that you got in your hand?

Spinks: That my office.

In fact, though, a real office, carpeted and with a view of Detroit's Congress Street, had been cleared for Spinks in suite 840.

Downstairs, in the National Bank of Detroit, an account for Spinks was set up. What remained of his cash was transferred from New York banks. Temporary checks were issued. Spinks' taxes were brought up to date. In 1977, his first year as a professional boxer, he had twice missed making quarterly tax payments on his fight earnings. When Top Rank sent him to a New York accounting firm, Leon showed up with a shopping bag full of cash receipts. But Spinks was now supposed to be catching on to fiscal complexities. When Bell and Hudson's tax specialist had asked the high school dropout if he understood why he had to document expenses more carefully, Spinks had answered, "You're talking 'bout my business partner [Uncle Sam]...looking over my shoulder...comin' in, saying, 'I'm not gonna let you get away with this.'"

Arrangements were made for Spinks to pursue a general-education degree. To improve his speech, he'd bought a tape recorder ("Not a little bitty box," he'd say, "a big box...made by Pioneer...that I know I can get the whole sound of my voice into it"), so that he could hear himself and learn from it. And then there was The Leon Spinks Calendar.

On white cardboard the size of fight posters, Spinks' monthly itinerary was recorded on The Leon Spinks Calendar. In Bell's office, and Hudson's, a calendar was prominently displayed. At a glance, either lawyer knew what the champ was doing.

Spinks' future engagements were marked in red and black inks—red for tentative and black for solidly booked dates. In the month ahead, Spinks was to receive *The Ring* magazine championship belt (4/4) in New York, lay over a night at the Hilton and travel to Philadelphia, where he would be honored by the city of Philadelphia and would tape *The Mike Douglas Show* (4/6). Then:

April 10-15 Miami, Fla. training

April 16-22 Carribean [sic] exhibition tour

April 23-29 Carribean [sic] exhibition tour

It was an impressive-looking document, except for one thing: its efficacy. Leon Spinks, who had only to catch a plane to Detroit, hadn't been up to it for three days running, a fact that jibed less with the blue-skies future that Bell and Hudson foresaw for Spinks than with events of the past weeks.

Then there was the information from my Spinks source, Whisper, that had the jagged feel of self-destruct:

"Leon is still Leon. That's the amazing thing. Still irresponsible. Wants to do exactly what he wants to do. He's got...something a little loose there, I think.

"Like, he doesn't have a driver's license and yet he continues to drive. A couple of days after he was arrested for driving without a license, he drove a guy I know to the airport. Like, it didn't faze him at all. With Leon, these things just happen. Very spontaneously. And he goes with it.

"Then last week, his bodyguard was expecting his wife to fly in to St. Louis from Des Moines. Since the wife was staying with Nova, Leon says there's a possibility that Nova might be on the same flight. If Nova's on the plane, Spinks says, the guy is to call up. It's like a little game with Nova and Leon. OK? Leon flies out of town. She follows him. She never sees him. Leon flies out of town again. She follows him. Like Marlene Dietrich in 'Morocco.'

"Sure enough, Nova's on the plane. The guy calls up to find out what to do. The problem here is that Spinks has a broad staying with him. So? What's the answer? Take the broad and stash her in another hotel? No. Too easy. They put Nova in the room Leon had stayed in. And Leon gets another suite, two flights up. Same hotel. Nova thinks he's not even in the building. The way it went, Nova's downstairs. The girlfriend is upstairs. And the news guy is trying to get Leon to sit still for an interview.

"Spinks, my friend, is going to drive you crazy."

That same afternoon, waiting in Bell and Hudson's office with car salesman Smit and others, I wondered if I *would* go crazy, as Whisper had prophesied. What I did know for sure was that I had a bad case of the fidgets. Three days of waiting to talk with the heavyweight champion.

The hoped-for vision of order was clearly down the tubes. Where was the artful dodger? Late that afternoon, a *St. Louis Post-Dispatch* reporter heard that Spinks was signing autographs in the ghetto and phoned Leon's bodyguard with the address. At that point, Nova and the bodyguard slipped away from the ex-cop from Detroit and went looking for Leon.

Spinks was where he was said to be. The bodyguard saw the silver Chrysler New Yorker that Leon drove when he was in St. Louis and told Nova that he'd retrieve Leon. Instead, he told Spinks, "Your wife is here, man," which gave Spinks and his St. Louis woman the chance to drive away. Back at the hotel, Nova knocked on the door of the ex-cop's room and told him that the bodyguard had screwed up.

At the time this was occurring, Smit was emerging from attorney Hudson's office in Detroit to say, "They're contacting a guy with the St. Louis police who knows Spinks. To see if he can dig him up. The word is: Be discreet.

A smile flickered across Smit's lips. Each screwy twist of waiting for Leon was a perverse entertainment for him. But that was ending. Smit left Detroit that afternoon, regretting he hadn't had a chance to try his pitch on the heavyweight champion.

"'Cause I know Spinks is a buyer," Smit said. "All I got to do is stick his ass in the seat. Boom! Thirty-five Gs. Cashier's check, if you please. All I need is five minutes."

On the chance that Spinks would slip into Detroit in the near future, Smit left the limousine with a relative of a fellow employee and made arrangements to have it driven back to Indianapolis if it turned out that Leon was on a sabbatical.

As for me, I thought of catching a flight to St. Louis but had the paranoiac vision of Spinks' plane passing mine in the night, with Leon flashing me a demonic jack-o'-lantern grin.

I took an evening flight to New York.

On his own, Spinks flew to Detroit the next day.

He hadn't much to say, except about the limousine. On that item, he did not appear to need Smit. Never mind the informed spiel on gear ratios or rear-axle options. Spinks saw the white

Lincoln Continental limousine with the gold striping. He saw the AM/FM stereo cassette player, the small-screen color TV, the digital clock, the bar, the sun roof, the phones for in-car communications and the two back rows of facing seats in crushed velour. He saw all that and knew what he knew. As Leon put it:

"That my motherfucking car. I'm buying."

From St. Louis, Nova phoned Detroit later that day.

"You tell Leon," she said, "that I'm going to sue him for divorce. I'm going to take all his money. And you tell him if he wants to discuss it, I'm going to my parents in Des Moines."

As she hung up, though, Nova, a woman of more than two hundred pounds, winked at the photographer from the *Post-Dispatch* and said, "I'm going right to Detroit. Just said that about Des Moines to throw him off my tracks."

When Spinks won the championship, the press wrote traditional copy about the ghetto fighter's transcending deprivation. A few unkind reporters carped about the slurred speech and fractured syntax and the dearth of feeling the new champion had for the press. Ali backlash, so to speak. But by and large, Spinks was warmly depicted.

The fact was, though, he was not O.J. black, not the establishment's kind of colored. He had the discomforting sound of the back-alley, muscatel-swigging black man, and a hard-edged look to go with it. So when incidents began to occur, the press was not disposed to go easy on him.

That did not surprise Spinks. From the start, he'd met resistance as champion. In some quarters, he was still regarded as a man whose triumph over Ali was a freak of timing, a fortuitous conjunction of fate and Muhammad's middle age. In dreams before the title match, Spinks had conjured up the image of his arms raised in triumph, but he never imagined the thorny times that would follow.

"Like, I remember," he said later, when we finally connected, "the first time I went back to St. Louis after I won the championship. I was in a club. I was supposed to meet the manager of the place. I was waiting there when a guy ran up to me, point a finger in my face, say, 'You ain't shiiit. You ain't nothing.' And, like, I almost went at him. You understand? 'Cause somebody say that...that's just like saying, 'Let's get it on, let's fight.' I got a heating sensation in my body. A burning sensation in my chest and neck. Like what I used to get when I'm out on the street. But I thought, No, man, that ain't you. Look at you now. I mean, even though he's hollering about how much he hates you...and what-ever...a lot of people around here do love you. Like the people in the club—they said to the guy, 'Who in the hell is you, nigger, to come to our champ like that?'"

The encounter in St. Louis was the first of several instances in which strangers accosted Spinks and bad-mouthed him to his face. His correspondence contained a percentage of hate mail, too, mostly provoked, it seemed by his victory over Ali, of whom he was genuinely fond. "What a joyful man Ali is," Spinks had said before the fight.

Compared with Ali, Spinks lacked the easy grace in public. At times, he could be a sunny soul, breaking into a grin that looked nearly equine in the close-ups that photographers snapped. At other times, he was perplexed by the people he encountered, partic-ularly those who stared dead in his face without speaking. For those cases, Spinks had acquired a line—"What's wrong with you, you ill or something?"—that had proved helpful. "When I say it, then everybody start laughing. Whatever." Whatever. It was not easy being the heavyweight champion.

For Spinks, the problem was compounded by a lack of educa-tion that had been exploited before. Barnes said that when Spinks joined the Marines, he was under the impression that it was for a two-year hitch rather than the four-year term stated in his papers.

Once, to clarify whether or not Spinks' brother Evan had an S at the end of his name, I asked Leon to spell it. He took two fal-tering stabs at the spelling and gave up with an exclamation of "Oh, wow!"

Spinks' ingenuousness invited an atmosphere of conniving and intrigue and produced the internal confusion that was built into the heavyweight champion's operation. Even friends tried to take advantage.

"Some of them," Spinks said later, "try to hit me up for money. I tell 'em, 'I fought hard and I worked hard to get where I got. Don't take away my gusto, 'cause *you* ain't got none. All you got to do is make it for yourself and then you have some gusto. And then you ain't gotta ask nobody for anything.'"

Spinks is a creature of contradictory pieces, eluding easy labels. Although he hasn't the glibness of Ali—his sentences often lurch and sputter—he sometimes strikes a rough poetic note with his words. "I broke out in a thousand tears," or "Nobody really finds hisself, 'cause if he finds hisself, he knows the future." Similarly, though he takes his image with what sometimes seems undue sobriety ("I don't want nobody to see me just like a Tom, Dick and Harry. I want to always keep an image as a nice neat man"), he reacted with boyish hilarity when TV had a laugh at his expense.

"What's that man," he asked, "that tells jokes...on *The Gong Show*...has a bag on his face? Yeah. Unknown Comit. He made a joke on me one night. Said, 'I'm going to do an image of Leon Spinks.' Turns around, took the first bag off, put another bag on his face. Had the whole front of the bag black, with two teeth missing. And he turned back around, changed his face mask back, said, 'You didn't know I was two-faced, either, did you?' That gassed me, man. I die laughing. I went in and holler out to my wife. Said, 'This fool is doing an image of me.'"

One moment Spinks would yank a cork from a bottle of champagne with his teeth. The next, he'd clutch a pillow to his chest or suck his thumb as he sat for an interview. The word man-child has been applied to him. Even Nova has been quoted as using it. It is a good word, evoking the contradictory forces within Spinks that make him difficult to pin down.

The odd angles at which Spinks sometimes carries his hands—reminiscent at times of the singer Joe Cocker—are part of a repertoire of body quirks signaling his moods. A bounce to his step indicates that he is in good humor. At those times, his erect carriage has a dancer's lithe quality. In foul moods, he draws in his neck and cocks his head to the side, which has an ominous effect.

But he can be sweetly attentive, too. "You know what I like?" he asked. "Meeting the mommas. All the mommas are big and fat.

They get excited when they see me. They be grabbing on me"—
Spinks twists his shoulders from side to side in recollection—"la
de la, la de la la la."

Flying to Detroit from Boston, Leon met a little girl, about
seven years of age, who had had a series of operations on her throat
that left her unable to speak at the time of the flight. "Her parents," Spinks said, "had just picked her up from the hospital. And
her birthday were coming up. So I sung *Happy Birthday* to her.
Yeah, I sung it to her. And I gave her my autograph. And then we
sit back there and...we writing notes. Was talking to each
other...through notes. We just talked about anything and everything. Anything that she asked me about, I would tell her. She
asked about boxing. She asked how a guy could get hit on the face
like that. I said, 'Well, baby, it's all in the job.'"

Spinks is a visceral person who is not afraid to express himself.
To the anonymous benefactor who'd flown his mother to the
Montreal Olympics, Leon said, "You know, it's the nicest thing
that's ever happened to us. We just love you for it." When confronted by LeDoux's dirty tactics, Spinks had asked in the ring,
"Why you cheat?" a remark that had struck LeDoux by its ingenuous inflections.

The most striking instance of man-child expressiveness
occurred the night Spinks talked to me of his ghetto upbringing,
the anguish and humiliation of which apparently were vividly felt.
At one point, as he paced his room in the Las Vegas Hilton,
growing more agitated, he stopped and, with a stricken expression,
said, "Get me out of here, get me out of St. Louis," which really
only meant he wanted to change the subject.

Spinks has what seems an obsessive tie to his past. His very
speech reflects it. His words do not falter or get jammed up at the
beginning of sentences when the subject is ghetto travail. It's as
though he's had the same thoughts many times before. "I was the
type of person who was quiet," Spinks said. "People could do different things to me and I'd come by and make my momma think
everything was all right. I would lock everything inside myself.
Because the hurt I felt, I always kept it to myself. I never did try to
explain to people what I had went through."

His father is at the core of his pained memories. Leon, Sr., separated from the family when the boy was young. What contacts Spinks had with him afterward were mostly disappointing—he remembers being ridiculed and whupped—and filled him with a desire "to be the man my daddy wasn't."

There is a darker side to Spinks that possession of the heavyweight title seemed to provoke. Whisper had a story in that regard:

"I knew George Foreman before he knocked out Joe Frazier. A real gung-ho nice kind of kid. Now, the morning after he knocked out Joe Frazier, he walked in to the press conference...and like this: 'Hey, get the hell off that couch, man....You, I don't want you sitting there.' He's rearranging the room. How to sit. How to take pictures. And you know who did the same thing the day after he won? I swear. Leon Spinks. 'Get off the couch,' he told news guys. He's barking commands as to who sits where. 'Clear that couch. Get out of the way.' Uncanny. Absolutely uncanny. Almost to the T."

The title conferred an elaborate celebrity of a peculiarly American kind, with its mix of grand and tawdry attentions—headlines and hotel suites and the *National Enquirer* asking Leon to by-line "WHY I LOVE AMERICA."

Being the heavyweight champion mattered. People simply did not worry about the "image" of champions in other weight divisions. The almighty shazam belonged to the heavyweight king. And with it went the recognition, concern and gaudy fanfares inherent. Snubbed at the door of Manhattan's chic Studio 54 when he was a challenger, Spinks was "olee olee in free" as the champion.

For Spinks, though, some measure of his newly acquired fame was the motion and commotion he could trigger. Bodies snapped to. That could be exhilarating for a young man whose background was filled with mockery and rejection. Spinks' whirlwind days, especially the ones he lived when he bolted, had people dashing about, worrying and wondering about him. That might appear selfish from close up. By the long view, though, it was a pay-back on a hard, cold past. As Spinks once said. "See, my dad said I'd amount to nothing. He would tell people that. And it hurt me to hear him say it. It stayed in my mind. Why'd he say that? What for? Call me a fool out of the blue. Not to my face but to people who'd tell it to me. And that became my thing—to be somebody."

Underlying all contradictions, it sometimes seemed, was a mad pleasure in the inappropriate moment, the attraction to which brought unanticipated twists: Spinks would experience seizures of laughter in the midst of a sober account of one of his St. Louis driving busts or while he analyzed his impromptu disappearances. They were great gurgling sounds—laughter shot through with an unhinged quality.

At those times, the phrase "inappropriate response" had flashed in my mind like the TILT light on a pinball machine, the laughter suggesting a self-destructive impulse of the kind that made tragic heroes.

Was Spinks' gusto just a bit bent? "He's got...something a little loose there, I think." Whisper had said of him. The words applied, though, to the whole shebang—the Spinks High Times and Soul Aplenty Caravan. It was a hard scene to get a fix on. There was the continuing sense of the whole works' being slightly out of whack, bent in a way no orderly vision could possibly straighten.

Welcome Leon Spinks
Heavyweight Champion
Of the World

read the marquee outside the DiLido Hotel in Miami Beach. It was April 11, the day of the news conference with Ali. I had accompanied Spinks from New Orleans to Miami.

Situated on the ocean, with its front entrance on Collins Avenue, the DiLido is a high-rise hotel with a spacious L-shaped lobby and walls covered with pastel murals of boats and trees and monkeys and birds. The aura is art-deco daft—a movie set out of a Thirties comedy. It appeared to possess the right cock-eyed charm for the Spinks entourage. The mood was high on arrival.

During the press conference in New Orleans, Leon had had this exchange:

Newsman: At the airport, you said you'd have something to say after you signed the contract. What do you have to say now?

Spinks: Santa Claus

He growled the words with a loving Satchmo sound, grinning as he did. Santa Claus: shorthand that meant the getting had been good—Spinks' signature assured that millions of dollars would be made. The pleasure remained. At the airport in Miami, when a TV sportscaster asked Spinks to describe how it felt to whip Ali, he smiled and did a soft-shoe routine, at the finish of which he extended his hand and said, "Like that."

Later, in Miami Beach, he walked Lincoln Road Mall, where he signed autographs, mugged for cameras, kissed women and shopped.

"How much those shoes?" he asked, pointing to a pair of size-12 Pierre Cardin loafers.

"Not too much," the salesman said.

"Then I'll take them."

From a thick wad of currency, Leon peeled off a $100 bill for the salesman.

"And what are these?" Spinks asked.

"Money clips."

"Will they hold a lot of money?"

"Yes, Mr. Spinks."

"O.K. Gimme one."

Spinks tried to insert his roll of bills, but it was too thick to fit inside the clip.

Spinks spent a sunny day in Miami Beach, grinning, dancing across streets, quipping to young women ("Whaddaya say, momma?"). That night, Spinks, a welterweight named Roger Stafford and I stood by a low stone wall at the end of Lincoln Road, watching the ocean break against the shore just below. Spinks was in a form-fitting maroon shirt and cream-colored slacks. He and Stafford were drinking California pink champagne. A gentle breeze blew.

"It gonna be good to hit some motherfucker again," said Spinks, putting his glass on the wall and inhaling a smoke.

"Yeahhh, I know," said Stafford, setting his drink down, too.

Spinks struck a fighting pose, bent at the knees, and let his hands go.

"Whap! Whap!" Stafford said, as he watched. Then Stafford was moving punches through the air, emitting small grunting sounds as he did. "That's the way I did it to that dude," he said, referring to a preliminary bout he'd fought that weekend on national TV. "All over the motherfucker."

"Yeahhh," said Spinks.

"I whupped that dude good——"

"Hey. My man." Spinks interrupted, addressing me. "Hey, you ain't gonna put in the ar-ti-cle that I *smoke*, is you?"

"Heyyy," I said, with an elaborate shrug that was not quite an answer.

"'Count of my image." Spinks said.

Spinks thought about it and then forgot about it and began to move sinuously, reducing his shadow punches to a stoned dance.

"Women," said Stafford. "Got to get women."

"Women," answered Spinks.

"Got to."

"Sweet nothings?" I asked.

"No. Lies," said Stafford. "Tell 'em lies."

"Liiiiees," crooned Spinks, his body rocking as he grinned. "Tell 'em liieees."

Stafford swayed in answer. "Liiieees."

"Tell 'em liieeees."

They doubled over in laughter, Spinks making plashing sounds with his mouth.

"Liiieees."

"Tell 'em liiieeees."

Minutes later, Spinks was gliding through the DiLido lobby, still sipping champagne, when a team of women bowlers from Terre Haute, Indiana, recognized him. Out came the cameras. Spinks obliged by posing for snapshots, drinking champagne refills as he did.

"Get out my pitcher," a pretty young black woman said. "Just me 'n' the man."

A bowler in pin curlers arrived. "We was dressed for bed and they come up and said Leon Spinks."

"Leon," a heavy-set woman said, "let me show you a picture of my grandchildren. They triplets."

"Where's the champagne?" another bowler wondered.

"It's on me," Spinks said, moving toward the hotel restaurant, waving his arm when the women hesitated. "Come on, ladies."

Soon after, the Spinks caravan was on the move. Up the road it went to Place Pigalle, a Miami Beach club whose all-girl revue and X-rated comedienne, Pearl Williams, were the attractions. Tuesdays, though, Williams was off. So, for this night, the strippers would do.

The Leon Spinks Calendar had called for Spinks to spend this second week in April training for his Caribbean tour. But the good times would roll instead. The sun was coming up when the heavyweight champ made it back to the DiLido.

A few days later, there was another incident that still lives in my mind. Spinks was standing in the DiLido penthouse number one, his $100-a-day lodgings, idling for a moment before plunging into another day. The sun streamed through a space in the drapes. His step had a loose, easy swing. Then suddenly he was holding up the index finger of each hand and, with a rhumbalike motion of the hips, he began to move, chanting in a comically falsetto voice, "Penthouse number one, penthouse number one"—and smiling. The style was Carmen Miranda's, but the pleasure was all Spinks'. Penthouse number one: top of the world, momma.

But with Spinks, the pleasure of being up there was never far removed from the trick impulses that could bring him down. And as the week progressed in Miami Beach, there were troubling notes. Complications caused the Caribbean tour to be pushed back a week, creating a gap in The Spinks Calendar that left Leon susceptible to demon whispers. A call from Lewis also augured problems. As he hung up, Spinks muttered, "One thing after another. Shit. Shit. Shit."

And a few days later, as Nova arrived in Miami Beach, Leon was on the run again, headed for St. Louis. There were problems there with Barnes. Barnes had agreed to take less than his customary thirty percent of the purse for the Spinks-Ali rematch, but he had grievances that could threaten the bout.

Lewis was to meet Spinks in St. Louis. Before Lewis left, he phoned the DiLido to check on Spinks' whereabouts. In penthouse number one, Nova picked up the phone, heard Lewis' voice and hung up. She figured he was to blame for Spinks' latest abrupt departure.

Lewis found Spinks and told him that a meeting in New York was planned to straighten out details of the Spinks-Ali rematch. The various interests—Barnes, Bell, Arum—would be there. Spinks agreed to the trip but kept delaying.

On Wednesday, April 19, Lewis urged him to leave St. Louis. Spinks seemed inclined to but asked, "Can I take my baby with me to New York?" a reference to his St. Louis woman. Lewis told him he could do what he wanted—just be on the flight to New York. Spinks' woman said she had to get her clothes. Lewis waited at the airport. When Spinks did not appear, he gave up and flew back to New York. That was on Thursday.

On Friday, April 21, he heard on the radio that Spinks was busted again.

"Has been released on a $3,700 bond. Spinks was taken into custody on charges involving suspected drug violations...and failure to produce a driver's license. He was booked on suspicion of two counts of violating the Missouri controlled-substance law by possession of marijuana and cocaine. Police say warrants will be sought later today. Arrested with Spinks was a 26-year-old woman companion."

A later report stated that torn $10, $20 and $50 bills were found in the trunk of Spinks' car.

With the heavyweight champion involved, guilty or innocent hardly mattered. Wheels would turn, deals could be made. In fact, the drug charges were later dropped. But...

Whisper called the next day.

"Battling Siki," he said.

"Who?"

"Battling Siki, my friend. Real name for Louis Phal. A Senegalese Negro. Won the light-heavyweight championship in

1922. Knocked out Georges Carpentier in six rounds. Paris, France. Siki was called the Singular Senegalese. And he came here a raw fucking African. We're going back over fifty years. Loved his wine, women and song. And belting guys in the chops. And wearing the grass-skirt-and-top-hat kind of thing. He's buried here in New York. Out in Flushing, Long Island. A couple of years ago, a boxers' association put a tombstone up...Died in a fucking bar brawl in New York City. December 15, anno Domini 1925. Look it up."

And he clicked off.

In 1992, Leon Spinks was making yet another boxing comeback at the age of thirty-nine.

LEON CALVIN: Death Outside the Safety of the Ring (1990)

The sign at the rear of the Northside Bombers Boxing Club says "In Harmony." When Charles Hamm, the fifty-two-year-old plumber who has run the place since 1978, first saw the sign, he liked the sentiment so much that he made sure the lettered poster board ended up on that wall of his storefront gym.

Harmony is a nice notion. But on St. Louis' West Florissant Avenue, where the gym sits, harmony is a pretty elusive objective these days. The street courses through blocks of boarded-up and damaged buildings, an urban landscape promising more poverty and violence than anything resembling harmony.

From the day he opened the modest gym, Hamm, who lives one floor up with his wife, Jeridean, recognized the trouble that was out there on the streets. And like a pied piper he fought it by cruising the North Side ghetto in his van, urging the youngsters loitering on the street corners to try boxing.

Some boys came to the Bombers gym for the challenge of the sport, others for the hamburgers that the mild-mannered Hamm would buy after a day's training was done. Leon Calvin was eight years old when he first showed up in 1979.

For the next eleven years, Calvin was a regular at Hamm's gym, learning enough about the manly art to turn pro in June. But on Sunday morning, July 21, Calvin's career was cut short when he was shot to death on a bridge connecting East St. Louis, Illinois, and St. Louis. Police found him in a car at 5:30 A.M.

The death of Calvin, the son of the former heavyweight champion Leon Spinks Jr., underscored not only the pervasiveness of inner-city violence but also the random nature of it, which makes the quest for success by the young inner-city athlete a bit of a roulette spin.

103

For Calvin, a 6-foot-1-inch light heavyweight who some thought had the potential to be a world-class boxer, the abrupt ending was, of course, a personal tragedy. But in the context of his famous father's difficult life, it stood as another sad twist to the chaotic Spinks tale. For Hamm, Calvin's death was a sorrow compounded by the time and attention he had invested in the fighter, a commitment that was never easy.

Back in 1979, when Hamm first encountered him, Calvin was a good-natured youth with a radiant smile, but possessed of a mischievous side as well. He tended to use the cuss words that Hamm forbade and sometimes hit other boys while just standing around.

"Even bigger boys," said Hamm, "he'd hit 'em pretty hard. Which irritated me. When you got a gym, you got to be careful. You can't let anybody get hurt."

Hamm, a former boxer who does not drink, smoke or use profane language, had to order the boy out of the gym on more than one occasion. Calvin kept coming back, though. And somewhere in that first year, Hamm found out that Calvin's father was Spinks, who in 1978 was the heavyweight champion of the world.

His curiosity piqued, Hamm began watching more closely to see whether this boy from the 1900 block of nearby East John Street had his father's spark for fighting. Calvin proved he did. As an amateur trained by Hamm, he won two St. Louis Golden Gloves titles. But the promise Calvin showed as a boxer was threatened by what he did outside the ring.

Like his father, who had been called "Neon Leon" because of his tendency to go partying when he should have been training, Calvin was something of a good-time Charlie. And he was an expert dancer. 'Around when he was fourteen, fifteen," Hamm recalled, "that's when you'd look out the window and see a crowd collecting. You'd figure there was a fight going on. But no, it'd be Leon just dancing, with the music coming out of what we call ghetto blasters—those boom boxes the kids have. Outside the gym, or over where he lived on East John Street, he'd have people watching him dance."

As Calvin grew older, he continued to dance, going to clubs and house parties. Hamm warned him about the late hours he was keeping, and the questionable characters, some of them gang members, who were part of that social circle.

He saw the night life to which Calvin was attracted—with its alcohol, drugs and occasional violence—as being at cross purposes to a fighter's more ascetic existence.

It wasn't long before Calvin was beset by the very complications that the older man feared.

Two years ago, while at a party, Calvin was shot in the abdomen by a friend who was aiming at somebody else. Surviving that, he was arrested in 1989 and charged with illegal possession of a handgun. The case was pending when Hamm persuaded Calvin to turn professional in the spring of 1990.

Hamm's hope was that as a professional Calvin might spend more time in the gym, away from his risky night life.

"At the time he turned pro, I set him down right in front of me at my house," said Hamm, "and I told him. 'Back away from those parties.' He told me, 'Mr. Hamm, it takes time. I just can't stop everything.' I told him, 'Just start doing it. That's all the time it takes.'"

On July 10, Calvin, 1-0 as a professional, fought Jordan Keepers in Merriville, Indiana. In the audience that night was his father. It was the first time that Spinks—who over the years had spent little time with his son—had ever seen him box. That absence accounted, in part, for the detached reaction Calvin had when Spinks stopped by the dressing room before the fight to wish him well.

Even when the former champion told his son that he would be ringside shouting advice to which he should pay heed, Calvin just nodded but would not speak.

But after Calvin scored a third-round knockout and a jubilant Spinks was the first man into the ring, the son was more receptive. He hugged his father and smiled.

"Later on," said Hamm, "the ring announcer called both of them back as father and son. They hugged again. After that, they were jolly-jolly and giving autographs."

Off that victory came an offer of a three-year promotional deal from Cedric Kushner, the New York-based promoter of the world champion welterweight Marlon Starling.

On Saturday July 14, a St. Louis mailman named Jim Howell, who with Hamm was co-manager of Calvin, showed the fighter the Kushner contract.

"He smiled that big smile of his," said Howell, "and told me, 'Quick, give me that pen before they change their mind.' Leon had made $200 for each of his first two fights, and up to that point I don't think he was aware that people could make real big money boxing."

At home now Calvin took to sashaying up to his brothers, Darrell, seventeen, and Corey, twelve, and, while throwing shadow punches, telling them: "They bring 'em here, I'll knock 'em out...They bring 'em here, I'll knock 'em out."

On July 21, the nineteen-year-old Calvin had a late afternoon workout at Howell's gym just outside the city limits. That evening, he went to a party, and around midnight, returned home. Not for long, though. When Darrell Calvin saw his brother head toward the front door, on the way to a nightclub, he told him not to go. "He had a fight coming up July 30," said the younger brother, "and needed to get his rest. But he told me, 'I ain't gonna stay out long.' He left by himself."

Leon Calvin never made it back to East John Street.

Zadie Mae Calvin grew up in the same Pruitt-Igoe projects in St. Louis that Leon Spinks Jr. did. Spinks was only seventeen when Ms. Calvin gave birth to her Leon, the first of the three sons she had by Spinks, whom she never married. In 1978, when Corey was born, Spinks, married by then to another woman, would upset Muhammad Ali and become heavyweight champion of the world.

In some of his earliest interviews back then, Spinks would make pained references to his past and in particular to a disappointing relationship with his father, Leon Sr.

Leon Sr. and his wife, Kay, were separated when Leon Jr. was young. The father's sporadic contacts afterward tended to disappoint and eventually alienate the son. "I remember I stayed with him one time and I did something," Leon Spinks Jr. said. "He hung me on a nail and hit me across the face with some cord of some kind. It put a long mark on my face. He told me he was sorry. But ever since then, I didn't like him. O.K., I had done wrong. But why'd he have to scar me up? I mean, I can take a butt-whupping. But you don't have to scar me."

The father was, Spinks said, "in and out of trouble all the time," and he affected Spinks' self-esteem, even from a distance. Like his father, Leon Spinks Jr., even as champion, would have his share of trouble. Within six weeks of defeating Ali, Spinks was sued by a motel for unpaid bills, sued for back rent in Philadelphia and arrested for driving the wrong way on a one-way street in St. Louis.

That turmoil would be constant in a pro career that saw Spinks lose the title in his first defense of it and then fight on until 1988. By then he was a chronic loser, boxing for a pitiful fraction of the millions of dollars he had made and lost. In contrast, his brother, Michael, who won the heavyweight title in 1985, would go on to earn $13.5 million in a 1988 bout against Mike Tyson.

Through those years, the Calvins of East John Street struggled. Their welfare payments were supplemented by what Zadie Mae's mother, Aline Pickett, earned as a nurse's aide while she lived with them.

"Zadie Mae was not able to work on account of her health," said Mrs. Pickett. "I worked at a nursing home and then at a hospital. I was bringing home $265 every two weeks from the nursing home. And when I went over to the hospital, $750 a month."

The relationship with their father was disappointing, Darrell Calvin said. Except for annual Spinks family reunions, Spinks was rarely in touch with them. Then, two years ago, after Spinks invited his three sons to spend time with him in Detroit, the visit ended badly. On his return, the story that Leon Calvin told was that when his father turned down a request for money and he pursued it with Spink's latest wife, Betty, Spinks got physical with him. Calvin's attitude toward his father hardened.

"He'd tell me," Hamm said, "'My daddy was heavyweight champion, and we ain't got nothing.' I wasn't the type to give him ill feelings, but I'd say, 'O.K., Leon, look at yourself.'"

This was a reference to the two children Calvin had fathered and from whom he remained mostly distant.

What male guidance the Calvin boys and their half-brother, Steve, received would come from Hamm, in whose gym all of them boxed. While Hamm was raising two sons and a daughter of his own, he was nurturing the Calvins.

"They would need boxing shoes and trunks, and we didn't have the money, so he bought it for them," Aline Pickett said.

Where many of Hamm's fighters who made a name as amateurs would move on to better-equipped gyms, Leon Calvin did not. He remained loyal to Hamm. But in a ghetto of often capricious violence, minding him was not easy.

Likeable though he was, Leon Calvin had an unpredictability much like his father's, that seemed to invite hard circumstances.

When, for instance, the police stopped a car he was driving and found a handgun inside—a weapon that, Hamm said, belonged to a friend of the fighter's—Calvin was drinking, in plain view, a bottle of beer.

Hamm tried hard, though, to keep Calvin on the straight and narrow, hiring him as a plumber's helper so that he would have spending money and maneuvering him out of the many jams in which he regularly got entangled.

But in East St. Louis on that Sunday morning, Leon Calvin got into trouble that Hamm could not fix.

Like the Illinois State Police, Hamm found the facts about Calvin's last hours difficult to ascertain. Questioning friends of the fighter who he thought would know what happened, he encountered resistance.

"I'd ask for details," Hamm said. "They didn't know. 'You lying,' I'd say. 'You know everything.'"

As he pressed for answers, the details of the final night began to emerge. Calvin, it turned out, was friendly with members of a street gang called the Crips. At a party on Saturday night, July 20, he had been present when a member of a rival gang, the Bloods, was badly beaten.

By Sunday morning, as the scene shifted to an East St. Louis club, there would be another fight involving the gangs that would be quelled, at least until the place closed at 5 A.M. At that time, as the youths spilled out into the streets, gunfire erupted. Calvin jumped into the car of a woman friend who drove hard toward the Dr. Martin Luther King Jr. Bridge, which spans the Mississippi River.

"There were two other cars with friends of Leon's that were being shot at," Hamm said. "Gunfire was ringing as they were going across the bridge. They forced the car Leon was in to the side of the road. The girl driving, she jumped out and ran, and the person in the other car went to shooting."

A few days after the shooting, Capt. Phil Kocis of the Illinois State Police said Hamm's version of the events was basically correct.

On the Thursday night after he was killed, Calvin's body lay in an open casket at the Foster Funeral Home—a Golden Gloves medal hanging from his neck, a pair of miniature boxing gloves on his chest. Leon Spinks Jr. did not want to go into detail about the relationship he had with his son.

"I loved him," he said. "I'm glad I got to spend time with him. It's too bad it got cut short, though."

More than two years later, the killer of Leon Calvin has not been apprehended.

TYSON AT NINETEEN (1985)

At the end of a dirt road in Catskill, New York, the white fourteen-room Victorian house sits on a bluff overlooking the Hudson River and mountains in the distance.

Were he in the mood for a picture-postcard view, it is what Michael Tyson, boxing's hottest new heavyweight (13-0, 13 knockouts), would see from the front porch of this house that has stood for more than a century. But on this cloudy yet mild November afternoon, his birds—the more than one hundred pigeons he has acquired since turning pro last March—are what preoccupy Tyson.

In a crew neck sweater and gray leather trousers, Tyson steps briskly across the front lawn to the coop built months earlier. Thirteen steps up a metal ladder, from a platform just outside the coop, Tyson shoos the birds and then watches them circle a nearby tree. In formation, the pigeons fly with a gentle whooshing sound broken only by the papery flapping of wings as one of the creatures breaks ranks and heads back to home base.

To make the birds climb higher, Tyson takes a red flag on a long wooden pole and begins waving it while he shouts, "Harrrh, harrrh!" He stands there awhile watching the pigeons' circling flights before turning to a visitor to say: "Doesn't that look beautiful?"

But a few minutes later, he begins to fret as he spies a hawk loitering close by. "Drop down," he says to his birds. "Don't let this guy get you." As the last stragglers slip back to the coop, he relaxes, knowing the hawk will not approach the coop. A bird is safe there. And in Tyson's awareness of this, there is a bit of irony. For like his birds, this ghetto kid who made his way here five years and countless troubles ago found—through an aging fight man named Cus D'Amato—that the place at the end of the dirt road was a safe home for him, too.

110

He is nineteen years old and is yet to be ranked by the governing bodies of the sport. Most of his opponents were men who will never advance beyond the agate print of their defeats. And not until his next bout—Friday against Sam Scaff in Madison Square Garden's Felt Forum—will he fight a ten-round match. Despite all that, the three major television networks are already after Tyson to make his network debut in February for them.

The reason is simple: Tyson punches so hard that opponents take the kind of half gainers to the canvas that leave a usually rational observer with only a comic-book vocabulary of wow-geez-&-ohmygod. Nine of his thirteen opponents developed arrested consciousness before the first round was over, and one of them, Sterling Benjamin, stated afterward: "He have a sledgehammer," which he meant apparently in a figurative sense.

At a time when heavyweight champions are, in the words of Tyson's co-manager, Jimmy Jacobs, "as interchangeable as flashlight batteries," Tyson, a squarely built man with a 19-1/2-inch neck and a rugged style that evokes memories of the Marcianos and Fraziers, may be the crowd-pleaser that the heavyweight division has lacked for so long.

With a schedule that has seen him fight thirteen times in little more than eight months and with interest in him growing daily, life is moving at quick time for Tyson. But the 5-foot-11 1/2-inch, 221-pound puncher from the Brownsville section of Brooklyn insists the attention will not distract him from his objective of becoming the youngest heavyweight champion ever, which was D'Amato's goal for him. Nor will it make him forget the hard road to that safe place in Catskill.

That road began in Brownsville where, at age ten, Tyson discovered that crime paid—in hard cash that he could convert into the high-priced clothes that made a peewee delinquent feel like a big-timer on the streets.

From petty theft and picking pockets, Tyson was graduated to stickups. "At first the other guys would have the guns," he says. "I'd go through people's pockets and take their jewelry." Criminal activity eventually led to his doing time in juvenile detention facilities, including, at age thirteen, a stay at the Tryon School in Johnstown, New York.

Bitter about being locked up there, he rebelled, making enough trouble to be put in a cottage reserved for hard-core cases. At that low moment, he met a Tryon staff member, Bobby Stewart, who had been a professional boxer. Tyson expressed a desire to become a fighter, and Stewart gave him his first hard lesson.

"I had a reputation for beating up other students," said Tyson, "and when we boxed he tried to humiliate me so that the other kids would see I was nothing. He hit me in the body and I went down. My air stopped; I thought I was dead."

Tyson fought back. In the weeks and months that followed, he hounded Stewart to teach him boxing's fine points. He absorbed his ring lessons so well that Stewart took him to D'Amato, who ran a boxing program in a gym over the Catskill police station.

D'Amato had once trained and managed the heavyweight champion Floyd Patterson, and trained the light-heavyweight champion Jose Torres. Now he was a boarder in the big white Victorian house, which was owned by a congenial woman named Camille Ewald, whose sister had been married to D'Amato's brother. Years before, D'Amato had battled the monopolistic International Boxing Club, controlled by a gangster named Frankie Carbo, and had been a major figure in the fight game. But he had come upon hard times. "He owed the Government more than a quarter-million dollars," says Miss Ewald. During his many years in Catskill, his rent would be paid by Jacobs.

Not long after watching Tyson spar in his gym, D'Amato told Jacobs, "Mike Tyson is going to be the heavyweight champion of the world." Jacobs, who knew D'Amato to be stingy with a compliment, was impressed—more than Tyson himself was when he heard D'Amato's pronouncement. "I didn't take Cus seriously," Tyson said.

That would change. Tyson spent two weeks with D'Amato living in the Ewald home before returning to Tryon. In September 1980, at age fourteen, he was paroled to D'Amato. Tyson moved back into Miss Ewald's house and, as he puts it, "My life begins here."

It was a life that took getting used to. Tyson was not communica-
tive at first, wary of D'Amato and others—an inmate's reflex reaction. In the gym, though, he proved to be a good student.
D'Amato's emphasis was on defense. He wanted his fighters, even
a puncher like Tyson, to be elusive. "So it was," says Tyson, "hours
of boxing with little and fast fighters, without being allowed to hit
them back and trying to make them miss. And if a 140-pounder
jumps up and punches you in the face, it's not going to tickle."

D'Amato soon had Tyson fighting on nonsanctioned fight cards
known as smokers in venues where the crowds, wagering on the
bouts, would scream epithets at the boxers and sometimes settle
their differences with knives and other persuasive instruments.

In such settings, Tyson had to learn to deal with wild-swinging
and often much older opponents—as well as with his own fear. In
his first trip to a Bronx smoker, he excused himself to get a pack of
gum. Standing alone in the street, in the shadows of elevated
subway tracks, he almost bolted. "I thought to myself: 'What the
hell am I doing here? These guys'll kill you.'"

He fought in smokers and more genteel amateur competitions,
with his progress closely monitored by D'Amato, who tutored him
in the mental phase of the sport as well, even addressing the fear
that Tyson confessed to experiencing, "Heroes and cowards feel
exactly the same fear," D'Amato would say. "Heroes just react to
it differently."

D'Amato did not neglect life beyond the ring either, trying to
educate Tyson to a world far removed from that of Brownsville and
juvenile correction facilities. It was not easy.

"At first," says Miss Ewald, "Mike was very rebellious, very
angry. He wouldn't listen. But Cus spent hours and hours
explaining everything. When he had to, Cus was the boss. He
would scold him. Then Mike would come to me for sympathy."

"In the beginning," says Tyson, "if I got upset, I'd get nasty.
Cus would take me aside to warn me. If I did it again, he'd warn
me out in the open—put me in my place. 'I warned you about that
already. You're not back in Brooklyn with those tomato cans.' I
wouldn't say nothing."

Eventually, D'Amato became Tyson's legal guardian. When the fighter's mother, Lorna, died, Tyson asked Miss Ewald if he could call her his mother. "After that," she says, "he'd introduce me as his mother and Cus as his father."

The fighter that Cus D'Amato wrought is, at 5-11 1/2, small for today's heavyweights—Marciano was 5-10 1/4; Larry Holmes is 6-4. And his loss in the 1984 Olympic trials to the eventual gold medalist, Henry Tillman, raised questions about his ability to handle slick boxer types. But the urgency of the bidding by the networks to land Tyson reflects a prevailing view that the fighter has come on very quickly in his brief career.

In the ring, there is nothing fancy with Tyson. He works out of a slight crouch, shoulders and head bobbing and when he strikes he is quicker on his feet than a man with his thick-legged, barrel-chested build ought to be. He has knocked down opponents with both hands but the left hook seems the more dangerous punch.

In person he is affable and responsive, a young man who professes a reluctance for the spotlight but is aware of his obligation as a public figure. There is, however, a sense of detachment that perhaps owes to his difficult past—and to D'Amato: "Cus would say, 'Talk and be nice to people, but be careful who you trust.'" Tyson claims to have no close friends. Only in his concern for his pigeons ("I love my birds. They're like my babies.") and in his feeling for the place at the end of the dirt road ("This is my home. It'll always be my home. I don't plan on leaving.") does he let his guard drop.

On November 4, he lost D'Amato, who died of pneumonia at age seventy-seven. "Coming back from Cus's funeral," says Miss Ewald, "he broke down and cried. He said: "Camille, I never knew what love was until now. He taught me so much.' It was the first time I ever saw him cry."

Less than two weeks after D'Amato's death, Tyson fought in Houston, taking with him a photo of D'Amato and himself. "And he told me," says Miss Ewald, "'A lot of people would think I'm crazy. But I talked to Cus. I talked to him every night.'"

TRAVELS WITH TYSON (1990)

From the boardwalk, you could see the big waves slap against the shore, their frothy caps bubbling upon the sand before the next surge of water washed over. By the calendar it was autumn, but the wind that blew up and down the beach already had a wintry edge on it.

For me, even at the height of summer, Atlantic City would never be confused for a tropical paradise. On its six-and-a-half mile boardwalk were soaring casinos with interiors full of baroque excess. But just beyond those gaming halls, out where the Monopoly-board streets of Atlantic and Pacific and Baltic lay was a city sagging and creaking from neglect, streets sunk in doom and poverty.

The best line I ever heard about this place was offered from stage by a brash and rotund comedian named Jackie Gayle, who squinted at the spotlight and then quipped: "The hotels here are worth millions of dollars. You look beyond, it's downtown Beirut."

That's a line that may keep brother Gayle from being invited to lunch by the local Jaycees, but for truth-in-advertising it works pretty well. For me, Atlantic City has always been a claustrophobic sliver of a boardwalk resort, flanked by a sea on one side and a ghetto on the other.

But it's also the place where—redeeming social value—I first caught a glimpse of an unknown fighter named Michael Gerard Tyson. The day was October 25, 1985, and Tyson was in a prelim of a card headlined by a pair of lively featherweights. Tyson's opponent that night was a good head taller, and built lean—an El Greco sort of a heavyweight named Robert Colay. Tyson was Tyson, who from adolescence has looked like the Incredible Hulk's kid brother. A phantasm of such menace was he that in amateur competitions

115

the opposition sometimes would take half gainers practically before Tyson hit them, and afterward their trainers would demand to see Mike's birth certificate.

It took less than half a minute for Tyson to lay the business end of a left hook on this Colay, who went down with his eyes spinning like the wheels of a slot machine. From flat on his back, Colay made it to a sitting position and—strange business—held both gloves against the sides of his head, as though he had an Excedrin headache.

It was not so much that Tyson finished the poor schnook in thirty-seven seconds. It was the authority the kid showed in doing it. Although he radiated a fury that soon enough would make him America's gladiator, Rambo in short pants, what an eye caught in that compressed moment of violence was experience and control far beyond the fighter's recorded history of ten fights, ten knockouts.

I didn't know it then that Tyson was no boxing beginner. He had been prepared for this spotlit life from the time he was thirteen. Even as an amateur he had sparred against young professionals like Carl (The Truth) Williams and Frank Bruno while being tutored in his trade by Cus D'Amato, who had been the manager and trainer of past champions, Floyd Patterson and Jose Torres.

Now I didn't intellectualize that first glimpse of Tyson with the sort of full-fleshed thoughts to which a wage-earning prose writer is prone. But the threads of what I have recorded here were surely present—it was just my reaction was more visceral. That night in AC I got the sort of flash I'd had watching an unknown named Bob Dylan at the Newport (Rhode Island) Folk Festival, or catching a young actress, Julie Christie, in a film called Darling— keen sense that what I was looking at was the real McCoy, a lasting star. A few weeks later—November 15, 1985, to be precise—I parked my car in the driveway of the fourteen-room Victorian house at the end of a dirt road in Catskill, New York, where Tyson had been raised by D'Amato.

That day I would hear from him of those Dickensian circumstances that had led him from street crime in the Brownsville section of Brooklyn to the nasty confines of the juvenile detention system and on to this house that sat on a bluff overlooking the Hudson River. Tyson was fourteen when, on September 2, 1980, he was paroled to D'Amato and moved into the Catskill house. As he told me that first time we met: "My life begins here."

What began there for me was the serpentine odyssey that reporters undertake when they get in on the ground floor of a big man's journey upward. Over the next four years I would be among the pack that followed Tyson east and west across this country, chronicling the glory and infamy of his dizzying life and, when he wandered abroad—to Mexico City, Moscow and Tokyo—monitoring his movements through sources. Through those years we were friends and not-so-friends, fluctuations that were not surprising given the very weird times that Tyson encountered and that I was obliged to report.

It's funny about fame and fighters. Back in 1985, at nearly the same time Tyson and I had our first conversation, I did a lengthy profile for my paper on a fighter named Livingstone Bramble, who was a sports-page exotic by virtue of his vegetarian diet, Rastafarian dreadlocks and a menagerie of pets that included snakes and pit bulls.

In September 1986, Bramble, the W.B.A. lightweight champion, was knocked out by Edwin Rosario, and like-that ceased being of consequence to those of us who patrol the boxing beat. By what factors his irrelevance was determined I'm not sure. No tom-toms beat a message that said lose him, but in a blink Bramble slipped off our radar screens.

Defeat, of course, helped make him our Judge Crater. Fighters are acquired tastes, and the ones that matter are those who win again and again—and do it with a particular luminescent violence. But celebrity, like a thumb print, varies to the man, and each pug's impact has its own incalculable shelf life. Go figure. While that loss to Rosario made Bramble virtually disappear from the sports page, other beaten fighters—Donald Curry, Bobby Czyz, Gerry Cooney, John Mugabi—for some reason remained newsworthy.

And not all winners, it turns out, are created equal either. In a matter of months, the kid Tyson, not yet a ranked contender, had caught the public's fancy. It was early 1986, and folks who usually didn't give a rip about the sport I cover would ask the question I would hear ever increasingly as Tyson's life became more and more entangled in complications and tumults. The question: *What's Mike Tyson really like?*

It was not hard to figure what compelled their interest. The Tyson they saw in the ring was a bobbing, weaving torpedo with an urgency about him that was impossible to miss. He was Robo-Slugger and damned if he didn't look the part. Just under six feet tall, he was all bunchy muscle—from a neck that measured more than nineteen inches around to the tree-trunk legs from which emanated the torque that gave his punches their authority. From certain angles he was so extreme a muscle mass that, with his slightly stooped shoulders and the arms hanging off to the sides, he evoked—indiscreet as it might be to say it—the primordial men who preceded the rest of us centuries upon centuries ago. That was the visual impact of all that body density. To act otherwise was to pretend.

But to the public that aura of invincibility contrasted with what it caught of a kinder, gentler Tyson—the Tyson of that soft and nearly sissified voice and of seemingly vulnerable moments. My first time up to Catskill, I'd seen glimmers of that side. That afternoon, he had led me across the front lawn to the elevated pigeon coop he had built months earlier. He climbed up a ladder and stood on the platform outside the coop, shooing the more than one hundred birds. "Doesn't that look beautiful?"

Maybe a year later, I saw a documentary on D'Amato that offered a revealing look at Tyson when he was fifteen years old. The footage showed a Tyson waiting to step into the ring for the finals of the junior Olympics, which he had won the year before.

On a street near the arena where the fight was to take place, Tyson, in a blue robe with a gold belt, began to pace back and forth. "Just relax, Michael," said his trainer Teddy Atlas, sensing his fighter's nervousness. "Just relax."

As Atlas put his arm around the fighter's shoulder, Tyson began to cry. On the soundtrack, amid his snuffling, only snatches of Tyson's conversation were audible. "When we first started...come a long way, remember? ...Everybody likes me....I'm proud of myself...."

It was, it turned out, but one of several crying jags Tyson had had while awaiting his title fight, and the only such moment that made it into the film. "What he was saying to me," Atlas would tell me later, "was that he had come a long way. 'People like me. I've done good. And people like to know me.' He was afraid of losing all that and he felt that if the guy beat him, he *would* lose that."

Well, he didn't lose his foothold on a new life. The public's curiosity about Tyson ran deep, and his constituency grew well beyond hard-core boxing types. Early on, I received this letter in my *New York Times* mail bin from a female reader:

"Dear Sir:

Is there something wrong with Mike Tyson?

I noticed, while watching his last fight...a nervous jerking of his head.

I have read numerous newspapers and have never seen any mention of this affliction."

Like Terry Malloy—the Marlon Brando character in *On the Waterfront*—he wanted to be a "somebody," and by God he got what he wanted—million-dollar deals with ABC-TV and Home Box Office and media exposure that he sometimes wished would quit. From New York, to points due north, south and west, I saw Tyson grope with his rising celebrity, reluctantly at first and then at times with the gusto of a bandit who'd just stumbled onto the penthouse master key.

In Atlantic City in January, 1986, after he stopped Mike Jameson in five rounds, Tyson wore to the post-fight news conference red-rimmed triangular sunglasses, of the sort one might see at a punk rock concert, and acted surly and indifferent toward the press. It was early in his career, and clearly he was divided on what he would allow himself to feel about it. But that reluctance to enjoy his VIP status changed. He began to dress the part of a heavyweight champion and, where earlier in his career he might show up at public functions in a denim jacket unbuttoned, Mandingo style, to the navel, now he wore designer-brand sports clothes and tailor-made suits.

In a financial statement of his that I saw for 1987, his accountants reported that Tyson had spent $178,314 on clothes and $219,819 on jewelry during that calendar year. The fighter who had once said that he only had to look into the mirror to know he was no Mr. Black America now was attracting women friends even while he pursued a few on his own. Once, as I was walking through the Las Vegas Hilton early one morning, Tyson saw me and waved me over to an empty blackjack table, adjoining an occupied one run by a female dealer. "Tell her," he said, smiling, "what a good guy I am." I told her, but she seemed to want more proof that he'd be worth the bother.

Whatever. Like certain cut-rate furniture stores, Tyson worked on volume. One afternoon, while he was still a contender, I watched him tug the pigtail of a young woman as he waited for a limousine to materialize, and smile shyly when she turned around. Later that night, I saw an attractive production assistant on the Letterman show slip him her phone number as Tyson headed out of the green room and into the city night. As Mel Brooks, in *History of the World, Part I*, said, "It's good to be king."

But even heavyweight kings get the blues, as Robin ("Michael loves me, and he loves my mother") Givens would prove. I was the first newsman to interview the newlyweds at Tyson's East 40th Street apartment in New York, a week after they traded vows in February 1988. I knew theirs had been a tempestuous courtship and mentioned that to Givens. A graduate of Sarah Lawrence College, she invoked the "law of entropy," which she said held that "a stable state is the most confused state."

"If molecules are all in a line, that's when they are most unstable," she said.

I hadn't a clue if any of what she said coincided with what existed in those science texts my schoolboy mind had recoiled from years before, or whether she was fabricating it wholesale right on the spot. But I liked the agility of the mind that could come up with the thought, even if her manner held a glibness that left a lingering doubt. But what the hell, I thought, she's young and she's an actress.

No point here in itemizing the lunatic turns of that marriage. That it got wild, and that it was a marriage made for tabloid page one goes without saying. But I suspect that I knew before you did where the balance of power in the marriage lay. I saw it up close and personal.

It was April 9, 1988. I'd just sent a story to the *Times* that the conflict between Tyson's manager, Bill Cayton, and Givens and her mother, Ruth Roper, was threatening to disrupt what had been, until then, a smooth-running and very profitable business. That night, I arranged to have dinner with Tyson, the women and Don King in Las Vegas to get a reaction to what Cayton had told me earlier that day: "Don King is making moves, I guess, to take over [Tyson]." At the Barronshire Prime Rib, Tyson insisted Cayton had it all wrong: "I don't know why he feels threatened. Bill sounds like he's worried I'm going to leave. I'm not a rat fink or a traitor." Well, you know how that went. Before the year was out Tyson sued Cayton not once but twice to void his managerial control. But we are speaking of that night in April. The telling moment for me came some thirty minutes into dinner when, without any cue from the conversation, Givens cut in to say: "Don King's never approached me or my mother."

It was a perfect non sequitur, meant to dispel speculation, I guess, that she and her mother had allied with King to encourage Tyson to defect from Cayton.

I wrote her words down, studying Givens for a clue as to what had prompted her to say them. As I did, Tyson said, "Oh, my wife is getting upset." With an elbow he nudged me in the ribs, saying, "Please leave. Please leave."

I looked over to Givens and did not think she appeared upset. In fact, suspecting it was a private joke, I hesitated to move, even as Tyson's elbow was prodding me. But when Tyson said, once again, "Please leave, Phil. Please leave," and as that persuasive elbow pressured my ribs, I began to realize that Tyson might be serious.

Still, I was hesitant to budge. I was on to a story that was taking an important turn, and like any reporter, I wanted to poke around it for as long as I could. Again, I eyed Robin, who still did not register the anguish Tyson appeared to think she felt, and at the other parties to see if their expressions would let me in on the joke. But there was no such encouragement, and Tyson's own pained expression seemed genuine.

I got up and left.

But there were instructive echoes in my dinner with the Tysons. When the subject had been dollars and cents—mainly complaints about Cayton's methods of doing business—Tyson had seemed rehearsed. The irony was that as rational as he sounded talking money, he was not as credible as when he spoke about and reacted to his wife, irrational as he might seem then. The image that came to me, as I headed out to my car was of dogs that hear high-pitched whistles the human ear can't register. That night I knew his marriage was headed straight for the crapper.

Right before Labor Day—a week or so after Tyson had punched the Little Richard of heavyweights, Mitch Green, on a street and busted his hand—I arranged to see Tyson at the Bernardsville, New Jersey, mansion where he and Givens were living. For a while now, I had been kept from Tyson by Givens and Roper, who apparently regarded me as not friendly enough to their point of view. But a breakfast meeting was convened so that Mme. Ruth and I could sort out our differences. At the conclusion, I was cleared for further contact with Tyson. But events conspired against me. Two days later, Tyson crashed a BMW into a tree in Catskill and, suffering a concussion, would plunge headlong into chaotic events that a month later would prompt Givens—now publicly declaring him a manic-depressive—to file for divorce.

The next time I saw Tyson was months later when I happened to bump into him at a twenty-four hour workout facility in Las Vegas. Tyson was stepping from a shower after an hour on a stationary bicycle. We exchanged pleasantries, then I tried to arrange an interview for later. "You gonna make me out to be some sort of psychotic killer?" Tyson asked.

"No, a manic-depressive killer," I quipped.

A joke. But Tyson's intent expression showed that the humor had escaped him. Not until I let the tiny smile play out at the corners of my mouth did the heavyweight champion "get it" and relax. But in using that word *psychotic*, Tyson seemed to suggest a certain weariness with fame, and a feeling that the Big Cigars of the boxing press were misconstruing him, blowing things out of proportion.

But that's a kneejerk reflex of any celebrity who has his masks stripped away in public. As Tyson came unglued in a bad marriage, we ink-stained wretches remembered the whispers and innuendos we had heard back in the days of the Cus-and-the-kid tale, of a Tyson more ornery and complex than we had been shown. Probing deeper now, we found that Tyson's unruly behavior with Robin encouraged previously reluctant sources to tell what they knew of the fighter's darker side.

They were not pretty tales. Tyson groped women, was self-centered, unreliable and mean to boot. He had a temper and a relish for violence that sometimes left damage. The TV that stood in the vestibule of Givens' Los Angeles home had no screen because Givens told people Tyson had kicked it in in a fit of temper. Yet she chose not to remove the wreckage. The TV stood there like some modern art irony, an objet de Tyson. Tyson's cornerman, Matt Baranski, who knew the champion from his first days in Catskill, once saw him kick a dog, an $864 sharpei he bought after he won the title. "I told him," said Baranski, "'You son of a bitch. If you weren't so big, I'd haul off and belt you. The thing's only a puppy.' He denied doing it. 'How can you tell me that? I just saw you do it.' Why'd he kick it? 'Cause it was in his way. That's how he is."

How he was was for a while a boxing reporter's *raison d'être*. We amassed all brands of Tyson miscellanea, some of it useful, some not. I could tell you, for instance, that Tyson

• liked Chinese food and Haagen Dazs vanilla Swiss almond ice cream.

• named a white pigeon of his Gerry Cooney.

• occasionally saw a hypnotist.

• would carry big wads of money, which he liked to flash.

• ate thirty-six steamed clams for dinner every night while in training for Tony Tucker.

• had in his New York apartment a black hefty bag full of autographed apparel from pro basketball players he admired.

But there were those more sobering anecdotes that ended up in notebooks too—-often contrary pieces that in their cumulation suggested a conflicted soul caught up in a brute's body. Good Mike/Bad Mike. As a reporter I'd been stood-up, stone-walled and subject to his changeable moods, but less often than I was charmed and intrigued by him. In front of the "boss scribes," as King sometimes called the big-city press, Tyson's behavior tended to be correct. But he was not a mannequin; over four years, sometimes for better or worse he let his guard down. When boredom overtook him at press conferences we saw him rest his head like a child on the shoulder of his late manager, Jimmy Jacobs. And throughout that stormy marriage of his, he played out his violence in public, in "incidents" that became Big News.

By this December, though, when Tyson and I sat one-on-one at the home he and King have in Las Vegas, the heavyweight champion seemed to be more philosophical about the tumults he had experienced. He spoke of the hurt he had felt from his wild and wooly marriage, and his disinclination to get deep into another relationship with a woman. To me, he now seemed a bit more detached about the complex business of being Mike Tyson than when he had wondered months before if I was going to make him out a psychotic. At the Leonard-Durán fight a night later he even stopped by press row and shook hands with some of the boss scribes toward whom he had a grudge. Was this a new mellow phase for Iron Mike? Or just the calm before another storm? Who can say?

But as he pillages the heavyweight ranks—and seems likely to end up an enduring legend in his business—the question before the house is still, can a man who has been in perpetual conflict with himself survive himself beyond the ring ropes?

TYSON TALES FROM THE DARK SIDE (1992)

Not long ago, as I walked through the lobby of Bally's casino in Reno, I saw a photo that stopped me in my tracks.

It was accidental art, a black-and-white closeup of Michael Gerard Tyson, made from a color original. It had been meant as a standard head shot, to be used to hype a closed-circuit telecast of Tyson's projected fight with heavyweight champion Evander Holyfield—the November 8 title match that was postponed in October after Tyson damaged his rib cage.

Anyway, a strange thing had happened in cooking down that pedestrian color shot to shades of gray. The picture turned into a stunning metaphor for the Tyson I had known since 1985, the year he began fighting professionally.

In that photo, one side of Tyson's face was hidden in a deep shadow that cast a broad hint of menace, while the other side, in light, portrayed him as alert, intense and forthright. The picture was a perfect expression of the schism in Tyson's nature that has made him so intriguing to the public and kept the boxing press more than a little busy for the last six years.

Long before Tyson stood accused of raping a beauty pageant contestant in Indianapolis last July—for which he is scheduled to stand trial at the end of January—he seemed a fragmented figure, alternately exposing a dark, troubled aspect with a gentler, kinder side. This was the Tyson who routinely handed out $100 bills to derelicts and a day later espoused the virtues of punching the tip of an opponent's nose "because I try to push the bone into the brain."

In the beginning he was afforded the benefit of the doubt, as new heroes are. What an impression he made as he padded into the ring—always without a robe or socks, wearing black trunks and black high-top shoes, the no-frills gladiator, oiled and greased and

125

ready to go. And he fought with a damn-all fury that registered on even the casual spectator and left his over-powered opponents, when asked what it was like to be hit by him, saying things like "He have a sledgehammer."

Yet in those early days, he seemed a user-friendly heavyweight. In part, that impression came from the lispy, whispery voice and from his habit of analyzing his brutal approach to the game in language that was crisp as a starched collar—an echo, some would say later, of the rhetorical style of Cus D'Amato, the veteran boxing trainer who became Tyson's mentor in the sleepy village of Catskill, New York. The rest had to do with the Cus-and-the-kid tale: old white guy takes a black hooligan and retools his felonious urges into the stuff of champions. We are all suckers, aren't we, for those boot-strap tales of reformed character?

In time, the tale would tarnish a bit as snoops in the press discovered that the reality was not quite so idyllic as the fighter's handlers wanted people to think. Tyson had had his share of problems in Catskill—trouble with teachers, "incidents" with coeds, even the occasional run-in with D'Amato himself. For those of us who covered Tyson, it didn't take long to combine those tales with our own impressions of him and then to wonder how well he would hold up if his career flourished and the clamor increased. By 1986, as he started to become big enough to appear on the *Today* show and on the cover of *Sports Illustrated*, it was clear he was struggling to cope with the furor he was creating.

There was never any accounting for his moods. The first time I interviewed him, in November 1985 in Catskill, he was articulate, expansive and interested. He was an engaging if shy figure. At one point, as I spoke with Camille Ewald, the woman in whose house D'Amato had raised him, he came into the room, sat on the arm of her easy chair and hugged her, saying, "Is Mr. Berger interrogating you, Camille?"

Yet some time later, in the Manhattan offices of his managers, Bill Cayton and Jim Jacobs—who had taken over as Tyson's mentor after D'Amato died in 1985—Tyson was antsy and so removed from the interview that he insisted on doing it while watching old fight films of Jack Dempsey on a small TV monitor. It was a curious interview, with Tyson's responses interrupted by his reactions to the events on the screen: "Wow! Boom! What was your question?"

His changeability would become routine in his relationship with the press and, it seemed, the world at large. Jacobs and Cayton made a point of accentuating the distance Tyson had traveled from his nasty origins in the Brownsville section of Brooklyn. They understood that if Tyson was ever to capitalize beyond the ring on his success, it was imperative that mainstream America feel comfortable with him. Although the public might marvel at the savagery with which Tyson dismantled opponents, it needed to be assured that he was, in a term sport executives love to use, "good people." Good people, and not another athletic creep.

That is why Jacobs and Cayton sought to defuse Tyson's first "incident," in June 1987, when he stole a kiss from a female parking-lot attendant in Los Angeles and then smacked her male superior for butting in. It cost Tyson $105,000 to settle that little problem and avoid the media circus that, his managers assessed, would have attended a lawsuit and trial.

In those days there was always a lurking sense of extremist edges to Tyson. That was what attracted the public to him. They saw him as larger than life in the ring, and that roused curiosity about his life outside it. In time that translated to the big-time celebrity of supermarket tabloid tales and a visibility that attracted the predatory fringe.

I remember Tyson telling me once about the "strange people" who managed to get his unlisted phone number in Catskill. "They call and we talk to them: we're bored," Tyson said. "Girls call. Nuts call to say, 'We're related from another world.' There was this one girl who called. She tells Camille she needs money for an operation. She's been in a bad accident and is paralyzed. She sends pictures showing she's crippled. I look at them and tell Camille. 'She's not crippled.' And you know what? I end up seeing this woman on the TV show about America's most wanted criminals. Turns out she's a con."

A strange world it was for Tyson, source of perpetual curiosity and the target of a multitude of schemes. Yet from the other end of the telescope the view seemed nearly as odd—and grew more so when he found himself in a bad and conspicuous marriage to the actress Robin Givens in 1988.

A week after he married, he was jolly as he boasted to me of how he had—in his words—"suaved" Givens, saying this even as she sat, in a housecoat and with a sleepy expression, sipping early-morning coffee. But in a matter of months, he was snarling and cursing at the press one day, and the next breaking into tears as he spoke of D'Amato.

Then there was the day in New York when he greeted me icily at a shooting session for a Diet Pepsi commercial, and an hour later saw me backstage and threw a bear hug on me and kibitzed. Could I account for either reaction? Hardly.

As the marriage came unglued, so did Tyson. You remember. There was the cockeyed bit of largess when he dented his $180,000 silver Bentley convertible and tried to give it away to a couple of New York Port Authority police officers. There was the early-morning street fight with heavyweight Mitch Green. There was the night Givens went on the TV show "20/20" and made Tyson out to be as volatile as Conan the Barbarian (and manic-depressive to boot) while he sat at her side with a sedated and dopey expression.

It was during this marriage that illusions about his combustible quality dropped away. That is why, I suspect, every transgression of his got big play from the news media. There was a sense now that Tyson was a clear and present danger to Tyson—that eventually he would land in the crapper.

The marriage lasted only eight months—from the civil ceremony in February to Givens's filing for divorce in October. But they were intense months—marked by turbulence and violence and ending in anger and rejection—that would have been traumatic for any twenty-two-year-old man, and especially so for one living them in public view.

John Hornewer, the attorney to a rising heavyweight contender named Lennox Lewis, happened to be on a Chicago street in 1989 when Tyson, his aides and his promoter, Don King, went shopping. "The whole group was in fur coats and they were in a store that had locked its doors to let them shop in private." Hornewer says. "Well, I got there as they unlocked the doors. King led the way. 'Out of the way,' he says, 'Here comes Mike Tyson, heavyweight champion and the greatest fighter of all time.' And the Tyson group kind of pushed its way through the crowd to a limo and off they went.

"I saw that and I thought back to March '87, the morning after Tyson defended his title against Bonecrusher Smith in Las Vegas. I came down to the hotel lobby and Tyson was standing there by himself. I congratulated him on the victory. He didn't know me, but he gave me a big hug and said: 'Thanks for coming. I'm sorry I gave such a bad performance.' He seemed like a such a happy, nice kid."

Those vignettes of Hornewer's capture the broad strokes of this contradictory soul—the vulgarian excess and the little-boy sweetness. Tyson's unsettled nature seemed to hold the increasing possibility that somewhere, sometime, he would detonate, and his sumptuous life would go up in smoke.

By January 1989, Jacobs too had died and Don King had usurped Cayton as the guiding force behind Tyson's career. King's approach, for all his flamboyance, was like that of the managers before him—accentuate the positive and let the lawyers clean up the problems.

So when Tyson gave out Thanksgiving turkeys to the poor, or made donations to charity, or received an honorary degree, it tended not to be kept a secret. The public-relations axis of the Tyson enterprise would swing into action.

The irony here was that Tyson in private was far more generous than he was in these public shows of philanthropy. He bought jewelry, cars and more for friends of both genders. Rock Newman, the manager of heavyweight Riddick Bowe, wandered into the Gucci shop at Caesars Atlantic City on the morning after Tyson knocked out Tyrell Biggs in October 1987, and noted the doors were locked while a group of young people were shopping inside.

"I counted twelve people," says Newman, "and they were: 'Give me two of these, two of those.' I said to a salesperson, 'What's going on?' She said, 'These people are guests of Mike Tyson. We're taking care of them, giving them what they want.' I watched. One person rang up $2,700 in 10 minutes."

Tyson himself quickly became an elite consumer. Under Givens he began dressing up and in time he would lavish as much praise on the style of Gianni Versace as he did on those gritty turn-of-the-century fighters he had studied under D'Amato and Jacobs.

After his divorce, he moved to Southington, Ohio, near King, and settled into a six-bedroom, 27,000-square-foot home on sixty-six acres, a place that had the lavish refinements only a man of monstrous success could afford. The living room had a one hundred-inch television screen and a 1,100-pound chandelier, and the balcony overlooking the room was bordered by brass railing.

"Brass and gold—if I was an architect, they'd be my trademark," Tyson said as he gave me a tour of the place.

Tyson's bed was covered with a fox-fur blanket replete with foxtails, and there were seventy-two pairs of size-13 shoes and sneakers in a walk-in closet that was the size of a small studio apartment. The recreation room had a slate-and-marble pool table that doubled as a craps table one night when Tyson won 60 grand from King.

But the most conspicuous show of wealth was in his driveway. Parked there were nine luxury cars—a Rolls-Royce, two Porsches, two Ferraris, a red Range Rover, a Lamborghini and two Mercedeses, including a four-door convertible that Tyson said was custom-made for him. When I noted the mileage on the odometers and did the arithmetic, the average came out to a little more than 4,000 miles of use per vehicle.

"Yeah," said Tyson. "I don't drive them much. I just like having them."

He said it with an affecting shyness, a boyish quality that strangers found endearing. The shyness was no put-on, but those who knew him better were aware of how fleeting his moods could be. A year after I saw the place in Southington, Tyson had occasion to drive from there to New York in one of those fancy cars of his.

That morning, at a news conference for his fight against Holyfield, when asked about the journey, he called it "a fly ride," and then added: "It's one that you'll never have."

What prompted that sudden peevishness was not clear to his interrogators. It was Tyson being Tyson—mercurial, a man who resisted easy understanding.

By his last fight, against Donovan (Razor) Ruddock in June 1991, hardly a day passed in which Tyson's civility was not impugned. While in training he had punched an ABC-TV camera lens into disrepair, and during a news conference to promote the bout he talked to Ruddock with brutishness uncommon even among fighters. He said Ruddock was best suited to be his concubine. "You're a transvestite," Tyson said at one point. "You know you really like me. I'm going to make you my girlfriend June 28. I'll make you kiss me with those big lips."

Yet later I stumbled into an instance of good Mike. While watching Tyson train, I saw a retired fighter, Scott LeDoux, sitting with Tyson's sparring partners. LeDoux, forty-two years old, was a heavyweight who fought in the late 1970s and early 1980s.

These days, LeDoux told me, he worked as a salesman for a freight company in Minneapolis. A year and a half earlier, LeDoux's wife had died of cancer. The medical care for her had left LeDoux and his two children in a financial pinch. Tyson had heard about LeDoux's situation and invited him to training camp nearly two months before the fight with Ruddock. While LeDoux was fit enough, he was now just a middle-aged fighter.

"Mike used him once in sparring early on," Tyson's trainer, Richie Giachetti, said, "and realized it wouldn't work. But he told me, 'Richie, keep him on. Keep paying him.'" Tyson's sparring partners routinely get $1,000 a week.

"I'll tell you this about Mike Tyson," LeDoux said. "He's got a lot more heart than folks give him credit for."

A month later he was charged with rape.

In the tumultuous eight months of Tyson's marriage, there were plenty of clues that Tyson was wired for his own destruction. In fact, there were enough to incite the doomsayer's impulse in me as

I finished a book on Tyson in that summer of 1988. As I wrote then: "A premonition crept upon [me] and wouldn't let go, that this was another Joplin or Hendrix—live fast and die. Dead or arrested before his time—that was the creepy intuition that played in [my] mind..."

Of course, the words flashed back at me this last July when news of Tyson's alleged rape of an eighteen-year-old contestant for Miss Black America moved on the wires. In September he was indicted in Indianapolis and two days later he was arraigned. That afternoon I was aboard the same flight from Indianapolis to Las Vegas that Tyson was on. One of the other passengers asked the flight attendant to get Tyson's autograph for him. "Tell him to sign it, 'To Steve,'" he said.

When the attendant returned with Tyson's signature on a piece of lined paper, the passenger turned to the man next to him and said, "If he gets sixty-three years, it'll be worth a lot more."

On Tyson's arrival in Vegas, fans waved and voiced encouragement as he moved through McCarran International Airport. "She's just trying to get famous off you, champ," one man kept shouting.

"You dick!" one woman screamed at him and raced ahead to harangue him again.

A Las Vegas TV sportscaster shouted at him: "How come you only answer the soft questions, Mike?"

Tyson appeared indifferent to the tumult. He stood tall and looked calm. He answered reporters' questions on the move, giving pat responses—"I'm okay...Looking forward to the [Holyfield] fight...I'm innocent and will prove it"—before making it to the ever-present limousine that swept him away.

But a few weeks later, when I returned to Las Vegas for three days, Tyson seemed more restless, as though the pressures on him had turned his focus inward. Word was he had not expected to be indicted in Indianapolis—King supposedly had assured him he wouldn't be—and Tyson had been stunned and angry when it hadn't turned out that way. In any case, he wasn't exactly in a chatty mood when we met up.

His expression was bland. His answers were neutered of emotion and detail. His words were robo-speak. The idea that Tyson is unaffected by the chaos that often surrounds him doesn't hold.

Just what Mike Tyson did in room 606 at the Canterbury Hotel in Indianapolis last July 19 is not for me to say. Sometime in 1992, a jury will weigh the evidence and then judge him. He faces a maximum sentence of sixty-three years in prison if found guilty on all four counts in the indictment: rape, two counts of criminal deviate conduct (digital penetration and oral sex) and confinement.

Should Tyson end up doing time in Marion County, Indiana, I for one will not lapse into shock. In the summer of 1988 when I imagined a grim ending for Tyson, I figured if it happened it would involve a woman.

After coming onto the boxing beat in 1985, I kept hearing stories that had as a common thread Tyson's playing women cheap. What was compelling was the diversity of sources who would mention, in passing, a nasty bit of misogyny involving Tyson—tales told mostly without my broaching the subject, unsolicited testimony that took on force in my mind.

A female photographer told me Tyson had walked up to her during a shoot and, without so much as a hello, had taken her breasts in hand and squeezed. A West Coach fight manager talked about overhearing Tyson at a post-fight party in L.A. propositioning women in the rawest, most direct way. José Torres, a former world champion who had been a confidant of the fighter and later wrote a book about him, related to me conversations in which Tyson expressed pleasure at "hurting" women, through anal sex.

In 1988, Tyson's amateur trainer, Teddy Atlas, told me that Tyson had had problems with women as a teenager. "He'd verbally, and a little physically, force himself on girls in school. There were a whole bunch of incidents reported, incidents by young girls in school. They'd say no. He'd get emotional. Wasn't good emotion. He felt he had a right to act that way."

After Tyson was indicted, I called Atlas, who declined to add to his previous accounts of Tyson's problems with women for fear, he said, that it would harm Tyson's case in Indianapolis. But Atlas stood by what he had said and corroborated back in '88, including the details of a run-in with Tyson over an incident with Atlas's teenaged sister-in-law.

She told Atlas's wife that Tyson had put his hands on her in school. When Atlas found out, he confronted Tyson—with, it was rumored, a gun in his hand. "I had something in my hand—let's leave it at that," said Atlas in 1988.

After his marriage crumbled, Tyson became entangled in several incidents involving women. By his own admission, he was drinking heavily and feeling forlorn. In December 1988, after Tyson spent a night at a New York disco, Sandra Miller of Queens, and Lori Davis of Bay Shore, New York, filed separate lawsuits charging that Tyson had fondled them. Miller eventually won a token $100; Davis settled her case.

In January 1989, at the Desert Inn Hotel and Casino in Las Vegas, Tyson gave a deposition in his lawsuit to void his management contract with Cayton. There was a moment toward the end of the two days of testimony when lawyers for both sides conferred about dates for future depositions.

As I and several other New York boxing writers watched on a closed-circuit television in an adjoining room, Tyson began speaking softly to somebody just out of camera range. It was obvious he was trying to be charming. Then he began to gesture—poking a finger through a circle formed by his thumb and index finger. It wasn't hard for the newsmen to guess he was coming on to Joann Crispi, an associate of Cayton's attorney, Thomas Puccio.

A day earlier she had told me during a break that Tyson had asked her out. "I told him, 'I'm the opposition,'" she said. "He said, 'So what. You're not doing anything.'"

When the second day's depositions ended, reporters sought out Crispi, who confirmed that, yes, it was to her Tyson had been talking on the closed-circuit screen. "I want to fuck you," she said Tyson told her.

Even as I lay out these tales, I know there are stories that make a better impression for Tyson. I have spoken to girlfriends of his who beat the word *gentleman* like a tom-tom and insist the untold story is the boldness with which many women approach him. They say he is more victim than victimizer.

What I have glimpsed of Tyson's interactions with women has often been tame enough. One time, as I walked through a hotel lobby, I heard a theatrical throat clearing. When I looked up, there was a smiling Tyson, with a good-looking woman on his arm, extending his hand for a high five. Yeah, I suppose that word *boyish* would apply there, as it did one time back in June 1987, when he was asked how things were going and he blurted out, "I'm in love"—referring to Givens—and then he blushed.

Of course, there have always been skeptics who say the two sides of Tyson are really the same, that the sweet side simply reflects the ingenuity that certain jailbird sorts have for ingratiating themselves, and that the real Tyson has always been mean-spirited to the core.

In Marion County, the jurors who look into Tyson's behavior of last July will have more than an opinion about how dark his heart is. They will have the ability to bring consequences.

On February 10, 1992, Tyson was convicted of one count of rape and two counts of deviant conduct, exposing him to a potential jail term of sixty years. His sentence is currently on appeal.

JAMES "BONECRUSHER" SMITH. © 1992 Anthony Neste/HBO.

Left to right: LOU DUVA, VINNY PAZIENZA, KEVIN ROONEY. ©1989, 1992
John R. Hornewer.

EVANDER HOLYFIELD vs. BERT COOPER, November 1991. © 1991 Tony
Triolo/HBO.

HECTOR CAMACHO. ©1992 John R. Hornewer.

BERBICK vs. THOMAS, March 22, 1986. © 1986 Jack Goodman/HBO.

LEONARD vs. DURAN III, Las Vegas, December 7, 1989. This was the first fight at the Mirage. ©1989 John R. Hornewer.

FOREMAN vs. RODRIGUES, June 16, 1990. ©1990 John R. Hornewer.

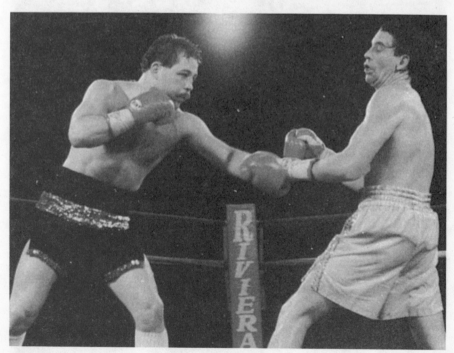

BOBBY CZYZ (left) vs. DONNY LALONDE, May 8, 1992. ©1992 John R. Hornewer.

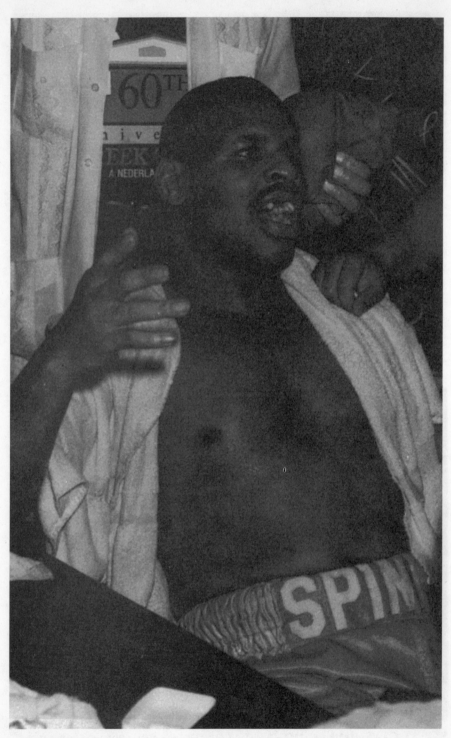

LEON SPINKS. ©1992 John R. Hornewer.

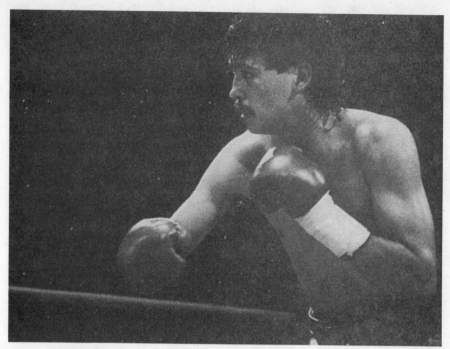

PAUL GONZALES. Courtesy of *Boxing Illustrated.*

AL STANKIE, trainer of Paul Gonzales. Courtesy of *Boxing Illustrated.*

MIKE TYSON and DON KING. Courtesy of Don King Productions.

Left to right: COONEY, KING, HOLMES. ©1982 Hollis Stein, Don King Productions.

TYSON. ©1989 John R. Hornewer.

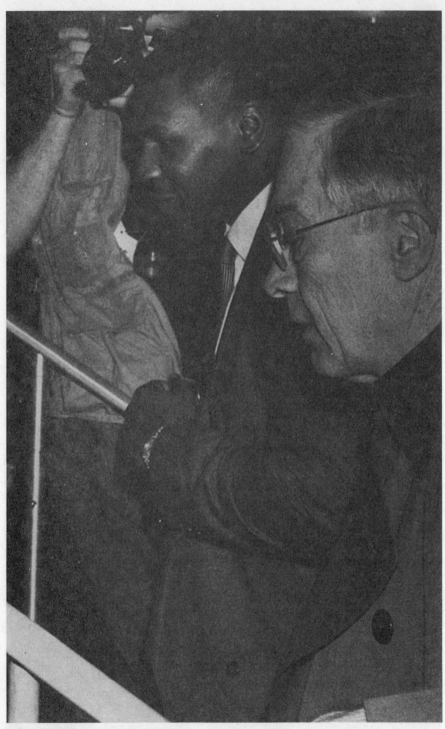

MIKE TYSON with Vincent Fuller on the way to the court room in Indianapolis for verdict and sentencing. ©1992 John R. Hornewer.

RIDDICK BOWE (standing) vs. EVANDER HOLYFIELD, November 13, 1992.
©1992 Phil Masturzo.

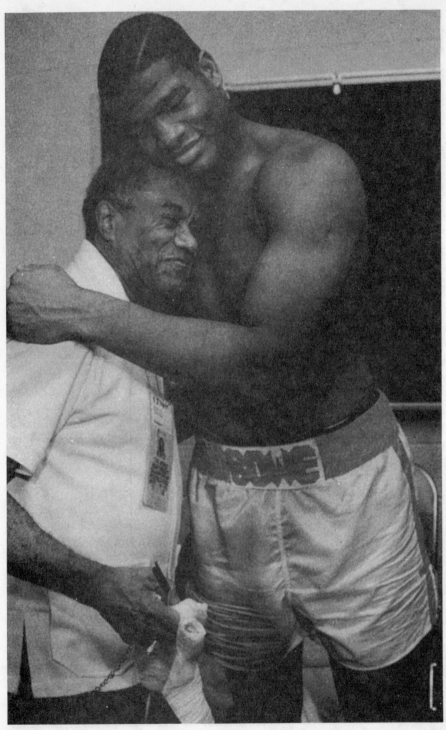

RIDDICK BOWE hugging EDDIE FUTCH after winning the heavyweight title:
November 13, 1992. ©1992 Phil Masturzo.

PART TWO: GUYS IN THE BIZ

They also serve who fine-tune and finagle.

RAY ARCEL AND FREDDIE BROWN
The Sunshine Boys (1980)

Freddie Brown is steaming.

The clock on the wall of Gleason's Gym on W. 30th Street is inching toward 1 p.m., and Brown is sneaking glances at the door and wondering where in hell is Roberto Duran.

The welterweight champion of the world is late for training. And since Brown is charged with getting the fighter into shape, he takes this tardiness personally. Yet such problems are routine for Brown. Over the eight odd years during which he has prepared Duran for his matches, the seventy-three-year-old trainer often has had an unwilling accomplice in Duran.

His job is complicated by Roberto's *manana* attitude toward training and the extra poundage he invariably brings to it. Duran, you see, has a weakness for food and drink that, to hear it from Freddie, leaves Roberto between fights looking more like William Howard Taft than a man in trim.

Sometimes Brown's eighty-one-year-old partner, Ray Arcel, is around to help him cajole Duran. But Arcel is still active in the metals business, and only in the final weeks before a fight does he assume a more conspicuous role. Until then, the real grind of getting Duran into condition falls to Brown.

It's why Freddie Brown is fuming on this day in Gleason's. He's standing in a black hat and black overcoat, the familiar cigar jutting from his mouth, and is muttering about his no-show fighter. That Duran is late for training, maybe even AWOL, with only seven weeks left before his rematch against Sugar Ray Leonard is a sacrilege to Brown, who regards a fighter's condition with the sort of single-mindedness which the Kamikaze forces gave the emperor's war effort. "This is an important week," he mumbles, the cigar tipping up toward his bent nose. "How's he gonna get in

139

shape? They were supposed to bring him over. Nobody does nothing. How the hell's he gonna be ready? The most important fight of his career."

He slips a dime in the slot of the pay phone on the wall and calls the hotel at which Duran is registered. No answer from Duran's room. That does it for Brown. He bolts out the door of Gleason's and on up Eighth Avenue, headed for the subway and a trip back home to the Bronx. "He don't even wanna train," he says, a wounded tone to his voice. "Well, fuck him."

While Brown is muttering darkly on Eighth Avenue about Duran, the champ's other trainer, Ray Arcel, is in Scottsdale, Arizona, for the annual convention of the Meehanite Metal Corp. Arcel is a purchasing agent for the firm. And though a fulltime salaried employee, he manages to slip away from the convention from time to time and phone New York for reports from the Duran camp on Roberto's progress.

Despite the squeeze that business puts on his time, Arcel plays his role with Duran. It was he who looked after Roberto while Brown was in Las Vegas training Larry Holmes for his heavyweight title match last month against Muhammad Ali. On weekends, Arcel traveled to Grossinger's, the Catskills resort at which Duran was lodged.

With his long years in boxing, Arcel knows the fighter's psyche—and what makes it flourish. "Duran," he says, "lives awfully hard. You know, he's from a small country (Panama) and is a kind of god there. His followers drag him and pull him. After a fight, he stops working and starts partying. We had to give him a couple weeks away from the hero-worshipers. They can destroy you. What we wanted to do at Grossinger's was to get Roberto into his preliminary training."

Early or late in his training, Duran can be intransigent about doing what his trainers ask. "Freddie and Roberto," says fight publicist/matchmaker Bobby Goodman, "fight like cats and dogs. Freddie is a taskmaster. Roberto will scream and holler and curse in Spanish. Then he'll come back and apologize and do what Freddie wants."

That this old-boy tandem of Brown and Arcel is handling a fighter as volatile as Duran seems, on the face of it, a mismatch—an imposition on two aged boxing souls. Do not be deceived. They are uncanny men—and easily up to the job. In Brown and Arcel, fight people swear, Duran has as savvy a pair of corners as a pugilist could want.

Angelo Dundee, who trained Ali and now works with Leonard: "One night I saw Ray Arcel do something. His fighter knocked the other guy down. And as the referee counted, Arcel climbed the steps to the ring and made like he was throwing the robe over his fighter's shoulders. What this did was divert the referee. He got confused with the count, and counted the guy out even though the guy had gotten up in time."

Tony Carione, the manager of former middleweight champ Vito Antuofermo: "Freddie Brown is one of the best. He's a guy who goes into detail with fighters. Every time a fighter makes a move, Freddie can give you a counter-move. A lotta trainers can't.

"Also, he makes sure his fighter gets in shape. He'll be with a fighter constantly. Wakes him up in the morning. goes to watch him run. Sits with him when he has breakfast. Walks with him after breakfast. Et cetera, et cetera. A lotta trainers are not as attentive as Freddie. They'll say, 'You run. I'll be at the hotel.'"

Through Arcel and Brown, Duran has the benefit of a cumulative century of boxing experience—years clocked in dingy arenas and big-time boxing palaces. Along the way, the two have become masters of righting body and soul in a fighting man.

Brown, for instance, is considered the finest "cut man" in boxing, which means he is adept at stopping the flow of blood from a gash on a man's face. Fights are lost for lack of a corner's skill in these between-round crises.

"He uses good stuff," says Carione. "It's like a paste. And if the cut is real bad, he'll use the swab stick to apply his stuff. And then put the Vaseline over it. The thing about Freddie is, he's cool in the corner. Some guys—they fumble and drop things. They get all excited. Not him. He don't get rattled. He told me that years ago he could stop three, four cuts in the minute between rounds. Maybe he's not as quick as he used to be with the cuts, but he's still okay in my book."

Arcel is regarded as a keen strategist. Duran has lost only one bout in his pro career, a non-title fight to Esteban DeJesus, who knocked Duran down with a left hook as Roberto started to throw his right. Arcel knew that Duran would be pumped to get back at DeJesus and feared he'd be waylaid again. With Carlos Eleta, Duran's manager, as interpreter, Arcel told Duran: "You want to go out there and kill him, I know. But he's expecting you to do it. You go right-hand crazy, he'll sit you on your duff. So you come out and you will box." Arcel waited until the 11th round before telling Duran: "Now." Roberto promptly kayoed DeJesus.

In Duran's last fight against Leonard, Arcel and Brown may have gotten Roberto an edge in how the bout was officiated. They vociferously objected to the choice of Carlos Padilla as referee, claiming he broke up clinches too quickly to allow Duran his infighting advantage over Leonard. Brown pointed to Padilla's handling of the middleweight title bout his fighter, Antuofermo, lost to Alan Minter last March as proof of Padilla's quick-break impulse. The lobbying they did for a different referee was calculated to make Padilla think twice about breaking the fighters prematurely.

And lest Padilla forget, Arcel and Brown were there to remind him the night of the Leonard bout in Montreal. As soon as he entered the ring, Brown wagged his finger at Padilla and growled: "You let my fighter fight. Don't do what you did to Antuofermo." Arcel took a more diplomatic tack: "Listen, Padilla. You are one of the best referees in boxing. Let these men fight. The whole world will be watching you."

Padilla allowed Duran the mauling tactics he'd denied Antuofermo against Minter. Some say that it made a difference in what proved to be a very closely-scored bout.

"One of the most touching things I ever saw in boxing came immediately after the fight," says Bobby Goodman. "There was a big crowd of people in Duran's dressing room. And I hear Roberto: 'Bobby. Bobby. Where Freddie?' I find Freddie, tell him Roberto wants him. And here's Duran, holding the championship belt. He gives it to Freddie, says, 'Here, Freddie. This your belt. You the champ.'

"Well, Freddie was so touched. Tears came to his eyes. Here's this old, gruff guy. Nothing ever fazes him. He looked at me, said, 'He give me the belt. He give me the belt!'"

They may be kindred boxing spirits—two men who have spent long years in the fight racket—but Arcel and Brown are an odd collaboration—more different than alike.

Arcel is a lean man, whose crisp diction gives him a professorial air not usually associated with fight trainers. Arcel attended Stuyvesant High in Manhattan—a school requiring stiff academic entrance exams—and at one point intended to be a doctor. His world is not restricted to boxing: Arcel moves in business and cultural spheres, counting among his interests art, opera and the theater. And yet in his career as a trainer, he has worked with 19 world champions, including Benny Leonard, Ezzard Charles, Abe Attell, Abe Goldstein and Duran.

Arcel retired from boxing in 1955 and came back to work with Duran only as a favor to Eleta. He tends no other pugs these days and agreed to be associated with Duran so long as Brown could work with the fighter on a daily basis.

With his flattened nose, squinty gaze and protruding cigar, Brown's is the look of a fully certified fight figure. And what you see, in Freddie's case, is what you get. He is a crusty, introverted fellow, on the smallish side, who puts all the force of his presence into training boxing professionals.

"He is," says matchmaker Teddy Brenner, "the closest thing to the Burgess Meredith trainer in the film *Rocky*. A loner, a guy who'd tell a fighter to get lost if he didn't do as he was told. I've seen Freddie a lotta times tell a guy—'Get another trainer.'

"Freddie doesn't bend. A fighter does it his way or not at all. It's why he's always in a bit of a hassle with Duran. A lotta trainers listen to what the fighters say. Freddie won't. 'The hell with him. Let him get somebody else.' And that's in his favor."

With a fighter's interest at stake, Brown can be testy. "Especially," says Goodman, "when it comes to the fighter's food. Walks into a place. 'Where's the food?' He doesn't like to have his fighters waiting. Five minutes after he's ordered: 'It's half an hour. Where's the food?' He rates the waitresses at the hotels where his fighters stay. From No. 1, the best, to No. 10. He walks in, he says, 'Gimme No. 1 (waitress). She's not working? Gimme No. 2.' Any edge he can get for his fighter."

RAY ARCEL:

"I grew up in an Italian section in East Harlem. We were the only Jewish family living there. Because of that, as a kid I was in a fight every day.

"My father, who was in the wholesale candy, nuts and fruits business, put the thought of being a doctor in my head. At Stuyvesant I studied Latin, French, subjects like that.

"But I started to hang around a gym on 116th Street, between Seventh and Eighth Avenues, called Grupp's. I used to work out there. And sometimes I'd fight these no-decision amateur bouts in gyms converted to fight clubs on weekends. They wouldn't weigh you. They'd look at you, point to another youngster and say, 'You and you fight.'

"What it was about boxing that attracted me, I'm not sure. I just became fascinated with the damn thing. After a while, I began hanging around two great trainers—Dai Dolling and Frank (Doc) Bagley. Bagley managed Gene Tunney. Before boxing was legalized in New York in 1920, they'd work in these clubs that had no-decision contests. And I'd be there too, in these smoke-filled places— back rooms, usually—swinging a towel.

"One time Doc had a kid boxing in New Jersey. He said to me, 'I'll send you over there to take care of the kid.' And the first thing I did was to buy a plug of chewing tobacco because I wanted to be Doc Bagley. Doc always chewed. Anyway, I got so excited during the bout, I swallowed the plug. And got sick as a dog. They had to call an ambulance. I've never touched tobacco since.

"In the old days, they didn't have dressing rooms as they do today. One big room—that was all. You got there early enough, you'd grab a nail to hang your clothes. After the fights, the fighters would talk about their experiences. Guys like Benny Leonard, Abe Goldstein. And you'd learn from one another. Over a period of time, I handled so many fighters that I began to pick up tricks of the trade.

"When Grupp got drunk, he'd make anti-Semitic remarks. So a bunch of us went to a place on 125th Street, near Seventh Avenue. There was something there called the Marshall Stillman Movement. Stillman was a millionaire who wanted to get the kids off the street and into the gym. He put in charge a retired policeman named Lou Ingber. People thought Ingber was Stillman and they'd call him "Mr. Stillman." And pretty soon he let himself be Lou Stillman. Eventually, he opened Stillman's Gym downtown—near the last Madison Square Garden on Eighth Avenue. That was where I met Freddie Brown."

FREDDIE BROWN:

"I grew up on the Lower East Side. Forsythe Street. Quit school in the eighth grade 'cause I had to make a living.

"My father had a horse and wagon. His jobs were, like, go here, go there. Today, the only horse and wagon is what goes through Central Park.

"As a kid, I was a good street fighter. That's how you become a fighter. In those days, we didn't use knives or sticks. Just fists. I used to win all the fights. Always come out on top.

"I took up amateur boxing. My parents objected. 'Go to work. Don't be no fighter. Learn a trade.' To them, a trade equaled money.

"I'd tell 'em, 'I'm not fighting, I'm not fighting.' Those days, a fighter was supposed to be, like, a bum. That's what people believed.

"I won sixty-eight of seventy amateur fights. Then I had a bad operation on my nose. And I quit. I started working in a shoe factory. And on the side, I'd train amateur kids. I worked with the amateurs for five years, and then I went with the pros. My first big fighter was Bob Pastor, who fought Joe Louis twice. Soon as I went with the pros, I quit the job in the shoe factory and never went back."

It's the day after Freddie Brown has cut and run on Duran, angry over his fighter's being late.

Brown is seated in Gleason's balcony, sipping coffee and looking down across the gym's two rings, toward the door. Waiting on Duran.

The gym is astir with the sounds of the trade; the thud of fists against heavy bags; the staccato beat of speed bags; the scuff of gym shoes against the canvas of the rings; the exaggerated snorts of fighters exerting.

Then Duran is coming through the door, amid the white blasts of flash bulbs—Duran with sparring partners and entourage.

Brown lifts up in his seat, his face registering a tiny note of pleasure. For an hour, he will watch as the fighter goes through his paces, salsa music blaring in the background. When Duran spars, Brown will be leaning over the ring ropes, occasionally rolling his shoulders to Roberto's moves and exhorting him: "...Don't drop your hands...give him a little fake, then boom boom boom....Move your head, move your head. That's it." As Duran spars he will steal glances at the trainer—as if to say: Am I doing okay? And Brown will give a curt nod: yes—fine, just fine.

When it is all over, when Duran has emitted his last odd grunt, a strange dolphin-like, high-pitched note he makes as he digs punches into his sparring partners, Brown will peel the yellow towel off his shoulder and mop the champion's face. Then, for the first time in two days, Freddie Brown will allow himself a hint of a smile. "Tomorrow," he tells the champ, "more work. More work. Heh?" Duran's eyes narrow, he fixes Brown with his fierce gaze. But in the end, he nods. More work, indeed. In this ring, at least, the old boys prevail.

Freddie Brown passed away in 1986.
Ray Arcel is retired from boxing.

GEORGE BENTON: The Ex-Middleweight Who Won Ali's Title (1978)

The fight was over. Muhammad Ali had lost the heavyweight championship. And no sooner did his conqueror, twenty-four-year-old Leon Spinks, jubilantly raise his arms toward the roof of the Las Vegas Hilton Pavilion than viewers everywhere began speculating about the surprising outcome. Theories ranged from the reasonable (that age finally had caught up with Ali) to the absurd (that the fight had been fixed).

But the insider's view was voiced by an Ali aide named Gene Kilroy. As he watched the new champion move past a crowd of well-wishers to his dressing quarters, Kilroy pointed to a trim, athletic-looking man in Spinks' group and said, "There's the guy who beat us."

The guy was George Benton, a forty-five-year-old trainer and ex-middleweight contender from Philadelphia. Benton had been summoned to Las Vegas eight days before the Ali fight by Butch Lewis, a vice-president of Top Rank, Inc., the promoter of Spinks' bouts.

Lewis knew that Benton had revived the careers of veteran middleweights Bennie Briscoe and Willie (The Worm) Monroe, and that his tutoring had aided a number of promising young boxers. Benton had been working as a trainer for ex-champion Joe Frazier's stable of fighters since 1974, following his lengthy recovery from a bullet wound that had ended his twenty-one-year-old fight career in 1970. Lewis ranked Benton at the top of his profession alongside veteran trainers Ray Arcel and Angelo Dundee. "George," said Lewis, "is like a specialist, a man who can give a fighter fine tuning. Like, you can have a mechanic in a service station—but George would be the one you'd take your car to if you planned to

147

put it on the track." Spink˙ ˙esperately needed Benton's expertise, Lewis felt. "I got to have you out here," he told Benton over the phone.

Benton had been called in for Spinks' previous bout against Italy's Alfio Righetti and asked to refine Leon's rough-house style. In camp for the Righetti fight, though, George had felt "unfriendly vibrations" from Spinks' trainer, a white-haired, rotund gentleman named Sam Solomon, who appeared to take Benton's presence as an affront to his own professionalism. It made Benton reluctant to get involved with Spinks again: "If you know a guy ain't comfortable with you being around," Benton said, "it makes you feel uncomfortable too." What overcame Benton's reluctance about returning to Las Vegas and Spinks again was not Butch Lewis' persuasiveness so much as Philadelphia's wintry climate. As Benton recalled: "It was snowing back here. I looked out the window and saw all that snow and figured, 'What the hell. This is as good a chance as any to get away.' So I told Butch Lewis, 'Okay, I'll come.'" On such quirks is fight history made.

For boxing observers who had seen Spinks muddle his way to a draw against journeyman Scott LeDoux last October and then eke out a narrow victory over Righetti in November, the Ali fight was a revelation. Leon Spinks suddenly had a touch of class. Where previously he'd fought with a disdain for the subtleties of boxing and relied on a furious expenditure of punches, against Ali he combined aggressiveness with scientific boxing. He bobbed and feinted and no longer was an easy target for punches.

"I told him," said Benton, "your main objective is not to get hit. You've got to make Ali miss. You can't let this guy hit you back. When he starts them flurries, get down, get down and make him miss, make them punches go by you. You can't get hit. Don't let him land on you. Because if you hit him three punches and he hits you one, he's winning with the officials."

That was only part of Benton's plan. The rest focused on neutralizing Ali's assets—the stinging jab and uncanny footwork for a thirty-six-year-old heavyweight.

From the opening bell on February 15, it appeared that Spinks had learned his lessons. Moments into the first round, Ali circled and Spinks came after him, mimicking Muhammad's footwork step-for-step. This was how Benton had told Spinks to cut off the ring against Righetti, but Spinks didn't care about scientific boxing then. But with the title at stake against Ali, Leon cut off the ring and carefully carried out Benton's other plans. Well before the end of the fight, it was obvious that Benton's message had gotten through to Spinks, and then to the Ali camp (which recognized Benton's work), and finally to the ringside press (whose postfight analyses credited Benton with a key role in dethroning Ali).

The sudden celebrity was the last thing Benton had anticipated in May, 1970 when he lay wounded in Temple University Hospital in Philadelphia, his boxing career over and his future looking bleak. Benton had been shot by a local character known as "Chinaman," who had struck Benton's sister Nettie in a bar and later been beaten in retaliation by Benton's brother Henry.

Looking to get even, Chinaman had returned with a .38 caliber pistol and fired at the first Benton to happen by, who turned out to be innocent-victim George. A few weeks after, an unknown gunman killed Chinaman. Benton took no satisfaction. He was in intense pain and facing several operations.

His recovery was slow and agonizing for a man used to expressing himself physically. It affected body and soul, and led George to have a strange, nearly mystical experience. "I'm going to tell you something I've never told to anybody else," he said. "I'm lying in bed one night in the hospital, and I heard a voice. It said, 'George, you've been a lucky man all your life. You were a good fighter. You were a good hustler. You never had it too bad as a young man. You could really take care of yourself. You've been in the limelight all your life. Now I'm going to take all this away from you. *Like that!*'"

Benton, who is given to saying "God works in mysterious ways," understood the voice to be challenging him to make a new life, a prospect that scared him: "I was afraid I just couldn't make no living once I got myself well."

Friends of George set him up in a small numbers operation briefly while he recuperated. It was not until 1974 that Benton found his true calling. That was when Joe Frazier, preparing for a bout with Jerry Quarry, called Benton and asked him to come by the gym while Smokin' Joe's trainer, Eddie Futch, was busy elsewhere.

"Joe knew I was hurting," Benton said. "And he knew I must have needed a little money. Instead of saying, 'George, put this in your pocket,' he was calling me to come into the gym, pal around with him, talk to him and maybe show him a few things. But after he saw that he was really getting a headful from me, he wanted me to stay on. I told him, 'Joe, I don't want to interfere. Eddie's your trainer.' When Eddie came back, though, Joe said to him: 'Eddie, do you mind if George works with us?' Eddie was glad to have me. We never had a moment's problem."

That Benton had a keen boxing knowledge to impart was no surprise. As a draftee in the Korean War, George took a nondescript Army boxing team and made it a champion. Earlier, as the sub-teenage protege of a Philadelphia trainer named Joe Rose, George had tended pros. "Joe Rose," said Benton, "used to leave me with his fighters when he'd go out on the road. And I'm a kid—only about eleven, twelve years old—but the fighters listened to me like I was the trainer. You, a stranger, not from Philadelphia, you'd say, 'How the hell did he leave a little kid there like that?'"

Ask Joe Rose that question, and he says: "George did the job. Are you kidding? I wouldn't have left him there if he couldn't. When I'd come back from the road, my fighters would be ready."

So too was Spinks ready against Ali, but the press' emphasis on Benton's work slighted Sam Solomon. The veteran trainer had been with Spinks since his first professional fight in January, 1977, and Solomon had gained earlier prominence for guiding heavyweight Ernie Terrell. While Benton was not responsible for news coverage of the fight, he apparently was seen by Solomon as having the recognition due Sam. The morning after the fight in Vegas, Benton chatted with newsmen while he awaited the start of a Spinks press conference. Solomon rushed in wearing pajamas and announced, "There will be no statements until Leon arrives," then directed a frosty glance at Benton. Feeling demeaned, Benton resigned from the Spinks camp and did so with no regrets, telling people he had plenty of work to do back in Philadelphia.

Every day Benton, the divorced father of four sons whom he sees regularly, drives from the modest frame house in which he lives to

Joe Frazier's Gymnasium in North Philadelphia. Amid the sounds of rope skipping, the rhythmic snorts of fighters shadowboxing or sparring in the elevated ring and the steady tattoo on speed bags, George Benton was working. He was throwing open-handed blows at a young white hopeful named Dieter Eisenhauer. The middleweight was rolling his body and head to elude the snapping blows, employing the defensive tactics and counterpunches that Benton had been teaching Eisenhauer ever since the youngster turned up at the gym several months earlier.

When Benton pawed at Eisenhauer's right shoulder, Dieter, as instructed, dipped low and fired a left hook that caused Benton to say, "No, no! Too slow. When you catch this"—he aimed another blow at the prospect's right shoulder—"it's like a button triggering the other hand to go. Try it again."

Eisenhauer's moves lacked the instinctive reflex—*React, don't think* is Benton's motto—that George wanted. "You're late. Too late," he said, in his calm, croaking basso.

"I can't," said Eisenhauer, "get the—"

"You *can*," Benton interrupted. "I don't give a damn for 'can't.'"

The fighter set himself in a boxing pose to try again. For a novice like Dieter Eisenhauer, the repeated reaction to shadow punches was what playing scales are to the beginner pianist. "Going to school," Benton calls it.

Benton himself began his boxing schooling at age ten, learning the craft from trainer Joe Rose. In Philadelphia's Diamond's A.C., Rose would strike at George with rolled-up fight posters and show him how to avoid being hit. Some afternoons, Rose brought in neighborhood youngsters to spar with George, demanding a quarter from his protege for every blow landed on him. "Collected damn few quarters," Rose recalled years later.

The training made Benton as clever a fighter as the Philadelphia crowd had seen in years. In 1952, at age nineteen, he upset highly regarded middleweight Holly Mims at The Met, a fight arena a few blocks from George's North Philadelphia home. "I remember," Benton said, "our names were on the marquee overhanging the street. BENTON VS. MIMS. Every five minutes, I'd run around the corner to look at it. I was thrilled."

In subsequent years, the thrill sometimes wore thin. Benton became a fighter who was too clever for his own good. Big-name professionals avoided him, and George's progress was stifled. Part of the reason, critics said, was that Benton was too cautious in big fights—not willing to risk enough. But even when he did record major victories, he could not seem to win a chance at the title. A typical Benton year was 1962. He knocked out Joe Louis Adair, Eddie Thompson and Rudolph Bent, and then beat Sam Solomon's fine middleweight, Jessie Smith, on a decision. The victory streak earned Benton a fight with Joey Giardello, whom he decisioned. That win was supposed to earn George a middleweight title fight with the champion, Dick Tiger. Instead Tiger fought—and lost the championship to—Giardello, who then figured that discretion was the better part of valor. "Why should I fight George Benton?" the new champion told Philadelphia boxing writer Gene Courtney. "I can't beat the guy."

Though he never did get a chance at the middleweight title, Benton remained a hero in Philadelphia. The local press used catchy phrases like "the Rembrandt of the ring" to describe the clever, stylish Benton. One man who was impressed by George's boxing skills was former major-league baseball umpire Shag Crawford. Years later, when Crawford's grandson Dieter Eisenhauer decided to become a boxer, Crawford recommended that he go see George Benton.

Under Benton, Eisenhauer said, he was acquiring a grasp of what boxing involved. "It's the body movements—the feints, the bobbing and weaving—that George teaches. Body movement is like your heartbeat. If your heartbeat is good, your body is going to be good."

As Eisenhauer worked on body movements on his own, Benton sat on a padded table across the room and drew on one of the Pall Malls that he would chain-smoke that day. He wore a camel-colored cap, blue denims, a green cardigan sweater and green turtleneck shirt. He was sitting to rest his back, which still contained the bullet from his shooting. Watching Eisenhauer intently, Benton turned to an onlooker, smiled and said, "Just a few months the kid's been at it. Can you believe the form he's got?" The trainer's enthusiasm was that of an aficionado. Making fighters function was not just a job to George Benton. It was his pleasure.

"He's concerned," Eisenhauer said later. "He'll keep showing you a move until you get it right. He breaks things down. Shows you how things are related. He really knows his stuff. I mean, if he told me to stand on my head, I'd do it."

In a sport filled with hype artists and colorful frauds, Benton speaks softly and to the point when he addresses a fighter. At times he instructs with humor, as Eisenhauer related: "When I first came around, I had trouble loosening up, doing the exercises that would make me flexible. George used to joke, 'We gotta get the white out of you. Keep stretchin', kid.'"

By late afternoon, Eisenhauer was tooling back to his home in Hatboro, Pennsylvania, thirty-five miles from Philadelphia. Frazier's Gym was filling with fighters, and Benton pulled a pack of Pall Malls from his calf-high sock and lit up a smoke as he watched Joe Frazier's son Marvis bang away at the heavy bag.

Marvis, a 6-foot-2-heavyweight, more classically proportioned than his father, wore green cutoff trunks and a blue T-shirt that read "The KO Kid." "Load up on the one you see," Benton told the powerful seventeen-year-old. "You're loading up on everything." Marvis nodded and became more selective with his heavier blows.

Marvis Frazier had worked under Benton for several years. "At the time I got involved with Joe," said Benton, "Marvis started coming into the gym. And Joe told me to go ahead, start working with him."

Marvis apparently learned his lessons from Benton. This past year, he won the Pennsylvania Golden Gloves heavyweight title. Benton withheld him, though, from national Golden Gloves competition, saying: "The kid's not even eighteen yet. He'd be facing fighters with men's bodies, men's strength. I don't want to mess with his confidence. Marvis has the potential to be a great one. The only damn thing that's holding him back is his age. We're shooting for the 1980 Olympics. After that, his father will decide what he wants."

Two of Benton's other young prospects are lightweights Charles Singleton, who won the National Golden Gloves title in March, and Greg Winston, who finished second in the Pennsylvania State Golden Gloves and won his first pro bout in April.

As the clock in Frazier's inched toward 6, Benton grew busier, here telling a fighter who wanted a bout ("I'm broke as a mutha, George") that he was not ready for it, there reproaching Willie (The Worm) Monroe for being diverted from the heavy bag by kibitzers ("Come on, Willie—get with it"). As he roamed the gym, correcting other fighters' moves, George still looked fit at 5-10 and 168 pounds. When he demonstrated a move, anyone could recognize the pro's fine edge. For all that Benton did not take himself too seriously. At one point, he kidded another trainer: "Hey, Rabbi, when you gonna start that dog-meat boxing?" In Frazier's Gym, even good fighters are needlingly called "dogmeat."

By 6:30, Benton was looking toward the front door, anticipating the arrival of Ernie Gladney, a junior welterweight of his. Gladney, with three wins and two losses as a professional, was fighting his first six-rounder that night at the Spectrum. There was a story behind the match.

About two years ago, a female probation officer brought Gladney to Frazier's and asked Benton to work with him. At the time, Gladney was awkward, hardly able, by Benton's account, to skip a rope or hit a speed bag. But he had good reflexes, quick jerky movements that in time made him a tricky boxer. Gladney fought briefly as an amateur, then turned pro. He lost his first two fights ("He run out of gas the first one," Benton said, "and got a bum decision the second"), then won his next three. The most recent was over Victor Pappas, a young pro from Upper Darby, Pennsylvania, who had been undefeated in four bouts, all of which he'd won by knockout.

Gladney, whose fights had all been four-rounders, then advised Benton that he was ready for six-rounders. "Got nasty about it, too," said Benton. "So I told him: 'Listen, you're not going to fight six rounds. You're gonna stay in four. And if you don't like it, we'll sit you down and you'll never fight.' Afterward, though, I thought about it and wondered where he got his six-round notions. Then it hit me. Someone was in his ear. 'Cause I happened to notice that this guy was around him all the time, telling him how great he was. Next day, I saw Gladney. I went up to him, said, 'You rotten sonofabitch. Hey, I done spent all this time with you, taught you how to fight. Now you giving me this boolshit.' I told him, 'Okay, you know what I'm going to do? I'm going to put you in six.' So I got him a six-round fight rematch with the white kid Pappas, who Ernie barely beat in four rounds.

"After that, Willie the Worm jumped on Ernie, and Bennie Briscoe jumped on him, cussed him out and told him how stupid he was. Now he come to me and says, 'George, you right. I'm sorry.' But I told him, 'You're still fighting the six-rounder.'"

At 6:31, Ernie Gladney entered the gym, wearing a fatigue jacket and denims rolled at the cuffs. With his sad-eyed, bemused expression, he resembled ex-heavyweight champion Floyd Patterson. Benton's eyes gleamed when he saw his fighter. "You been crying for six rounds, right?" he teased. Gladney made no response.

Minutes later, behind the wheel of his recently repaired 1969 Oldsmobile, Benton puffed on a cigarette and told Gladney: "Okay, okay. You know how this guy fights. He'll be comin' at you, right? Swarming. You know what I want you to do. From the first round, hands up high. Don't go to the guy. He's coming at you. So just move in a circle, left or right, understand? Sticking and stabbing. Keep sticking and stabbing. Inside, tie him up. He'll be fresh early. He might want to wrassle—don't you do the wrassling. Let him sling you—tire himself out. You just keep nailing him as he's coming in. Bap, bap. Then get the hell out. You can stick 'n' stab him all night." In the back seat, Gladney listened in silence.

Gladney's fight opened that night's Spectrum fight card. In contrast to Gladney's lean sinewy figure, Pappas had the compact build that fit the brawler's image Benton had conjured. And from the start, Pappas lowered his head and rushed Gladney, swinging looping blows as he came.

Gladney knew his job, though. Repeatedly, he stepped away, planted his feet and whacked Pappas short crisp blows—bap, bap—

as Benton had prescribed. Circling clockwise, Gladney deftly employed his left hook to halt Pappas' charges.

Pappas tried to adjust in the second round, charging in a crouch. Gladney kept slipping the punches and driving short blows into Pappas' face, causing Benton at ringside to nod and smile.

In round three, Pappas' wild swings began landing, a sign that Ernie was tiring. After four rounds, Gladney was ahead in the fight, but the snap had gone out of his punches.

Down the stretch, Gladney was too weary to exploit Pappas' mistakes. Though Gladney still eluded punches with savvy moves, he lacked the strength to discourage Pappas with counterpunches. Over the last two rounds, Gladney mostly feinted, bobbed and clinched. When he couldn't, Pappas popped him. Gladney lost a split decision.

In the dressing room afterward, as Gladney stared at his shoe-tops, a corner man snapped: "Ducking and hiding, Goddammit. You could have beat that chump." Exhausted and pained by his night's work, Gladney licked his lips but did not speak. He seemed embarrassed.

Then George Benton came in. "Hey, Ernie," he said. "I guess I know what I'm talking about, right?"

"Yeah," Gladney whispered.

"You understand I was trying to take care of you, huh?"

Gladney nodded.

"Ready to listen to me from now on?"

"Mmm."

"I ain't going to have anymore hanky-panky from you. I know a four-round fighter from a six-round fighter. Those last two rounds you gave him. You gave the fight away."

Gladney raised his head and studied Benton. His expression did not argue the trainer's point. Benton paced a few steps, then turned to Gladney and said, "You going to be all right. Now that you got your head on straight." Later, George Benton gave Gladney the trainer's share of the night's wages.

---

*George Benton has gone on to train world champions
Pernell Whitaker, Meldrick Taylor and Evander Holyfield.*

ANGELO DUNDEE: Champ of Corner Men (1981)

September 16, 1981: The twelfth round has just ended in the fight to determine undisputed possession of the welterweight title held jointly by World Boxing Council champion Sugar Ray Leonard and World Boxing Association champion Thomas Hearns. Leonard retires to his corner with the flesh beneath his left eye discolored, swollen and threatening to obscure his vision.

Leonard does not know he is behind on the scorecards of the three judges sitting at ringside at Caesars Palace in Las Vegas. Nor does his corner man, sixty-year-old Angelo Dundee. But Dundee senses that Hearns, who had almost been knocked out in rounds 6 and 7, has rallied behind his long left jab and now stands a chance of winning.

Toward the end of the one-minute rest between Rounds 12 and 13, Dundee leans toward his fighter and, in a voice full of urgency, shouts: "You've got nine minutes. You're blowing it, son. You're blowing it. This is what separates the men from the boys. You're blowing it."

Leonard comes alive in the thirteenth round. He hits Hearns with a right-hand punch that snaps his head back and has him staggering along the ropes. Before the round ends, Leonard has registered a knockdown and taken the fight out of his opponent. In the fourteenth round, the referee stops the match and raises Sugar Ray's hand in victory.

The role of the corner man is one of the most intriguing in all of boxing. In his sixty seconds between rounds, the corner man enforces or revises his fighter's strategy. He is the "cut man," doing a surgeon's work with Q-Tips and bismuth, able to staunch the flow of blood or suppress the engorging bruise. On the corner

157

man's instincts and advice, championships have been won and lost.

Today, after thirty-three years and nine world champions—including Sugar Ray Leonard and Muhammad Ali—Angelo Dundee is a corner man without a peer. Even his critics—who give him only an average rating as a teacher of boxing technique—concede that Dundee is the best there is in aiding a fighter between rounds. "In that one minute," say Ferdie Pacheco, a doctor, who for more than a decade worked corners with Dundee, "Angelo is Godzilla and Superman rolled into one."

In the Godzilla capacity, Dundee has a still-expanding arsenal of physical and psychological weapons with which to goad and assist his fighters in the ring. He flatters or berates as necessary. He pinches; he slaps; he insults. He drops ice cubes in trunks. He thinks positive: A fighter once complained, after a punishing round, that his legs were killing him. "Good," said Dundee. "It means you're getting your second wind."

Dundee, who will be in his familiar corner role on December 11, when Ali is scheduled to fight Trevor Berbick in the Bahamas, is a master at "knowing styles." To boxing insiders, this is the ability to analyze the progress of a fight and then create the strategic adjustment that undercuts the foe's fight plan.

"Angelo's aware of the mistakes you're making," says Ali, "and also of the way to take advantage of the other guy's mistakes. You come back to the corner and he'll say, 'The guy's open for a hook,' or this or that. If he tells you something during a fight, you can believe it. If Angelo hadn't been in my corner, I wouldn't be where I am today. I might have made it to the top, but not as quickly. As a corner man, Angelo is the best in the world."

It is this kind of talk, from this most self-centered of champions, that has helped to feed the Dundee legend. While others among the men currently licensed to work fighters' corners are highly regarded—Eddie Futch, Lou Duva, George Benton, Goody Petronelli and Victor Valle, for example—Angelo Dundee is the most respected. For good reason, too. Among active fight people, no one has been associated with success the way Angelo has been.

At Angelo Dundee Inc., on Northwest 167th Street in Miami, one whole wall is reserved for photos and illustrations of the champions with whom he has worked as trainer or manager or both (Ali, Leonard, Jimmy Ellis, Willie Pastrano, Carmen Basilio, Luis Rodriguez, Ultiminio (Sugar) Ramos, Jose Napoles and Ralph Dupas). The Allen Park Gym in North Miami Beach, where Dundee works, is like an audition hall for hopeful young boxers, and Angelo himself has become a minor celebrity, doing promotions, making personal appearances and endorsing products.

"It's gotten to where," says boxing publicist Irving Rudd, "Angelo's aura of success jacks up a young fighter. A kid who has Mr. Dundee in his corner thinks he's got an extra dimension going. And sometimes that's half the battle, isn't it?"

The Hollywood prototype of a corner man tends to be a hard-boiled, tough-talking loner with a lifetime cigar. Dundee runs against type. Angelo is a small man—5 feet, 7-1/2 inches—outgoing and upbeat, a man who likes company. A "mixologist" he calls himself, referring to his sociability. In crowds, he is a chronic kibitzer, trading jokes and insults with fighters and anyone else up to it. ("You know, dear," he says to a coffee-shop waitress before a fight, "I've heard a lot of compliments on the coffee. All the guys who smoke say it takes away the nicotine.")

It would be a mistake, though, to take Dundee, affable as he is, as just a goodtime Charley with little on his mind. Angelo has used his engaging personality to make his way in boxing. His sunny disposition allows him, in his words, "to blend" with a fighter, creating a rapport that will make his man produce. "A happy situation is a good situation," he says. "I don't believe in mystery."

Recently, Dundee traveled to Rosemont, Illinois, to try to gear up an undefeated (20-0) twenty-four-year-old heavyweight named James (Quick) Tillis in his challenge for the W.B.A. championship held by Mike Weaver. Tillis had never fought for the title before, and Dundee, who wanted his man "loose as a goose" for the match, set out to create a happy situation through several days of ego boosting, gentle ribbing (Tillis' hometown, Tulsa, Oklahoma, was described as, "Population 327...and that's counting the cows") and worse jokes ("When you were born," he told Tillis, "you were so ugly the doctor slapped your mother").

On the day of the fight, as Dundee and the young heavyweight walked off a meal, the trainer's methodical campaign to build confidence moved into high gear. "Mike Weaver," Dundee confided to Tillis sincerely, "he doesn't have the glow of a guy who's ready to win. You glow."

But that night, at the Rosemont Horizon, the luster began to fade from Tillis. Dundee's strategy was for Quick to circle Weaver, hit him—bang bang—and retreat before the champion could unload his heavy punches. Stick-and-move is what fight people call the tactic.

But by the ninth round, Dundee sensed that Tillis was fighting too defensively, that he had to risk more if he wanted to persuade the judges that he was dominating the fight. For Dundee, the time for being companionable was over. "Go to work, for chrissake," he hollered. Tillis, however, continued to play safe.

Before the tenth round, Dundee screamed at him: "Weaver ain't got nothin'. SHOW ME! SHOW ME! You got to push him." He slapped the fighter's legs and shoved him into the ring. For the rest of the fight, Dundee berated and beseeched Tillis. "Fight him, Quick. Fight him, goddammit."

Between rounds, he smacked Tillis' face and legs and cursed him for his inaction. Sweat streamed from Dundee as he tried to galvanize his man. Down the stretch, Tillis landed stinging blows on Weaver but failed to follow his advantage. In the end, Tillis' caution cost him the fight. Weaver won a unanimous decision.

Back in the dressing room, Dundee told Tillis: "You're a baby, son. You'll get better and better." But moments later, he was muttering: "He could've won it. He could've won it."

While Dundee is relentless in his ringside efforts to rouse his fighters, he can go just so far against a boxer's stubborn resistance. When Leonard fought Roberto Duran for the first time for the W.B.C. welterweight crown and lost, Sugar Ray failed to heed Dundee's advice to use his footwork to confound Duran. "He wanted to fight that guy," says Dundee. "And I couldn't take it out of him. Emotionally, he wanted to do a number on Duran because of the vulgar gesture that Duran had made to his wife before the fight. See, there's a lot of love and closeness between Ray and his wife, Juanita. They grew up in school together. I tried to make him box. But he heard what he wanted to hear. In my line, you get into a guy's head, but only so far.

"After the first Duran fight, Ray was brokenhearted," Dundee says. "He wanted to quit because he was disappointed in himself. But eventually we went back to work and we showed him things that would help against Duran. One thing that was wrong for Ray was to lay against the ropes: What he was doing every time he was against the ropes was spreading his feet and losing his mobility. I told him, 'When your right calf touches the bottom strand, slide off the ropes in one direction or the other.'

"The other thing was that, when Duran punches, he lowers his head and uses it as a weapon. You've got to step back to avoid his head. And that plays right into his hand. Duran likes to back people up. I told Ray, 'Push his head with either hand and then hit him.' Off-set his head, offset the ropes and keep Duran turning—that was the strategy. And it worked in the rematch. Ray got back the title."

In his constant search for an edge for his fighter, Dundee has been known to resort to guile. He laughs about the time he discouraged an official's between-rounds inspection of his fighter's bruised eye by nudging him away with his hip. Another time, he distracted a referee who was counting over a floored opponent by producing a robe to throw over his own fighter's shoulders. The referee reacted by hurrying his count, which made it short of the requisite ten seconds and led to a futile protest from the other man's corner.

When Ali fought in England against Henry Cooper in 1963, a left hook floored him at the end of the fourth round. He was on his feet when the bell rang but dazed. Between rounds, however, Dundee made an issue of Ali's glove being split. The maneuver bought time—new gloves had to be found—and allowed Ali to clear his head. He knocked Cooper out in the next round.

For the Hearns bout, Angelo tested a newly developed device. Shaped like a miniature flatiron and chilled in an ice bucket, the "doohickey," as Dundee calls it, produces an intense and therapeutic cold that reduces swelling. He used it in the fight when

Sugar Ray's eye began to swell and may have prevented the injured eye from closing.

These edges can favorably affect the outcome of a fight, and Dundee's search for them continues on fight nights. "Whatever you see during a fight is me, period," he says. "I don't know what I'm going to do. I work according to what the situation calls for, spontaneous-like."

Dundee seems genuinely fond of his fighters and, out of the ring, has had good times with them. Years ago, Dundee became so close with Willie Pastrano, the light-heavyweight champion from 1963 to 1965, that he hired another trainer as a buffer so that he and his fighter could get distance from one another. It helped, but it was never easy for Dundee to be "strictly business" about Pastrano.

Angelo describes his efforts to keep the impulsive Pastrano from undermining his own chances. "Willie," he says, "was a degenerate for water fountains, which gave him problems making the 175-pound weight limit." To discourage him, Dundee would stick lighted cigars in Pastrano's water glass at the training table. Willie retaliated by having his mother smuggle root beer to him.

"With stuff like that," says Pastrano, now forty-six years old and on the staff of Democratic State Senator Leonard J. Chabert of Louisiana, "I drove Angelo crazy. But most of it was in fun. Like Angelo is deathly afraid of snakes. So, one time, doing roadwork, I found a broken fan belt. Angelo was up ahead, waiting for me. I picked up the fan belt and shook it so that from a distance it looked like a snake. Then I started after him. Angelo panicked. He was wearing an overcoat and smoking a cigar. He ran—and the smoke rose up from his head, his overcoat was flapping. What a sight."

Even with Pastrano, whom Angelo began training in 1952 (when Willie was sixteen) and worked with through his last fight in 1965, Dundee put friendship aside with the outcome of a fight at stake. In 1964, light heavyweight champion Pastrano was matched against Terry Downes in Manchester, England. Through ten rounds, Willie's performance was so lackadaisical that before the eleventh round Dundee let him have it, screaming, "You're blowing your title. You're giving it away."

As Pastrano rose from his stool to start the eleventh round, Dundee twisted his fighter's face and then belted him hard on the backside. Angered, Pastrano swung around and shook his fist at Dundee, who snarled: "Hit *him*, not me, you S.O.B." Pastrano, known more as a clever boxer than as a puncher, knocked out Downes that round. "Angelo," says Pastrano, "knew how to channel my energy. He knew me better than I knew myself."

One of Dundee's most dramatic and fateful decisions in the corner occurred in February 1964. Cassius Clay, as Muhammad Ali was then known, was scheduled to fight the heavyweight champion, Charles (Sonny) Liston, in Miami Beach. To the sporting press gathered there, Clay, a brash, highly quotable young man, had only one chance of beating the champion: with a tire iron. The odds-makers had made Clay a 7-1 underdog.

And yet in the early going against Liston, Clay displayed foot speed and ring cunning that kept him largely out of range of the champion's blows. Through four rounds, it was a near-even contest. But then, after the fourth round, Clay returned to the corner, his eyes burning, his vision impaired. He was in a panic. "Cut the gloves off," he told Dundee. "I can't see."

Dundee, convinced that the condition was temporary, refused: "This is the big one, daddy," he shouted. "Jab and keep circling until your eyes clear."

As the bell sounded for the fifth round, Angelo raised his fighter off the stool and pushed him across the ring. By the seventh round, the bout was over. Liston was on his stool, complaining of an injured shoulder, and Clay was the new world's champion.

Dundee had guessed correctly that Clay had somehow gotten liniment in his eyes, which would wash out.

Angelo began to work with Ali in October 1960, after Muhammad had rejected his first professional trainer, former light heavyweight champion Archie Moore. "Archie planned to train me for a year or so," says Ali, "before he'd get me a good fight. I wanted to start right away. He also had me, like, on the side—just one of the boys in camp. I wanted to be Number One. The last straw was when he showed me his style—the way he fought, the way he threw punches. I wanted my own style. And when I went to Angelo, Angelo let me be free."

Dundee found that Ali didn't like being dictated to, which obliged him to use indirection to make his point. "Like I'd say to him after he'd sparred," Dundee recalls, "that left uppercut was dynamite.' Well, he had never thrown a left uppercut. But the next day in the gym, he'd be working a guy and he'd throw left upper-cuts."

In the early stages of Ali's career, the fighter listened to Angelo, who treated him like a younger brother—mixing affection with sound advice. As Dundee's older brother Jimmy recalls: "After one fight in the early 1960's, a few friends of Muhammad's stopped by the dressing room. At that time, Angelo had almost total control. Ali asked him for some money. Angelo gave him five dollars. Muhammad said, 'But I'm going out with friends.' Angelo said— and no scolding...more as an equal: 'They're friends, and you don't drink. Five dollars is enough.'"

The authority eroded as Ali's stature grew. "The relationship with Angelo," says boxing promoter Bob Arum, "changed psycho-logically. It went from Angelo the boss to Angelo the functionary. In 1965, which is when I first got involved promoting Ali's fights, Angelo would tell him the exact time for roadwork and the exact number of rounds to spar. Gradually, Ali began calling the shots, and Angelo only played a role on those occasions where Ali felt himself in trouble—against, say, a Joe Frazier or George Foreman. And those occasions became fewer."

Fight manager Cus D'Amato remembers what it was like in the years after Ali came back to boxing, in 1970, following his loss of the title for refusing, on religious grounds, to be drafted. "I remember the day in training camp when Angelo told him to do four rounds of sparring. Ali just ignored him and did eight rounds. It was terribly embarrassing. I would have quit."

In the mid-1960's, as Ali's entourage filled up with militant Black Muslims, racial friction was reported in the Ali camp. Arum, as the promoter of Ali's fights, remembers hearing lines like,

"Watch the white man"—meaning Dundee—"he's going to poison your water." Or, "The white devil's going to get you to lose the title." Others confirm the racially charged atmosphere.

In time, the Black Muslim rhetoric disappeared, but the habit of bad-mouthing Dundee did not. Many of Muhammad's aides-de-camp were freestyle opportunists with ghost functions—one man would taste Ali's sweat to divine how his conditioning was going. Ali's response to those who wondered how he could have a white man as a trainer was a lighthearted one. Angelo, he would say, was not a white man but an Italian, and everybody knew that when Hannibal went over the Alps, he spread a lot of black blood.

What bond there is today between Muhammad and Dundee is complicated by the grand figure Ali has become and Angelo's long history with him. He can remember Muhammad from the late 1950's, when he was just an amateur fighter talking his way up to the Louisville hotel room where Angelo was keeping an eye on Pastrano before a fight. Dundee had never heard of Cassius Clay then, but the young man took the occasion to assure him he would in the future. Turned pro under Dundee, the boyish Ali would do show-business imitations with Angelo as they strolled up Eighth Avenue to the old Madison Square Garden for a bout. That innocence was blown with the passage of time—and memorable fight moments. A few weeks ago, as Dundee was preparing to join Ali in the Bahamas, he seemed less insistent than Ali that there was a boxing future for the fighter. The attitude appeared to be one of resignation. "I'll get to the Bahamas a few days before the fight," Dundee said. "No point to showing up much earlier. What am I going to do at this stage, show him a new punch?"

Dundee's role—and his financial returns—varies from fighter to fighter. With Carmen Basilio, who won both the welterweight and middleweight titles in the mid-1950's, Dundee was a corner man employed on a fee basis, his cut purportedly never exceeding $2,500. Later, with heavyweight Jimmy Ellis, whose career was floundering in 1965 when he wrote Dundee saying he was thinking of quitting the sport, Angelo acted as manager, entitled to the traditional 33-1/3 percent cut that managers receive.

Though he has the title of manager of Sugar Ray, Dundee was hired in 1976 strictly to recommend opponents for the fighter and then to appear a week or so before each bout and help trainer Dave Jacobs put the finishing touches on Leonard's fight plan. During each match, Dundee was—and still is—the man in charge of the corner, giving Leonard between-rounds advice. For this, Angelo reportedly received 15 percent of the fighter's purses. This arrangement was altered after Leonard won the W.B.C. welterweight title from Wilfred Benitez in November 1979, and was replaced by a fee system less remunerative to Angelo.

"Angelo's contract expired," says Leonard's attorney, Mike Trainer, "and, yes, the basis of payment did change." Trainer declined to give the specifics of the new arrangement. Arum's claim that Trainer told him "Nobody is worth 15 percent" is disputed by the attorney, who concedes, though, that Arum did enter into the negotiations over the new Dundee contract as a mediator.

While boxing people consider the move an insult to Dundee, who deftly maneuvered Leonard through the welterweight ranks to his title shot, Angelo himself will not discuss the subject. "One thing I put bars on is what I make," he says. "Whatever comes, comes."

In truth, Dundee "puts bars" on any utterance that might stir controversy. Says Bob Arum: "Angelo seems a simple, charming, naive, frank, open guy. But it's more complex than that. He's really a great diplomat. He carefully guards what he says—and stays out of trouble because of that. A lot of us in this business, particularly with the popularity of Angelo, would have gone to the media screaming when they changed the way they paid him for working with Sugar Ray. Angelo continued to work with Leonard, picking up nice fees, but nothing like what he would have been entitled to under the old setup. Fifteen percent of, say, $10 million"—Leonard's reported purse for his fight with Duran—"is $1.5 million. If Angelo gets $150,000 instead as a fee, it's a nice payday, but it isn't the deal he started with."

Yet, as Arum suggests, Dundee is not one to make waves. Whatever comes, comes. For all the politics of big-time boxing, Dundee has shown a survivor's knack. He has waded through the verbal put-downs and fiscal comedowns. He has outlasted the con-nivers and hustlers.

"Even though," says Arum, "a fighter and trainer have a tight bond, there are people who can work crazy things on an athlete's mind, which, if a trainer or manager is not clever, can break the bond. An example is Sugar Ray's original trainer, Dave Jacobs, who started training him in the amateurs and was with him the night he beat Benitez for the title. Jacobs and Ray had an amazing bond."

There are conflicting versions of why Jacobs broke off with Leonard. Published reports say that money was the issue—that after Sugar Ray became champion, Jacobs wanted a bigger cut of Leonard's purses. Jacobs denies this, saying he left over a boxing issue—he did not want Leonard to take an immediate rematch with Duran after Sugar Ray had lost his title to the Panamanian. When the return match was made, Jacobs says, he made the deci-sion to leave: "I had Ray Leonard at heart."

Mike Trainer dismisses Jacobs' version, saying: "After the Benitez fight, Dave came in with a lawyer and asked for money going back to day one. That was resolved. What he quit over, really, was ego—that he wasn't calling the shots. This whole thing with Dave Jacobs has been beaten to death. It's like the wart on Sugar Ray that people want to find."

For his part, Dundee has been able to roll with the punches. His tenure in Ali's camp is viewed by some as a Ripley Believe-It-or-Not item. They put it to Angelo's tact—and to his unflappable nature. Says Ferdie Pacheco: "Angelo has what the Spanish call *la vista gorda*. It's like seeing through thick glasses. Spanish wives have that about their husband's cheating. Angelo becomes so involved in boxing he doesn't see the other stuff and doesn't let it affect him."

A more critical view is offered by Cus D'Amato: "Money is the reason he puts up with Ali's shenanigans. I once asked him, 'Angelo, why do you put up with Ali's nonsense?' He told me, 'Cus, everyone thinks I'm his trainer and manager. And that's how I get my fighters.'"

Dundee: "I never said that to Cus. And the truth is that from 1960 to 1964, I made very little with Muhammad. When he won the title in 1964, the Louisville Sponsoring Group that Ali was contracted to gave me a $20,000 bonus—my first real money with him. Money was never my reason for being with Muhammad Ali. Because when he paid people off after fights, I was at the end of the line."

Bob Arum saw this continue in later years. From April 1972 to January 1974, while promoting Ali's fights, Arum says he also paid the fighter's staff, on Muhammad's behalf. He remembers Dundee's fees being cut "drastically" when members of Ali's entourage complained to Muhammad that they were not being paid enough.

"Money," says Dundee, "was not why I stayed with Muhammad. I was pleased to work with a great fighter. To this day he is my friend. I was oblivious to a lot of things that went on, just as long as I could get the job done."

He was born Angelo Mirena Jr. on August 30, 1921, in Philadelphia, the son of Angelo Sr. and Philomena.

Angelo was the youngest of the five Mirena brothers—there are two sisters. When his older brother Joe began to box professionally in the 1930's, Joe took the name "Dundee," as did Joe's corner man, brother Chris. Angelo, too, began to use the name Dundee a few years after he got into the fight business in 1948 and moved to New York.

In those days, Angelo slept on the sofa in Chris' Capital Hotel office. Chris had promoted boxing in Virginia and then had gone on to manage a string of competent fighters. Among them was Ken Overlin, who won the middleweight championship in 1940. Angelo spent mornings in Chris' office, writing letters to promoters for his brother and watching how he operated. Afternoons, he went to Stillman's Gym, which was to boxing then what Gertrude Stein's Paris salon was to literature in the 1920's—a place where a newcomer was exposed to the craft.

The boxing business in the late 1940's was concentrated in one place—New York—in a way it has not been since. In those days, there were small fight clubs operating throughout the metropolitan area, with fight cards six nights a week. Angelo carried the "spit bucket" for veteran trainers like Ray Arcel and Chickie Ferrara and learned the basics of his trade, some nights working for as little as $20 in smoke-filled arenas like Ridgewood Grove and Eastern Parkway. Occasionally, he would see a trainer's guile make the difference in the outcome of a bout. One night a fighter who had been knocked to the canvas looked to the corner for advice. Ferrara signaled him to stay down. The trouble was that Chickie was working the other man's corner. The floored fighter realized his error a beat too late, just as the referee's count reached 10.

In late 1950, Chris Dundee moved to Miami Beach, where he became that city's exclusive fight promoter for more than twenty-five years. The move coincided with the decline of boxing in New York. By contrast, Miami Beach was beginning to boom, and the boxing business profited from it.

Angelo arrived in Miami Beach in 1951. He was married in February 1952, and he and his wife, Helen, have a son, Jimmy, twenty-seven, who is an optician, and a daughter, Terri, twenty-four, who is a teacher. Immediately after he married, Dundee left for New Orleans with Bill Neri, a fighter he managed. That was how it went for him in the early 1950's. He took fighters all over the world, usually for short wages. Occasionally, Chris would slip him a few bucks extra, but mostly Angelo relied on his own hustle to make out.

What Dundee learned in his lean years serves him well now. That his experience can make a difference is recognized well beyond the prizefight world. These days Angelo is more than a boxing figure. He is a celebrity too, right down to the obligatory television commercial—in his case for Natural Light, a low-calorie beer. Dundee has even hired an agent to look after speaking engagements, book contracts and other fringe incomes.

On a day not long ago, Angelo's Miami office was a scene of frenzied activity. His agent, a former British television comedian named Mike Winters, turns up early in the morning. Winters' business gets squeezed in between the nonstop phone calls that Dundee fields (answering one in the fluent Spanish he learned handling fighters in pre-Castro Cuba) and the voluminous correspondence he keeps up with newsmen, fight people and ordinary folks who write him for everything from his counsel on a doctoral treatise on boxing to an autographed photo. With his secretary, Angelo goes over future travel arrangements (Nova Scotia, Las Vegas, Atlantic City) and then tries to decipher names and phone numbers from the doodles on his memos.

Most of the scribbled entries refer to boxing matters. The fight game is still what makes Angelo, at age sixty, run. Oh, there are dates lined up for subsidiary dollars, but Dundee has a way of easing those opportunities off his calendar to keep up with his busy fight itinerary—Angelo has worked roughly two fights a month in 1981. At present, he is involved with eighteen fighters, ranging from past and present champions like Ali and Leonard, to contenders like Tillis and lightheavyweight Vonzell Johnson, to prospects like heavyweight Jimmy Clark, light heavyweight Young Joe Louis and flyweight Ian Clyde of Canada. Returning to Dundee from a ring sabbatical is heavyweight Lee Canalito, who played opposite Sylvester Stallone in "Paradise Alley."

After thirty-three years in the boxing business, Dundee is still challenged by his profession. "No two fighters are alike. You never meet the same guy twice," he says. And for him, finding the key to bringing out the best in a man is an objective that, in his words, "gets me juiced."

"The crowd," says Dundee, "can be screaming, but I don't get caught up in the excitement, because then I can't be 100 percent. I may look as if I'm going a little nuts. But really, I'm not. I'm trying things. Angling. Scheming. Creating situations. And that's what the kick is: stepping into the unknown and making it work for you. Believe me, my friend, there's nothing like it."

Since this article was written, Angelo Dundee has trained three more champions, to make a grand total of twelve world champions who have had Dundee their corner man.

DON KING: Despite Many Storms, He Lands on His Feet (1990)

There is a story Don King tells about himself:

It was January 1973, and King had gone to Kingston, Jamaica, to watch a heavyweight title fight between the champion, Joe Frazier, and a challenger named George Foreman.

King, a former numbers operator from Cleveland, had recently finished serving a four-year term for manslaughter at the Marion (Ohio) Correctional Institution. He had gone to Kingston at the invitation of Frazier, but during the weeks leading up to the bout he would manage to befriend Foreman, too. King, just a fan then but one with grander designs, encouraged the challenger's dream of becoming champion, while also making airport pickups for the fighter when Foreman's relatives arrived in Kingston.

The night of the bout, King rode to the arena with Frazier in a limousine that was escorted by siren-blasting police motorcycles, and took up his front-row seat in Frazier's corner.

"The first round," King said, "George hit Frazier with a devastating punch that sent Joe leaping into the air. Every time he'd strike Frazier, I'd move closer to the end of the row, toward George's corner. By the time the fight ended, a second-round TKO, I was *on* George's corner. When the fight was stopped, I'm into the ring, saying to George 'I told you.' And George said 'Come with me.' He took me to his room. Same thing. Motorcycle cops. Sirens blasting."

King pauses and chuckles as he finishes the story: "I came with the champion, and left with the champion."

If ever there was a metaphor for the basic business precepts of the fifty-eight-year-old King, that night in Kingston is surely it. In the years since then, King has shown that same knack for insinuating himself into the lives and dreams of a succession of heavy-weight champions—including but not limited to Foreman, Muhammad Ali, Larry Holmes and Mike Tyson—never missing a beat while moving nimbly from old titleholder to new.

That long run as the power brother of the heavyweight division seems no accident. Even his most bitter rivals credit King with the intelligence and cunning to survive in a cutthroat business. "He's a master showman, a master manipulator," said Dennis Rappaport, a fight manager and promoter. "He's a workaholic, who takes the posture that he doesn't understand the word 'no.'"

In spite of his relentlessness—and ingenuity—King has stumbled from time to time. An ABC-TV tournament he promoted in the mid-1970's was found to be scandal-ridden. Fighters have loudly denounced him for cheating them of money. The Government brought a tax-evasion case against him, and he was acquitted of the charges. Yet through all these contretemps, somehow King keeps managing to land on his feet.

When Buster Douglas shocked the world by knocking out Tyson last weekend in Tokyo, there stood King not far behind Douglas in the postfight television interview, with a smile on his face that struck some observers as being odd for a man who professed to love Tyson as dearly as a father loves a son. While Tyson was headed to the dressing room a vanquished man, King was still in the picture, the possessor of "quite a few" options, as he put it, on Douglas's future fights.

But in the events that followed Douglas's victory, King's devotion to Douglas would come to seem somewhat less than steadfast. While King later presented himself as a kind of detached observer, seeking only to find justice—the Lone Ranger of boxing—Douglas's stunning victory would be threatened by forces that critics of King said the promoter incited for his customary self-interest.

In the hours after Douglas's tenth-round knockout of Tyson, once again the methods of the powerful King would come under close scrutiny, in particular his relationship with the sport's governing bodies, organizations that in addition to rating boxers and sanctioning title fights supervise the championship matches. The sweat on Douglas's brow was hardly dry when the World Boxing Council and the World Boxing Association, the governing bodies at ringside that night, announced that they were suspending the result of the fight, because of the long-count controversy surrounding Tyson's knockdown of Douglas in the eighth round.

(Unlike the W.B.C. and the W.B.A., though, the International Boxing Federation, the third of boxing's governing triumvirate, recognized Douglas as champion right away.)

When Jose Sulaiman, the fifty-eight-year-old president of the W.B.C., was reached in Tokyo some eleven hours after the bout, he would tell a reporter that "someone" in Tyson's corner—he didn't remember who—had protested to Gilberto Mendoza, president of the W.B.A., and him between the eighth and ninth rounds about the long count.

On Tuesday, at a news conference in New York, King said it was he who had registered the protest at that time. That Sulaiman did not remember it was King who first approached him on the long count seemed curious, given not only King's recollection, but also the account of Dean Gettleson. Gettleson, a promoter and attorney from Los Angeles, was at ringside in Tokyo, a vantage confirmed by Larry Rozadilla, one of the bout's judges.

"Immediately to my left," said Gettleson, "were Jose Sulaiman and Gilberto Mendoza and directly behind them, in the first row of spectators, were King and Donald Trump. After Douglas got up from the knockdown, King started yelling at Sulaiman."

According to Gettleson, King's tirade, which he said was laced with obscenities, went as follows:

"Look at what you've done. What kind of ref did you bring me from Mexico? You're going to get my man beat."

"King was yelling at the top of his lungs," Gettleson said, "and Sulaiman's face was getting redder and redder. And King yelled: 'Stop the fight. The fight's over.'"

At that moment, Gettleson said referee Octavio Meyran Sanchez walked to that side of the ring to hand the judges' scorecards to Sulaiman.

"And King, again using obscenity, screamed: 'What were you looking at? You should have known the man was out. You should have counted him out.'"

Last Tuesday, King said that John Horne, a Tyson aide, had filed the formal protest with the Japanese Boxing Commission that led to the governing bodies' suspending the result while considering the possibility of a mandated rematch. That version gave King distance from the events, but Gettleson's account put the promoter in the thick of things.

"After the fight," Gettleson said, "we were all going back on the official bus to the hotel. We were where the buses and limos were parked. Well, King called Meyran off the bus and then started yelling at Sulaiman, 'I want a press conference. I want this straightened out.' He pulled aside a Home Box Office technician to get a tape of the eighth round and, with Meyran and Sulaiman, went into a closed room to look at the tape. It was one hour after the fight. After a while, King, Sulaiman and Meyran emerged from the room. Everybody was very somber-faced."

King denied addressing his remarks directly to Sulaiman, insisting he had spoken to the group of officials at ringside. "The count was long," King said. "The fight was over. I'd have done the same thing for Buster Douglas. I see something wrong, I'm a stickler for the rules."

The actions threatened by the governing bodies against Douglas created an uproar. Back in the United States, there was a renewed cry for a Federal commission to take control of boxing. And in Dallas, Steve Crosson, a real-estate appraiser and treasurer of the W.B.C. and a good friend of Sulaiman's, resigned from the W.B.C. after reading the critical news reports.

"The damage to the W.B.C.'s credibility was huge," said Crosson.

So huge that both governing bodies—the W.B.C., based in Mexico City, and the W.B.A., based in Maracay, Venezuela—retreated from their positions. Later on Tuesday—as King revealed Team Tyson had withdrawn its protest ("Buster Douglas put on a magnificent performance," he said)—Sulaiman was contending that he had never intended not to recognize Douglas as champion. While the public was puzzled at how the organizations and King could presume to challenge a result that seemed so clear-cut as Douglas's victory had been, boxing insiders were used to the vagaries of the "alphabet-soup boys," as the organizations are known—the sometimes illogical ratings, the bent rules, the favoritism.

"The thing you have to understand," said Rappaport, the pro-moter of Tim Witherspoon and former co-manager of Gerry Cooney, "is that whatever rules there are, you can change them."

Indeed, the W.B.A. has its notorious Rule 19, which, in effect, says that in certain situations all the existing rules may be ignored. In that atmosphere, the powerful and persuasive do well, no sur-prise given the economics of the governing bodies. The organiza-tions' money comes from their sanction fees on title matches—up to $150,000 of each fighter's purse and as much as $6,000 from a bout's promoter.

King minimizes the impact he has on the organizations, saying, "I don't maneuver or manipulate the governing bodies. My power is from my fighters. I have good fighters, and I have my enterprise and intellect. I don't try to take advantage of nobody. Give me fair play, that's all I ask."

But through the years, King, with his stranglehold on the heavyweight division, has acquired a reputation as a Mr. Fixit with the governing bodies, and particularly so with the W.B.C. because of his friendship with Sulaiman.

Sulaiman denies that King or any other promoter has ever used improper means to influence him.

Sulaiman's critics maintain that his friendship with King knows no boundaries. When Rappaport's fighter, Mike Ayala, was made the mandatory challenger to the W.B.C. superbantamweight champion, Jaime Garza, according to the rules that mandatory position meant Rappaport did not have to give Garza's promoter, King, options on Ayala's future bouts. And by those rules, Rappaport could insist the fight go to competitive bids among pro-moters to get the best deal.

"But no date was set for the purse bids," said Rappaport. "It kept getting put off. And when I asked Sulaiman, he told me King had to be given a single option. I became enraged, to the point where I said things to Sulaiman I shouldn't have. The funny thing is I like Sulaiman, and Jose in all other situations has been more than fair to me."

Before the Ayala-Garza situation was straightened out, Garza was knocked out by Juan (Kid) Meza and lost his title. King obtained options on Meza and Rappaport agreed to give King a single option so that Ayala could get a shot at Meza's title. Ayala was stopped in six rounds by Meza on April 19, 1985.

King is a persuasive individual, a man with virtually evangelical fervor for whatever notion it is that he happens to be floating. The bald-faced power grab that he nudged into motion the night Douglas beat Tyson was another bit of the old hard-sell and was in keeping with what he has been doing since he came into the fight game: taking good care of Don King. This task he has always managed with a certain flair.

Don Elbaum, a promoter who teamed up with King when King began in the business as a fight manager, recalled an instance of King's persuasiveness from the early 1970s, when King had a managerial share of Earnie Shavers and wanted to buy out another shareholder, the major-league pitcher Dean Chance, for $8,000.

"Then," said Elbaum, "he told me he wanted the eight grand back from his other partner, Blackie Gennaro, a very wealthy paving contractor. I told King he was crazy and that Blackie wasn't going to give him the money. I was so mad at King I ran down to Youngstown and told Blackie, 'Absolutely don't give the money back.'"

A meeting was convened. King painted a rosy picture of Shavers' future and of the brilliance of all those involved with the fighter.

"Then he told us," Elbaum said, "he needed $16,000 to implement his vision. Sixteen grand. No one said a word. They gave him $16,000. It was unreal."

But for Elbaum life-with-King got even stranger on a night in those early 1970s when King turned up at his office and set a briefcase on his desk.

"It was eight o'clock," said Elbaum, "and as King drops the briefcase and heads out the door, he tells me: 'Don't leave.' So I waited for him to come back. Eleven o'clock, twelve o'clock. I'm blowing my top. I get on the phone trying to reach him. I stayed all night. Eight A.M. he shows up. He opens the briefcase. It's filled with money. 'Where's my coat?' he says. He pulls money—big bills—out of one pocket, and then the other. 'Now I know I can trust you,' he said. I wish I could say the same for him."

LOU DUVA: A Long Way from the Primrose Diner (1991)

He is sixty-nine years old, and by now Lou Duva has become as recognizable in public as his fighters. There's the white hair and that face of a battle-wise munchkin, a crinkled expanse with blunt dark brows and a pug nose that got that way from taking a few too many punches.

That was back after World War II, when Duva, an ex-G.I., was a welterweight who fought with more enthusiasm than finesse—and certainly with less preparation than he would allow the world-class fighters in whom he and his son Dan now have a proprietry interest.

Duva's idea of road work was to take a shower so he would look wet enough to convince his trainers he had sweated his miles. Given that slacker's habit, it was inevitable that he was soon an ex-fighter. He built a trucking business to support his wife, Enes, and their five children: Dan, Dino, Donna, Denise and Deanne. Not coincidentally, the profits from trucking helped sustain his lifelong addiction to the fight game.

For many years the 5-foot-7-inch, 230-pound Duva scuffled on the fringes of the boxing scene. He was a bucket-carrier, a cornerman, a manager and a promoter, a man buoyed by love of the sport more than by the financial returns.

But things have changed. Duva, who survived a 1979 heart attack and an angioplasty procedure for blocked arteries earlier this year, is no longer odd man out. Today, Lou and Dan Duva's Main Events Inc. in West Paterson, New Jersey, is a multimillion-dollar operation. The star attraction is the heavyweight champion, Evander Holyfield, who was guaranteed just over $8 million when he won the title last October from James (Buster) Douglas, and $20 million when he successfully defended it in April against George Foreman.

177

As Holyfield has prospered, so have the Duvas. Main Events reportedly received just under $1 million from the Douglas bout and in excess of $2 million from the Foreman match. Holyfield is not the Duvas' only asset. Pernell Whitaker, the undisputed lightweight title holder, and Meldrick Taylor, the World Boxing Association welterweight champion, are both promoted by Dan and co-managed by Lou and Shelly Finkel, a rock concert promoter. Hector Camacho, the World Boxing Organization junior welterweight champion, has a promotional deal with Main Events but is not managed by the Duvas.

Through the 1980's, the Duvas recognized that the ability to expose a fighter on television would give them clout in the game. Their strength as boxing operatives was bolstered in the last year by their association with Time-Warner Sports, which includes Home Box Office, the pay-cable service, and TVKO, the pay-per-view entity by which viewers may subscribe for a single event.

Last December, Main Events struck a multi-fight, multimillion-dollar deal with HBO for the rights to televise the matches of Whitaker, Taylor and Camacho. More recently, Main Events signed a three-year deal with TVKO that guarantees the company five pay-per-view dates a year, with a promotional fee of approximately $250,000 per date.

That conjures up a sunny future that makes Lou's distant past in boxing far easier to joke about.

For Duva, the hard times started in Paterson, New Jersey. As a fifteen-year-old, he boxed in bar-room smokers for five dollars a fight and worked jobs delivering newspapers, shining shoes and setting up pins in a bowling alley.

"I'd set up pins til two, three in the morning and fall asleep in class the next day. One teacher kept hitting me on the head and telling me I'd have to make up my mind whether I wanted to go to school or not."

Duva made up his mind: He doctored a birth certificate, changing his age, so he could join the Civilian Conservation Corps, and he headed west, to Oregon.

"It was 1938," said Duva. "The C.C.C. would send $25 home to my family and leave five dollars for me. In Oregon and

Washington, they taught me how to be a truck driver and I learned one other useful skill: how to shoot craps."

Back in Paterson at the outbreak of World War II, Duva enlisted in the Army and ended up as a boxing instructor at Camp Hood in Texas. Mustered out in 1944, he joined his parents in Florida, where he assisted his father, Salvatore, in the family's restaurant business and delivered pies for a cousin's bakery. In between, he boxed professionally without much distinction.

"I was doing everything wrong," said Duva. "No roadwork. I wasn't training. I'd take fights on two days notice."

But the love of boxing lasted longer than his nondescript ring career did. While Duva grew beyond his welterweight's dimensions he built a trucking business (from three trucks to thirty-two) in Paterson and dabbled in boxing. He operated a gym, promoted small-time fight cards and eventually began managing boxers.

"But boxing in those years," said Duva, "was strictly a sideline."

Back then, Lou's children would man the box office, erect and dismantle the ring, staple fight posters to telephone poles and keep a wary eye on their old man as he hurled another obnoxious drunk out the arena's back door.

"We didn't make a lot of money, but we had fun," said Donna, now office manager for Main Events. "Sometimes fighters would fall out and we'd have to comb the streets of Paterson that day to find a replacement.

"After each promotion, we'd be in the back room, everybody yelling at each other. Dino would pay the fighters. I'd do the box office. The money would never match the receipts. We'd have one of those bank bags and we'd throw it in the trunk and head for the diner."

For the elder Duva, it was considered a good night if a promotion provided enough revenue to cover the tab at the Primrose Diner on Route 46.

The penny-ante scale of the Duva operation did not change until Dan unexpectedly decided to become more than a casual participant.

In 1977, Lou was working as matchmaker for the promoter Bob Arum. In that role, he met Mitt Barnes, the manager of Leon

Spinks, a fighter under contract to Arum. Barnes feared he was about to be disenfranchised as manager and asked Duva who, like himself, had been a Teamster official, to recommend a lawyer.

Lou introduced him to Dan.

"I agreed to represent Mitt in return for ten percent of his thirty percent managerial share," said Dan. "Six months later I'd made $600. So I told Mitt it wasn't enough money—I needed more. He said, 'I can't afford an hourly fee but rather than ten percent I'll give you thirty percent.'"

It turned out to be a fortuitous adjustment. In only his eighth fight as a professional, Spinks fought and beat Muhammad Ali for the heavyweight title in February 1978. In a rematch that September, Spinks lost the title.

"For the first Ali fight, Spinks' purse was about $350,000 to $400,000," said Dan. "Mitt got about $100,000, which meant I ended up with about $30,000. For the rematch, Leon made $3.5 million. That meant Mitt got one million dollars and my share came to about $300,000. That was it. I was into boxing. I told my father, 'There's no magic to what Don King and Arum do. We can do this too.'"

And they have, in tandem. Lou handles the fighters, collaborating with trainer George Benton on training and strategy. Come fight night, Lou works with his emotions close to the surface: he has harangued referees, and once—at the final bell—exchanged punches with a champion named Roger Mayweather, who was an opponent of a fighter of Duva's. The thirty-nine-year-old Dan and Finkel take care of the business end.

Finkel came to boxing by accident. In 1977, a next-door neighbor died, leaving a wife and son.

Finkel began spending time with the boy, trying to help him recover from the loss of his father. One night Finkel, who is the father of three children, took the youngster to the Golden Gloves at Madison Square Garden, on a card in which middleweight Alex Ramos fought and won and made an impression on him.

Finkel began following Ramos' amateur career and developed a friendship with the fighter that would result in his becoming Ramos' manager in 1980.

By then, Finkel had met the Duvas and agreed to become partners with them.

"The idea was I would get the fighters and Lou would know what to do with them," Finkel said. "In effect, Lou was involved in the training and matchmaking, and Dan and I were on the business end. I was the one who recruited the fighters."

In 1980, the year of the Moscow Olympics boycott, Finkel persuaded Ramos, Tony Tucker, Mitch Green, Tony Ayala and Johnny Bumphus to sign with Main Events.

Four years later, Finkel got Mark Breland, Whitaker, Taylor, Tyrell Biggs and Holyfield—gold medalists at the Los Angeles Games—to entrust their futures to the company.

Breland remembered liking Finkel's approach on money. "He was the only one who talked about what I could do to hold on to my money," Breland said. "The other guys recruiting me didn't care; they were just concerned about their money."

Father and son the Duvas may be, but their styles couldn't be more different.

"Dan is so serious, so dedicated," said Seth Abrahm of TVKO. "Sometimes telling a joke can break tension in negotiations. Dan doesn't laugh.

"You can see things about people in their body language. A guy like Don King uses his size. He puts his arms out—he has a big wingspan—and he's very theatrical. When he reaches out, it's like the wingspan of a condor. Arum moves around a lot and uses his hands, almost like he's calculating with his hands. As for Dan, he sits there and never moves or fidgets. No nervous mannerisms. He sits there like the Lincoln Memorial and just does his business."

By contrast, Lou's is a dervish presence—and a lot more touchy-feely than Dan's.

On Tuesday as Whitaker prepared for his title defense against Poli Diaz in Norfolk, Virginia—he ended up winning by decision— the champion embraced his co-manager outside a radio studio. That show of affection came just after Lou had handed Whitaker a shopping bag full of college basketball uniforms—Pernell is crazy for such attire and Duva has never met a shopping mall he doesn't like.

A day or so later, at Wareing's Gym in Virginia Beach, Virginia, Duva was everywhere as Whitaker and other fighters went through their workouts. Here he mopped a wet patch on the floor, there he plotted to steal the ultra-thick eyeglasses of a foreign reporter and then substitute junior lightweight Eddie Hopson for Whitaker for an interview. Duva posed for pictures, signed autographs, dispensed advice to the fighters and supervised the trainers.

Hopson finished his session, showered and then came by to borrow two dollars from Lou for a nutritional drink.

"I'll give you two dollars if you Simonize my car," said Duva peeling off a five dollar bill for Hopson.

"What a guy," said Hopson.

"Don't give me that stuff," said Duva. "I might as well get adoption papers on you."

LORDS OF THE RING (1989)

The neon lights blink non-stop on the Strip in Las Vegas, Nevada. From twilight to the first glimmer of morning, those lights make a firedance against the sky, their pulsing colors seeking to entice money to the tables. That is the game in Las Vegas—excite the wagering man to pass through a casino's door, and then let the mathematics of chance work for the house. In places like this they speak forever of the daily "pit drop"—defined as the cash and/or markers put into circulation, exclusive of slot machines. The goal of every Vegas casino is to increase the pit drop.

A Vegas casino routinely wins eighteen to twenty percent of the play. It does not take a Wharton School of Finance grad to fathom the beauty of volume. The more players, the heavier the pit drop. So get the jokers in the building and let the percentages thrive.

Boxing matches are the best action Las Vegas has for luring the "preferential customers," the euphemism casinos use for high rollers. Nothing excites the high rollers quite like the mano a mano of boxing. Bob Halloran, who booked the big matches into Caesars Palace for a decade, recalls what a casino host named "Wingy" used to say any night Caesars had a hot fight on its docket: "He'd tell me, 'Kid, this is like New Year's.' And everybody knows New Year's is as good as Vegas casinos do...Except when a really big fight is on the boards."

Where once the major bouts were staged in smoky arenas, now they land in the boxing venues of casinos. The arenas may have the B-movie tradition but these days the casinos have the kick. They can, and do, pay more in live-site fees than other venues. Pay more by the millions, and end up generating pit drops much larger than ordinary play would. "Three, four, five times greater," says a Vegas

183

casino operator. "There is nothing like boxing to impact that drop." Vegas casinos are not obliged to reveal their gaming figures, as New Jersey requires its casinos to do. But what Atlantic City reveals—and the same holds for Vegas—is that boxing is New Year's-plus.

Take the Tyson-Spinks bout of June 27, 1988 in Atlantic City. According to Gary Selesner of Trump Plaza: "The week of June 26 to July 2, when Tyson fought Spinks, Trump Plaza did a pit drop of $32 million. A year later we did $17.3 million and came in second among casinos here. Atlantic City as a whole did $221,154,000 during that week of Tyson-Spinks, and a year later, without a big fight, it was $155 million."

If the casino business is a numbers game, John V. Giovenco, president of the Hilton Nevada Corporation, is suited to play. For fifteen years he was a certified public accountant with the Chicago firm of Pannell Kerr Forster.

"It was the biggest hotel accounting firm in the country, and I was a partner in the Chicago office," said Giovenco. "But in 1972, when the Hilton corporation bought the Flamingo Hilton and the Las Vegas Hilton, Barron Hilton asked me to join the company as vice president-treasurer for the Hilton Hotels Corporation."

Giovenco moved up the Hilton corporate ladder and, by September 1985, was asked to shake up things at the Las Vegas Hilton.

"This property is the largest in the world—3,174 rooms," said Giovenco. "The previous guy's idea was to increase convention business, and mid-line gambling. That meant there were no comps, and the appeal was to the paying tourist. Caesars Palace, on the other hand, had gone almost completely high-line. I looked at our numbers against the other place, and the discrepancy led me to make changes. We needed to increase the excitement level in our building."

A crucial part of the makeover strategy was boxing, a sport with which the fifty-three-year-old Giovenco was acquainted. At Cathedral High School in Chicago, he had been a varsity athlete in baseball, football, and basketball, diversity that had encouraged him to try it one year as a featherweight in the Chicago Golden Gloves.

"It seemed like a good idea at the time," he said. "I thought I was fast and elusive and it turned out I wasn't, and I proved it by getting KO'd in the first round. The guy I fought used to lift cement blocks from trucks. Geez—I can still remember the size of his muscles. And the mouse I had under both eyes afterward. And my parents' reaction: 'You've got to be out of your mind!'"

Giovenco's return to boxing proved a happier experience. The Hilton's first bout in his regime—Donald Curry vs. Milton McCrory for the undisputed welterweight title in December 1985—did what fights are supposed to in Vegas: it brought out the high rollers.

"And fortunately for us," said Giovenco, "a couple of players lost a lot of money. It demonstrated what we could do with boxing."

The next year, Giovenco signed a multi-fight deal with promoters Don King and Butch Lewis that made the Hilton the site of most of Home Box Office's heavyweight unification series, including four bouts featuring Mike Tyson.

"The HBO series," said Giovenco, "was very good for us. We made money. But you know what? The best fight from a profit standpoint was the Thomas Hearns-Iran Barkley fight of last June [1988]. It brought out five of our biggest players and all five bit the dust."

Giovenco's involvement with the HBO series, he says, kept him in a perpetual stage of ready alert.

"That had to do with the way Don King and Butch Lewis do business," said Giovenco. "Take their rival, Bob Arum. He's a very straightforward guy. He comes from a law background. He's the most logical and easy of the promoters to deal with. He comes in with a contract. You negotiate several points and that's it. He has an organization that follows up with press conferences and promotions. It's a much more normal business relationship. Like you'd have with the promoter of any superstar.

"But Don King and Butch Lewis are in constant chaos. Neither of them has an organization worth spit. The people who work for them can't make a decision without Don or Butch putting their imprimatur on it. And when you sign a contract, you've just begun negotiations. You start out with a specific number of comp rooms and tickets for the promoter—and somehow by the time you reach fight day they have to have twice as many tickets or rooms or the fight won't take place. No one threatens anything, but they are continually manipulating.

"Butch especially was constantly crying about not getting treated properly. And the only reason we were treating him this way, he'd say, is because he's black. Like: 'There's no soap in the room. Don't you think black people use soap?'"

In 1987, Lewis was sued by the Hilton Nevada Corporation for breach of contract after his fighter, Michael Spinks, was banished from the HBO series for signing to fight Gerry Cooney without Cooney's guaranteeing to join in the series in the event he won. In a jury trial last year, the Hilton lost its case.

As for Lewis, he says that it was while he and King, as Dynamic Duo, Inc., co-promoted the HBO series that "King would make requests in both our names, which I was unaware of."

Then, said Lewis: "There came a time during the HBO series when John had to make a choice between King and me and he chose King. He was conned. But what the hell, Don King is the best there is at that. I told John, 'Don't feel bad. King's the master.'"

Lewis says that later when King and he had a falling out during the HBO series, he was obliged to buy a ticket "to my own promotion."

"And rather than a comped suite," said Lewis, "they wouldn't let me and my people into a room unless we put up a credit card. That's where that bar of soap came up. But it was an associate of mine, Don Hubbard, not me, who said it kiddingly. Said to Giovenco, after we checked in, 'You don't mind if we have a bar of soap in the room?' And we all kind of laughed."

For years, whenever Bob Arum staged a major bout, Rich Rose would be ringside as a fight publicist, aiding and abetting the working press.

Rose would urge photographers to remain beneath the lowest ring rope when they shot so as not to obscure the view of the writers behind them. And if a bout ended in a knockout, he would hurry into the ring to get the exact time of stoppage. Then he would lean through the ropes and shout that time to the guys on deadline so they could insert the information in their leads.

Rose worked hard on fight night and he worked hard during the weeks leading to the bout, and made an impression, apparently, on the casino community. For when Halloran defected from Caesars to become the "boxing guy" for Steve Wynn's Mirage, the thirty-nine-year-old Rose was appointed his replacement, as president of Caesars World Sports.

Like Giovenco, Rose had an early interest in the fight game. His grandfather was a vice president for Gillette, the razor manufacturer that for years sponsored the Friday Night Fights on TV. On the old man's weekend visits to the Rose household in Chappaqua, New York, watching those televised bouts was a regular routine.

As a teenager, Rose was intending to become a doctor, but by the time he went off to Syracuse University, he'd changed his mind.

"I was always a frenetic kid," said Rose. "I questioned whether I had the patience for ten years of education and interning. It was not fear of work. I just realized that maybe my temperament was not right for it. Sports was my great love."

And public relations became Rose's way to be part of the sports world. He worked at first for other publicists. Then, in 1984, he and Jacqueline Lapin founded their own public relations firm and built it into a successful business. "Lapin & Rose," he said, "did gross billings in 1986 of more than $700,000. And twenty percent of that was from boxing."

While Rose often worked for Arum, he was also a regular on fights of Gerry Cooney, with whom he survived a shaky start to become friends.

The first Cooney bout that Rose worked was against the heavy-weight champion, Larry Holmes, in June 1982. "Gerry didn't know me from Adam," recalled Rose, "and was very skeptical. He thought I was 'a Don King spy,' and he kept arm's length from me. The first day there I set up an interview for him—an *Inside Sports* cover story—and, when I told him, he spun about on his toes and pointed at me. 'You know,' he said, 'I don't like you and I don't trust you. The only people I trust are Mike Jones and Dennis Rappaport [Cooney's managers], and if you don't watch yourself, you'll be out.' I told him, 'You want me out, I know where the door is.' Fast forward to minutes after the fight had ended. Gerry was dejected and was staring at me. I told him, 'You've got nothing to be ashamed of. You went thirteen rounds in 110-degree heat and you fought well.' He looked at me and said, 'I don't like you, I don't trust you...' Then suddenly he throws his arms around me and laughs. Ever since then, when Dennis and Mike couldn't get hold of Gerry, they'd call me for his whereabouts."

Now that he is president of Caesars World Sports, Rose—or "Little Caesar," as friends jokingly call him—is charged with acquiring events that will draw the casino's biggest players into the building.

"I looked at all kinds of events," said Rose. "Billiards, tennis, Robbie Knievel jumping the Caesars fountains on a motorbike. While some of those other events do well for us, none of them works to the degree boxing does. We'll get 2,000 customers for a fight. Plus, when you do fights, you know that other people will be pouring into the city and they'll want to come to Caesars to be where the action is. To see Ray Leonard, or Don Johnson, or who-ever is rattling around the building."

When Rose's pal, Jay Larkin, a public relations man at Showtime, was appointed the executive who would make the boxing deals for the pay cable network, Larkin had occasion to talk to Arum. As Rose recalled: "They were talking fights and Jay told Bob, 'Wait a minute. That's not going to work. Let's do it this way.' Arum, who can be blunt, said, 'What do *you* know? You're a bleeping PR guy.' Larkin exploded with laughter."

The story underscores the shift from business accomplice to exec that Rose, like Larkin, has made, and the doubts that some boxing men have that he is up to the job.

"Like the time I made a deal with Dan Duva to do Evander Holyfield vs. Pinklon Thomas," said Rose. "Duva calls back a few days later and says, 'We got a problem. It's Don King.' King was Thomas' promoter and was trying to get more than double what I'd agreed to pay for the fight. King calls me, and says 'It's a big, big fight coming up. Worth a lot of money, especially to Pinklon. I replied, 'What about it? The last time anybody remembers Pinklon he was on his butt.'"

That was a reference to Thomas' knockout loss to Tyson in May 1987.

"'I've been offered twice that for him to fight in Atlantic City,'" Rose quoted King as saying. "I told him, 'If you can get it, take it.' King says, 'I'll be back to you.' I then called Duva and told him, 'In ten days, when he's finished blowing smoke, we'll still have a deal.' Ten days later, we finalized our deal."

While Rose's Caesars Palace and Giovenco's Hilton have dominated boxing in Las Vegas, there are new players waiting in the wings.

One of them is Steve Wynn, who turned the Golden Nugget, at its downtown location, into a thriving operation and now is bent on giving The Mirage a gloss of excitement to match a building so posh it has 14-karat gold electroplating between sheets of glass on its exterior. But that, as game show hosts like to say, is not all.

"The Mirage," said Wynn, "will be a self-contained tropical environment in the midst of a dry, barren Las Vegas desert."

In December 1989, when the Mirage opened for its first bout—Ray Leonard vs. Roberto Duran III—the sign said the white tigers would not be on display in their casino habitat this night. But at the new Mirage Hotel there were other sights to see.

In the lobby, behind the registration desk, was a wall-length 20,000-gallon aquarium. Not far from there, along a winding carpeted path, there was a tropical garden with royal palms and South Seas' foliage.

Outside the hotel entrance, behind a metal fence, was the showpiece, a tree-shrouded lagoon with a towering waterfall from which plumes of fire erupted every so often. The effects unfolded with enough whooshing energy that the Vesuvian spectacle drew applause from the gaping crowds.

The path to Wynn's high-profile Las Vegas existence goes back to 1952 when his father, Mike, a bingo-game operator, first brought him to the desert city. To Wynn, ten years old at the time, the place seemed "glamorous and wild."

"The Silver Slipper, where my dad ran the bingo game, had a Western Village, with a saloon and livery stable," said Wynn. "Each day I'd rent a horse and ride with my dad. There were no roads then, just desert. I was not allowed into the casino, so I didn't know my father was a craps shooter and a high roller. I just thought he was an important guy. Everybody paid attention to him. He loved Las Vegas. And I just saw it through his eyes."

Wynn's father died when the son was a senior at the University of Pennsylvania. After Wynn graduated with a bachelor of arts degree in English literature ("I started out as a pre-med, but the smell of fetal pigs and formaldehyde....") he became a partner for a while in his father's bingo-game operation.

By the mid-1960's, he had sold his share of the bingo-game business for $25,000, borrowed $10,000 and invested the sum in the Frontier Hotel and Casino in Las Vegas. There he managed the slot-machine department and issued credit.

In 1967, the Frontier was sold to Howard Hughes, at no profit to Wynn, who was dismissed when the Hughes regime took over.

From 1968 to 1972, Wynn operated a liquor distributorship in Nevada. Then, with a loan from a supportive banker, Wynn and another man bought a piece of property from Hughes for $1.2 million.

"I sold it ten months later for $2.25 million," he said. "I owned two-thirds, the partner had the other third. I paid taxes on my profit and bought Golden Nugget stock in 1972."

The Golden Nugget that Wynn bought into was what he called "a grind joint", a low-margin setup that did not cater to high rollers. In 1973, when Wynn became president and chairman, he redesigned it, aiming at and eventually getting an upscale clientele that has enabled him to add the Mirage to his empire.

"The Golden Nugget in 1973 had assets of $12 million," Wynn said. "Today, the assets are about $1 billion."

Before he landed at the Mirage, Halloran staged boxing's biggest bouts over the past decade at Caesars, using headliners like Ray Leonard, Muhammad Ali, Larry Holmes, Aaron Pryor, and Marvelous Marvin Hagler.

Halloran's entry into the casino business occurred in the midst of a nineteen-and-a-half-year career as a radio and TV sports broadcaster in Miami and New York.

"About 1977," Halloran said, "I happened to be skiing in Aspen and while there met the then chairman of the board of Caesars, Cliff Perlman. While I was having an apres-ski cocktail at his condo, Perlman got a call from Don King about a fight—I think it was Larry Holmes-Ossie Ocasio. Well, he put King on hold and began asking me a bunch of questions."

Perlman must have liked what Halloran had to say because when he went looking for a director of sports for Caesars World, Halloran was his man.

Halloran saw boxing soar as an attraction during his decade at Caesars. "Casinos were paying, maybe $50 grand, $75 grand for fights when I first came around. For Hagler-Leonard I paid in excess of $7 million."

Halloran also turned the fights into a special event for the preferential customer. "I put into effect a VIP section," said Halloran, "on one side of the ring. Before that, the press had occupied all four sides of the ring. I saw the value, as a marketing tool, of seating our best customers next to stars like Burt Reynolds. Then they could go home and say, 'Guess who I sat next to?' We ended up taking a lot of our customers from different parts of the country and made them fight fans."

Halloran probably will not be the only new casino dealmaker competing for the super bouts. The ubiquitous Donald Trump earlier this year set up the Trump Nevada Corporation and appointed thirty-five-year-old Michael Rumbolz to run the operation.

Rumbolz's job? Find a property that can launch dealmaker Donald's Nevada casino business.

Until now, Trump has run casinos only in Atlantic City. Through one of them, Trump Plaza (which adjoins the Convention Center) Trump became a big man in boxing's casino wars, an involvement not really premeditated. Trump says that while reviewing the daily pit drop reports, he noted what he refers to as "blips," the disproportionately high numbers the casino did on days it staged fights in the 2,500 seat ballroom on the Convention Center, or on its own premises.

"What I began to see over a fairly short period of time," Trump said, "was there is a direct relation between a high roller in the gaming sense and a boxing fan. Boxing, more than any other sport, brings out the highly-competitive person."

Trump took the logical next step, staging major fights in the Convention Center's larger facility, which can hold between 12,000 and 20,000 fight fans. Spinks-Cooney, Tyson-Biggs, Tyson-Holmes, and Tyson-Spinks followed, and suddenly Trump was a force in the boxing business.

If and when Trump expands to Nevada, Rumbolz will be at his side. A graduate of the University of Southern California Law School, he began his career as a practicing attorney in Las Vegas. But when an opportunity to run the state attorney general's Gaming Division arose, Rumbolz took a $3,000 cut in pay and the new job.

"In Nevada," he said, "if you want to practice administrative law, the most cutting edge is in the gaming industry. It's where the most important decisions are made."

In 1985, Rumbolz moved to a position on the three-man Nevada Gaming Control Board. Some two years later, when the board's chairman retired, the then thirty-three-year-old Rumbolz replaced him.

When he left that position last year, Rumbolz was courted by several Nevada casinos *and* law firms. But after Trump flew Rumbolz to Aspen for talks, Rumbolz chose to go to work for Trump Nevada.

While he keeps his eyes peeled for the right casino property, Rumbolz is charged with sifting through the multitude of offers that filter down to his desk.

"Because he's Donald Trump," said Rumbolz, "everybody figures Donald's Midas touch will make them rich too. I mean you should see the offers I turn down. Like 4,000 to 5,000-acre parcels in the desert on which he can build Trump City. Crummy motels on the Strip offer to sell. And there was even an ice cream-on-a-stick that was proposed. Called 'Trumpsicle.'"

PAPA SMURF, A.K.A. EDDIE FUTCH (1992)

It was January 1989, and the fight manager Rock Newman needed a trainer for the heavyweight he had just signed, Riddick Bowe. The one he had in mind was Eddie Futch, the soft-spoken knowledgeable man who had trained champions like Don Jordan, Smokin' Joe Frazier, Ken Norton, Larry Holmes and Michael Spinks. Futch had made a vivid impression on Newman back when Newman was managing a light heavyweight champion named Dwight Braxton (later known as Dwight Muhammad Qawi).

"In March 1963, Futch was the trainer for Michael Spinks when Spinks and Dwight fought a light heavyweight unification bout," said Newman. "That was as close as I've ever come to seeing a strategy do as much to beat a fighter as the fighter himself."

Futch's plan for that bout was simple. Braxton had a habit of baiting a foe into throwing the right hand by dropping his left hand. "As the man threw the right," Futch explained, "Braxton would roll and take the right on his shoulder and fire back with his right. He did that real well."

Not against Spinks. As Newman recalled, "I kept waiting for Michael to throw the right."

So did Braxton. But Futch had instructed Spinks to use his left hand—jab and hook—and never throw the right until Braxton did. The brawl that the public had anticipated never materialized, as Spinks fought and won a strategic victory.

"And after, everybody said, 'Braxton didn't do much,'" recalled Futch. "But that was because Spinks didn't let him do much."

Newman was sure that Futch was just the man to work with Bowe and reform the heavyweight's reputation. As an amateur, Bowe was widely regarded as lackadaisical, primarily because of the passive resistance he had offered to Lennox Lewis in the heavy-weight gold-medal final at the 1988 Summer Olympics in Seoul, South Korea. When he turned pro after losing that bout, the fighter was disparagingly called "Riddick-ulous."

The line on Bowe was that he just didn't care, that he was a head case. Newman insisted that Bowe had fought with serious injuries at the Olympics and had been misperceived.

Newman's view was one that Futch didn't share, at first.

"The reports on Bowe were more or less negative," the eight-one-year-old Futch said recently. "His heart was questioned after the '88 Olympics. On the basis of the information I came by, I told Rock no."

Newman, a former car salesman, went into his hard-sell and persuaded Futch to evaluate Bowe, a Brooklyn native, for himself.

"I never told Bowe it was just a look-see that Eddie agreed to," said Newman. "Eddie asked me not to. He wanted to see what Bowe would do on his own."

In February 1989, Bowe flew to Reno, where Futch was working with the light-heavyweight titleholder Virgil Hill. Futch's first impressions of Bowe were favorable.

"I did a drill with him where I told him I would jab to the body and show him how to parry it," said Futch. "Actually it was just a way I have of testing a fighter's reflexes. And Bowe's reflexes were impressive."

Later, Futch sat down and talked with Bowe.

"In talking to him," Futch recalled, "I realized that because he was a big fellow—six-foot-five, 230 pounds—people assumed he was a man. But I saw he was still a teenager, even though he was twenty years old going on twenty-one. A fun-loving teen who acted as though he wanted to be Muhammad Ali when he was actually looking for Riddick Bowe.

"At that stage, he was kind of floating. His feet were not on the ground. Not because he was a bad kid. He just needed someone to direct him and have him follow a straight line. He hadn't known a father for many, many years."

Bowe took to calling Futch "Papa Smurf", after the cartoon character, an affectionate nickname that has stuck.

"In the Saturday cartoons, Papa Smurf was a small, quiet man and very knowledgeable," said Bowe. "Come a crisis he was calm, cool and collected. Those were the characteristics of Mr. Futch."

One day in Reno, Futch told Bowe that he had to go out of town and wanted Bowe to continue training on his own.

"I had no intention of leaving. I just wanted to see if he'd follow instructions," Futch explained. "The next morning it was snowing and cold and I drove out on the route Bowe was supposed to run."

Bowe was there, dutifully covering the six-mile course in sub-freezing weather.

"At the end of the run Papa Smurf was waiting in his jeep," said Bowe. "I had icicles on my head and he had a little smile on his face."

At that point, Futch said, "I told myself, 'This kid is O.K. He's worth devoting time to.'"

Eddie Futch has been devoting time to educating fighters for most of his life. But his road to boxing was a circuitous one. As a youth growing up in Detroit his passion was basketball.

"I was a starter with the Moreland Y.M.C.A. Flashes," said Futch. "In 1927, we played the Savoy Big Five out of Chicago, which would become the first edition of the Harlem Globetrotters. The Flashes were a semipro club."

Futch married when he was seventeen and gave up basketball soon after. Through a friend, he became interested in boxing, not intending, though, to do more than hit the speed bag and skip rope. But after he was persuaded to spar, he joined the Detroit Athletic Association at the Brewster Community Center and began competing as an amateur lightweight. Among his teammates was Joe Louis.

"From 1932 to '36 I fought as an amateur," Futch said. "I won the Detroit Golden Gloves in 1933. These were the Depression years and I was lucky. I had a job. I worked as a waiter at the Hotel Wolverine in Detroit. Fifteen dollars a week and tips.

Futch's amateur career was halted when, in a prefight physical, a doctor discovered a heart murmur. Futch, who was training fighters at the time at a local Y.M.C.A. on a casual basis, became more serious about his future when he was named the boxing coach at the Detroit Athletic Association.

During World War II, Futch worked as a spot welder at the Ford Motor Company while training his first pro contender, Lester Felton, a welterweight. In 1951, he moved to Los Angeles and continued working with fighters there. When Don Jordan beat Virgil Akins for the welterweight title in 1958, Futch had his first champion.

Bowe—seeking to be Futch's latest champion—was no easy case.

"It took a lot of doing to get him to stop aping Muhammad Ali," said Futch. "I didn't give him my reasons why he shouldn't. But I had reasons. Ali in his prime was around 215 pounds and he had come up to that weight. Bowe was 230 and was going to get bigger. I couldn't envision a 230-pounder on his toes for twelve rounds.

"Plus, Bowe had greater power than Ali, and I wanted him to be able to use that."

Futch's insights were a revelation for Bowe. "I had the amateur in me when I came to him," said Bowe. "I was always excited. I threw a lot of punches. Papa Smurf showed me patience and a lot more. He showed me how to set up a guy—how to make him run into my punches. He told me I didn't have to knock out everybody."

Newman saw Bowe's faith in Futch generate confidence.

"Bowe executed better because he believed in his teacher," said Newman. "He had supreme confidence. If Eddie says it, that's the bible. And Bowe feels and believes it and it makes him a better fighter."

While the twenty-five-year-old Bowe has other aides—Dick Gregory, the former comedian, is his dietician, and Mackie Shilstone is his conditioning coach—Futch remains the voice of authority. And in the countdown to Bowe's upcoming title challenge of Evander Holyfield, Futch had to raise that voice, to keep Bowe from peaking too soon.

"Sometimes when he's doing road work, I follow in a golf cart," said Futch. "The other day he was supposed to go to a certain point and turn back. Well, he went past that point and pretended he didn't hear me when I said turn back. So I told him again. 'Bowe, turn around here.'

"See, this is the most important fight of his career and there's a tendency for the fighter to feel he's not doing enough. He figures if work is good, more work is better. It's not so, though. Sometimes you have to back off, so the fighter takes into the ring everything he's got and doesn't leave it in the gym or on the road."

And Bowe knows: when Papa Smurf speaks, a fighter listens.

ROCK NEWMAN IS ONE PART GIBRALTAR, AND ONE PART AVALANCHE (1992)

Rock Newman was sitting at the long oak table in his living room in Washington, D.C., doing what a man does when he manages a new heavyweight champion of the world: keeping up.

The black push-button phone was ringing like clockwork, bringing Newman and his fighter, Riddick Bowe, the usual offers and excitations that go with glory in the arena. An invitation to a screening of "Malcolm X." A business proposition from a man whose merchandise benefits black colleges such as Howard University, Newman's alma mater. A discussion of arrangements for a parade today for Bowe, which began in Prince Georges County in Maryland and proceeded into Washington before thousands of onlookers.

It is a crazy, exhilarating time for the forty-year-old Newman and comes just days after Bowe had beaten Evander Holyfield for the title. Days after the crowning moment, years after hard times. Back in January 1990, Newman was obliged to sell his beloved 1988 BMW for $25,000 to keep Bowe solvent while the both of them avoided entangling commitments to promoters.

When that money ran out a few months later, Newman succeeded in persuading a group of local businessmen to give him a cash infusion of $250,000.

The investors have been paid off, and early Wednesday morning Newman deposited in the Citizens Bank of Washington a check for more than $4 million from Bowe's victory over Evander Holyfield last Friday. He anticipates earning another $3 million to $4 million from the bout.

What a pleasure it must be to have your faith vindicated as he has. For when nobody else did, Newman saw a future in which

199

Riddick Lamont Bowe would be heavyweight champion. Saw the future and went after it hell-bent to fulfill it.

He talked up Bowe to anybody who would listen, appearing regularly on radio in New York with WFAN's Don Imus while cajoling mentions of Bowe from newspaper reporters. He did what he had to so Bowe would get attention, once even dressing him up in Batman regalia. He pushed for his man with the governing bodies of the sport and, when there was any controversy involving Bowe, Newman was in the thick of it. In one instance, he shoved a rival fight manager, Marc Roberts, during a television interview. In another, he climbed onto the ring apron and flipped Elijah Tillery over the ropes when Tillery kicked Bowe several times during a bout in 1991.

Newman's involvement in boxing goes back more than a few years. After graduating from Howard University in 1974 with a liberal arts degree, he worked as a car salesman before, as he explains it, a guilty conscience sent him looking for other employment.

"I sold a car to an elderly black couple at sticker price," Newman said. "These people didn't know they could have gotten it for less. I was making a good living, but that sale and my $600 commission haunted me because they were people of very meager means. The next day I spoke to a vice president at Howard and told him I wanted to do something with more impact and substance."

Newman became a counselor at Howard.

"I spent five of my most rewarding years there," Newman said. "I dealt with academic problems, homosexuality, serious drug addiction and with folks who were suicidal."

In 1980, a friend of Newman bought a Washington radio station and changed the music format to all talk. When a snowstorm kept the host of one show from making it to the studio, Newman walked two miles through the city's streets to fill in.

He did so well in his debut that he began filling in for other hosts until he eventually got his own show.

It was in that capacity that he met Dwight Braxton, now known as Dwight Muhammad Qawi, soon after he won the World Boxing Council light heavyweight title in 1981.

"The station's limo picked up Dwight in Baltimore; I rode along," Newman recalled. "I remember, as we talked, he told me he didn't own a car. Here was a world champion, and no car. I told him, 'I'll get you a car.'"

Newman arranged a promotional deal that landed Qawi a new Chevrolet in return for personal appearances at the dealership. Before long he was Qawi's de facto manager.

That was followed by a stint as a spokesman for the promoter Butch Lewis and, when Lewis chose not to pursue Bowe after the 1988 Olympics, the role as Bowe's manager.

In the beginning, even the fighter lacked his manager's conviction.

After a dispiriting loss at the 1988 Olympics to gold-medalist Lennox Lewis, Bowe—married and with two young children—had just about given up on the idea of a pro career.

"After the Olympics," said Bowe, "I was very displeased. So displeased that I was thinking about going into the military. Then Rock said, 'I believe in you.' He didn't seem to be shucking and jiving. Other guys would say, 'We'll give you a look-see' and wouldn't mention money. Rock said, 'I know you have kids—and the kids have to be taken care of. We'll get you a certain amount of money.'"

Newman's faith eventually translated into a hefty bottom line, and the amounts are about to escalate. Although he gave three options on Bowe's future fights to Dan Duva, Holyfield's promoter, to land the title shot, make no mistake about it: Now that he has the champion, Eugene Roderick Newman means to be in charge. He didn't do all that scuffling—sometimes paying Bowe's opponents in order for his man to stay active—so that when the spotlight hit he would duck into the shadows. And if his hard-sell style gives you a headache, Newman will tell you, "Brother, that's your problem."

"'Cause I'm not a meek, docile black man," said Newman. "Quite the contrary. I can be loud and forceful. And I wear kufi hats without apology, and other kinds of African garb, and say what I mean and mean what I say and don't laugh at jokes that aren't funny. I'm already detecting a real sense of resentment for the position we have gotten in and for the way I've gotten to that position. I'd be much more easily accepted if I hung my head and didn't look people straight in the eye and say what I mean."

What he means to do with Bowe is get the fighter his money's worth. On that oak table this morning was a fax from Lewis's manager, Frank Maloney. On October 31, in a World Boxing Council elimination match in London, Lewis knocked out Razor Ruddock in two rounds, a victory that was supposed to guarantee him a shot at the winner of Holyfield-Bowe. The letter from Maloney offered Bowe a guarantee of twelve million dollars to fight Lewis in London early next year.

For Newman, the offer constituted comic relief.

What Newman has in mind is straight out of the managerial primer, or as Holyfield's manager, Shelley Finkel, puts it: "Most money for the least risk."

Following that precept, Newman is trying to promote Bowe against George Foreman in Beijing, contending that there's a potential twenty million dollars in it for his fighter. Lewis? Well, Newman would have Bowe face him next if Lewis agreed to a guarantee of between two million and three million dollars.

Is this scenario—and Newman himself—good for boxing? If Lewis stonewalls and doesn't agree to fight Bowe under Newman's terms, chances are the W.B.C. will strip Bowe and fragment the heavyweight title.

"Look," said Ross Greenburg, of Home Box Office, "what Rock is doing is within boxing custom. When someone captures the heavyweight title, he doesn't immediately jump into the 'big one.' The Lennox Lewis fight will be there and will only build over the next year. As far as the average fight fan, I'm sure he's lusting for Bowe-Lewis. But there is nothing wrong with letting him drool for six, seven months."

Newman had other managerial duties on Wednesday. He accompanied Bowe to a three-acre site in Fort Washington, Maryland, where Bowe is intending to build his $1.3 million dream house.

As Bowe conferred with the builder, Newman and his wife, Demetria, walked off. Bowe chose that moment to ask the builder,

Mariano Flaim, about another house in the area, a $200,000 model he had seen months earlier.

"It's sold," said Flaim.

Bowe frowned: "I wanted to surprise Rock and buy it for him."

Bowe asked about a lot near the sold home.

"It's available," said Flaim.

"Maybe one day I could come down and look at the house, and see if it's compatible for the Newmans."

Then the heavyweight champion of the world said, "I wouldn't be here if it wasn't for Rock."

PART THREE: THE BIG GUYS

Heavyweights are forever. It matters not that there may be smaller men who have more élan, more skill. For the masses, there is nothing quite like the sight of two big guys punching the bejesus out of one another. The appeal is in the brute force that the uninitiated can sense, like seismic waves on the nerve ends, and the average Joe can only fantasize about.

TREVOR BERBICK: The Fighting Preacher (1986)

In the summer of 1985, Don King, the boxing promoter, was in Las Vegas, Nevada, feeling apprehensive and lowdown about a tax evasion case the Government was about to bring against him.

Yet he would later recall a glimmer of hope that was provided to him on a daily basis.

"Every morning at 6:30 A.M. there'd be a knock on my hotel door," King said, "and here would come Trevor Berbick, carrying a Bible and a cross.

"'While everybody may be your enemy, the Lord is on your side,' he'd tell me. I'd be sleepy and half groggy while he'd preach. Two, three weeks in a row, he'd be there first thing in the morning, reading the 91st Psalm: 'He that dwelleth in the secret place of the most High shall abide under....'"

For King, the gesture showed a side of Berbick that boxing people—King included—sometimes are hard-pressed to reconcile with the World Boxing Council heavyweight champion's more erratic and self-involved behavior.

King refers to Berbick as "The Three Faces of Eve"—an allusion to the changeable nature of a man who goes into his defense against Mike Tyson in Las Vegas as a 5-1 underdog.

Yet while Berbick is sometimes indecipherable under ordinary circumstances, and buccaneer in his business practices, he can be an engaging character with a shrewd sense of boxing's backstage maneuvers.

As a boxer, he is subject to the same changing winds that move him outside the ring, in some bouts fighting with a bumbler's tools, in others using his rough-edged style to his advantage.

The question, however, is which Trevor Berbick will stand up in the ring against Tyson, who, at age twenty, is seeking to become the youngest heavyweight champion in boxing history.

Will it be the Berbick who against just average opponents has sometimes stumbled: He was knocked out by Bernardo Mercado in one round in 1979, and the same year fought to a draw against Leroy Caldwell. And in 1982 he suffered successive losses to Renaldo Snipes and S.T. Gordon.

Or will Tyson be up against the Berbick who, though never an overpowering puncher, has a durability that enables him—when he is right—to command the late rounds of a fight and muscle his way to victory.

Berbick, with his 31-4-1 record, has made a habit of raising the level of his talent when least expected. Against favored opponents—John Tate in 1980, Muhammad Ali in 1981, Greg Page in 1982 and, last March for the W.B.C. title, against Pinklon Thomas, the 6-foot-2 1/2-inch, 220-pound Berbick prevailed with pressuring tactics that eventually wore down his big-name foes.

Berbick is a curiosity to boxing people, who marvel that ten years into his career a man with apparently limited resources is not just a factor in the heavyweight division but one of its champions. And from day to day, like Berbick's opponents, those who traffic in the boxing business can never be sure which Berbick will show up.

"He is a strange figure," said Mort Sharnik, boxing consultant to CBS-TV. "Nobody has ever been able to get a grip on him. The most clever, the most ruthless in the sport, none of them have been able to tie him down. He seems to be impervious to threat, or anything."

"A likeable rogue," is how Dennis Rappaport, co-manager of Gerry Cooney described him. Rappaport, who tried to induce Berbick to bolt the Home Box Office heavyweight unification series and fight Cooney instead, said: "He's unpredictable. During a period of negotiations, he's on the verge of a breakdown, talking to himself. But, by the same token, Trevor can be very charming. He's bright, though capable of a lot of con."

But the more exemplary Berbick, the one who provided spiritual comfort to King, said a religious awakening at age sixteen led him to preach the Gospel—these days at the Moment of Miracles Church in Las Vegas and outposts beyond—and to live a life of relative simplicity for a world champion.

That Berbick, who said he is thirty-two years old and, in publicity releases, is listed as thirty-three, does not smoke or drink; he is said by those who know him to be a dedicated family man (he has two young daughters and a son), and he can sound like Henry David Thoreau when he extols the virtues of picking fresh fruits from the trees in his backyard in Miramar, Florida.

On his two and a half acres grow oranges, grapefruits, grapes and sugar cane, and it is there that Berbick feels closest to his origins: He grew up in Port Antonio, Jamaica, where he would climb coconut trees for the fruit and dive in nearby waters to haul up fish from nets and traps.

But the Berbick who wanders beyond home base in Miramar has been known to act in ways that strain the straight-edged image of "The Fighting Preacher." When, for instance, he won the W.B.C. title from Thomas, Berbick told Larry Merchant, a television interviewer: "Well, Mr. Merchant, I say this to you. That many people don't understand what mysteries I've been through. But I think right after this fight, and pretty soon....I won't say too much, but when I build my church and the gates of heaven, hell will not prevail against it. You don't understand that. People will understand it soon."

That response followed a straight-forward comment by Merchant that few had expected Berbick to beat Thomas.

In September, at a news conference to announce the Berbick-Tyson bout, Berbick described the strategy he expected Tyson to use against him by saying: "He is going to attack me. If he attacks me, he's going to attack a wall." Then, for reasons not clear, Berbick started to laugh, and when he stopped said: "I love this. I love this," grinning while his audience stared blankly. Then he added, "Justice will prevail."

When Rappaport met Berbick for the first time last June to discuss the possibility of Berbick's fighting Cooney, Rappaport said the fighter's opening words were, "I need money, a $100,000 deposit."

"I said, 'What?'" recalled Rappaport. "And he said, 'I got a message from God. He said to ask you, and you'd give it to me.' I said, 'When did you speak to God?' He said, 'About twenty minutes ago.' I told him, 'Trevor, He changed his mind. He spoke to me about five minutes ago and said not to give you $20.'"

Berbick acknowledged asking for the $100,000, but said what he had told Rappaport was that if he wanted the Cooney-Berbick match as much as Berbick did, then that meant God wanted it too.

Berbick came to boxing relatively late in his life. After he graduated from high school in Jamaica, he went to Miami to work as a cruiseship waiter, and soon after moved on to a series of jobs at the United States Naval Station at Guantanamo Bay in Cuba.

"I spent five years at Guantanamo," Berbick said, "and that's where I started boxing. I entered an all-base tournament, and afterward began fighting amateur."

According to Berbick, he had only ten amateur fights—a 7-3 record—but he ended up representing Jamaica at the 1976 Olympics in Montreal, winning one fight and losing the next. He stayed on in Canada after he lost in the boxing competition and, fighting out of Halifax, Nova Scotia, he turned pro.

From 1976 through 1979, Berbick boxed mostly in Halifax. His big break came when Bob Arum, the promoter, phoned Berbick's manager, Don Kerr, and asked, "Do you still handle that bum, Berbick?" That was Arum's lead-in to offering Berbick a shot against Tate, who had won the W.B.A. title, then lost it to Mike Weaver on a fifteenth round knockout.

Berbick knocked out Tate in the ninth round, and then declined to renew his contract with Kerr when it expired soon after. Kerr said that he and his business associates went $250,000 into debt to keep Berbick's career afloat, and called Berbick's refusal to re-sign "desertion."

For his part, Berbick said that if there were losses, which he doubted, they would amount to a tax write-off for Kerr and his colleagues and that, nice man though he was, Kerr had neither the time nor connections to get a fighter big-time purses.

In pursuit of financial security, Berbick has had a history of signing and then renouncing contracts, sometimes amending the purse to his advantage. Before going into the ring, he demanded, and got, a letter of credit from the promoters of the Ali-Berbick fight when their finances turned shaky, and more than once has improved his original purse for bouts under King.

Berbick has signed with and then shed a brigade of managers, advisers and attorneys, many of them leaving in disharmonious and even litigious circumstances usually brought on by Berbick's reluctance to pay. Yet Berbick not only endures for his unorthodox tactics, he continues to profit from them.

Before Tyson came into the HBO series, Berbick's title defense would have been worth $750,000. Once Tyson was the opponent, the fight became more valuable and the champion's purse was sweetened to $1.1 million. But after Berbick read about the millions of dollars Tyson was supposed to make if he reached the unification finals he felt duty-bound to play Rappaport and King against each other and try to force his price up. At one point, Berbick flew to Las Vegas on a plane ticket provided by King to negotiate with him at the Hilton Hotel and Casino, and instead registered at a rival hotel under the alias Tom Brown and resumed talks with representatives of Rappaport.

In the end, Berbick raised the price for fighting Tyson to $2.1 million. According to Berbick, that is how it should be. As he put it: "Big fight, big money."

For a man who once said that his one-punch knockout loss to Mercado proved "I could take his best shot," big-fight, big-money probably would qualify as advanced thinking.

Trevor Berbick lost his title to Tyson and, though he continued boxing, he never returned to center stage. In 1992 he was convicted of rape and is now serving time in Florida.

COONEY'S BURDEN (1980)

Sometimes the letters to Cooney are a little weird. There is, for instance, the correspondent who uses red, white and blue inks and includes cartoons of prizefighters in action. Invariably one pug is black, the other white, and the slug line has editorial intentions. Where the white man is depicted as the victor, the word "GOOD" is scrawled under the cartoon. Where the situation is reversed, the word "BAD" appears.

Other letters read like this:

Dear Gerry, America needs you. God bless you. We've got to have a white champion. Our race is deteriorating.

Or sometimes Cooney will pick up the telephone and a stranger on the other end will tell him: "Do it for *us*, Gerry," the "us" amounting to white folks, as distinguished from black folks, whose fighters have had the kind of lock on the heavyweight title that in other enterprises might prompt brisk application of the Sherman Antitrust Act.

But in the world that Gerry Cooney inhabits, no such thing happens. For in boxing, talent is what counts, against which there is no legalistic counter. Things get simple inside the ropes. It is beyond the squared circle that complications arise. For Cooney, the World Boxing Association's number one-ranked heavyweight (who was scheduled to fight yesterday at the Nassau Coliseum), his burden is the White Hope hype that accompanies the rise of any male Caucasian with boxing license and a few televised victories. "After a while," the 6-foot-5, 224-pound Cooney says, "you hear it and hear it, and you'd just as soon be another fighter—and not be labeled, you know, a 'white hope.'"

Like it or not, Cooney, who was raised in Huntington Station, Long Island, and now lives in East Northport, seems to be stuck with the tag. History has made it so. The last great white heavy-weight champion was Rocky Marciano, who retired undefeated in 1956. Sweden's Ingemar Johansson won the crown in 1959 when he knocked out champion Floyd Patterson, but Johansson relin-quished it nearly a year later when Patterson defeated him in the rematch.

The best of the "hopes" was Jerry Quarry, who occasionally beat big-name foes but failed whenever he bid for the champi-onship. With Duane Bobick, the white heavyweight became a punch line in Johnny Carson monologues. Bobick caused this when, as an undefeated heavyweight prospect, he was flattened in fifty-eight seconds by Kenny Norton in a prime-time TV bout in 1977.

It is Bobick's legacy that has plagued white heavyweights. "In fact," says Dennis Rappaport, co-manager of Cooney, "a kind of reverse racism has arisen. Because of it, Gerry has had tremendous unwarranted criticism from people who've said that he can't fight. From early on, they jumped to conclusions based on the stereotype of the white heavyweight. It's added to the pressure. It's like every-body's ready to pounce—waiting for him to blow a fight. People will say, even though Gerry's only twenty-three, 'If you lose this one, you're finished.' Finished! And that's how people make him feel. That's the burden, the pressure he's under. And I don't mean the pressure's been just lately, either. By his third or fourth fight, people were saying, 'Why doesn't he fight Earnie Shavers?'"

In truth, the caliber of the early opponents whom Rappaport and Mike Jones matched Cooney against was bound to promote skepticism. As *Boxing Digest* recently reported: "His [Cooney's] fifth fight was with Joe Maye, who currently has a 3-42 record! In his eighth match, Gerry was paired with Terry Lee Kidd, who boasts an 0-9 log and looks like a big thalidomide baby."

On the surface, Cooney's early progress seemed a calculated "buildup," but while Gerry was beating set-ups, he was learning his trade in Gleason's Gym in Manhattan. There, trainer Victor Valle, who fought professionally as a featherweight, worked out the kinks in Cooney's style.

The left hook is Gerry's big asset. It is a punch that earned him two New York Golden Gloves titles, but, as Valle saw it, the left was not enough. "When Gerry first came to me," Valle says, "his arms were too open, he hopped about like a kangaroo. I taught him boxing and self-defense. I'd get in the ring with him and show him how. 'Cause I'm a guy who believes if a fighter has no defense, he has no future. He gets confidence when he knows he's not going to get hit."

Cooney is deceptive. He is not a fighter with flash. Because of his size, Valle has taught him to be economical in his movements. He stalks and then unloads punches, with a degree of studied caution. Earlier in his career the spare movements made him seem ungainly and bloodless. Because of that, he became the butt of critics' gibes, and opponents' too. A few of them learned better.

"We matched Gerry against S.T. Gordon in March '78," says Rappaport. "At the weight-in Gordon says to him, 'You big white motherbleeper. I'm going to beat you up. No white man's going to beat me.' Gerry told him, 'You got a big mouth. Let's see what happens in the ring.' In the ring, Gerry hit him a left hook in the second round. After that, the guy didn't stop running. In fact, the ref bounced him [a fourth-round disqualification] for not fighting. Gerry was ticked. It was one of his first exposures on TV, and the guy wouldn't fight. He saw S.T. later in a coffee shop at our hotel— almost went for him: 'If you didn't want to fight, you yellow bastard, you shouldn't have accepted the bout.' The guy said nothing. Gerry shut his mouth good."

The Concord Hotel, Kiamesha Lake, this past spring. Cooney, preparing for his first TV main event, against Jimmy Young, is in the front seat of the shuttle van taking him to his training facilities.

Suddenly, he puts his index finger to the driver's head—as if it were a gun—and screams, "Keep moving! Don't stop! Keep moving!" His eyes are wide, his body tensed. Abruptly, he relaxes, turns around and grins.

This is the fighter's prankster side. In person, he turns out to be a sunny, accessible individual, with a straightforward outlook accentuating traditional values—God, family, concern for others. It avoids being sanctimonious only through the impish good humor of the athlete.

Cooney has been known, for instance, to impersonate women friends of Rappaport over the phone; to do his roadwork in the buff for a laugh; or, without warning, to wrestle trainer Valle to the ground.

Cooney has the right attitude about his profession, too. In an age influenced by Ali's theatrics, Cooney is a departure, shunning self-promotion and braggadocio. He depicts himself as a boxing acolyte, doing his darnedest to learn the brutal intricacies of the business.

The intensity is evident in an afternoon workout at the Concord. During a sparring session, a mouthpiece drops to the canvas and Cooney shouts for another: "Mouthpiece, mouthpiece, mouthpiece"—and reacts with annoyance ["Son of a gun"] when it is not immediately produced, agonizing over ten or fifteen seconds of lost training.

"When it comes to boxing," says Valle, "Gerry is very serious. He dreams about being the champion. Not about the money. He's got a lot of pride. If he has a bad day in the gym, he thinks about it. Even in training, he'll say, 'Did I win this round?'"

In his earnestness and diligence, Cooney is reminiscent of Marciano, who was noted for his dedication. Like Marciano's trainer, Charley Goldman, Valle is refining a fighter with raw strength and considerable punching power, teaching him the subtleties that maximize his weapons.

In Cooney's case, his trainer, whom he sometimes calls Pop, occupies a larger, nearly paternal, position. "The first time I met Victor," says Cooney, "we hit it off. There was a feeling I felt, a warmth. It wasn't just a business transaction with him. And he was brutally honest. Early on, I saw him tell fighters of his to their face that they couldn't make it in boxing. It scared me. I asked him, 'Would you do that to me?' 'Damn right I would,' he said."

Valle mixes stern authority with a glint of humor and outright sentimentality at times. Without much coaxing, he will launch into a tune he composed to the melody of Al Jolson's "Sonny Boy."

The song has become a kind of anthem for the Cooney camp. *Come along with me, Gerry boy./Come along with me, Gerry boy./You were sent from heaven. You were sent from heaven./For me, Gerry boy./While there's those gym days,/I don't mind the hard work./For you are my son, Gerry boy.*

Those who know him harp on the essential decency of the fighter. "Truly sensitive," says Rappaport. "We were preparing for the Eddie (Animal) Lopez fight January '79 in Miami Beach. A day or two before the fight, Gerry saw a pelican out on the sand with a fish hook caught in its mouth. We weren't too crazy about his fooling with the bird—you know, he could get injured or something and blow the fight—but he spent an hour til he got the hook out.

"Another time, I thought of nicknaming him Candy Kisses Cooney and hiring a midget, dressed as a leprechaun, to throw Hershey Kisses to the crowd after Gerry had won. We did it one fight, but I guess Gerry felt it was a bit too much. He didn't want to hurt my feelings, though. So he told Mike Jones—maybe we could use something else to promote him."

There was a time in his career when Cooney resisted all efforts to promote his boxing progress. This was back in 1976 when his father was dying of lung cancer and Gerry was pointing for the Montreal Olympics; "My father—we called him 'Tony' even though his name was Arthur—was tough on us. He was physical with the boys—smacked us or used the strap. (Cooney has three brothers—Tommy, Mike and Steve—and two sisters-Eileen and Maddy). He was a big man—6-foot-3, 220 pounds. A construction worker. Very strict—set in his ways. At the time his health started to deteriorate I had moved out. I felt I was causing him more aggravation than he needed. Too many arguments. Over my having my hair short. Or coming home early."

Over Tony Cooney's objections, Gerry decided to bypass the Olympics. After his father's death, the son stopped going to the gym. "I just didn't care to box," he says. "I wasn't ready yet. I wanted to cool out. I had to be around my mother. There were a lotta family things. We have a close family."

PUNCH LINES / 217

Cooney still grieves for the love that was so hard to express between father and son. For Gerry, boxing was a means to conquer feelings of inadequacy. As a teenager he was called "Stringbean" behind his back and felt, as he puts it, "like I was funny-looking: tall, knock-kneed, skinny...I had a complex." Once he took up boxing in his teens, his father drove him; sometimes, it seemed, harder than was necessary. Tony Cooney monitored his son's road-work, often rising at 6 A.M. and running with him to make sure the mileage was covered. Evenings, he insisted on early curfew, a stricture Gerry was known occasionally to circumvent, usually by waiting until the old man was asleep and then going AWOL.

"My father was a good man," says Cooney. "At that time, he was rough. I just didn't realize he was trying to make me better. It wasn't until I worked construction with some of his steelworker friends that I found out how he'd talk about his sons, about how good they were doing. I love my father very much. When he was alive I couldn't tell him that. I realize now how stupid I was for not being able to. I wish he was here now to see what I'm doing."

Part of Cooney's burden, then, is to live up to his father's standards. He is preoccupied by his parent, delving without prompting, into that part of his past, exploring it with almost obsessive concern.

"His father," says Rappaport, "is an inspiration to him. He believes his father's there and tries to make his father proud of him. Early in his career, he sat down for an interview. As he talked about his father, tears came to his eyes. All of us got caught up in it; nobody said anything about his crying. We just went on talking as if nothing happened. But it was a very sad moment."

Dennis Rappaport has the pre-fight jitters.

He's pacing the lobby of the Boardwalk Regency in Atlantic City, New Jersey, this past May 25, and chain-smoking Newports, a few hours before Gerry climbs into the ring against Jimmy Young.

Young is the heavyweight who was slick enough to beat ex-champion George Foreman and win everything but the decision from Muhammad Ali in a title match. In recent times, Young has

tended to put on weight, enough so that on occasion the only difference between Jimmy and Kate Smith was an octave. That and a
few losses have tarnished his once lustrous image.

For the Cooney bout, Young has slimmed down and is looking
fit, evidently aware that the big money stops here if he loses. The
thought of a possibly revitalized Young does not—contrary to
Rappaport's worst fear—have Gerry Cooney on edge. He lies
relaxed in his bed in Suite 500, with a religious tract on his chest
and a Tarzan movie on the TV screen.

After a while, Cooney looks up to see the bind that Johnny
Weissmuller, as Tarzan, is in. Locked up in a cage on circus
grounds, Tarzan fears that Boy has been kidnapped and knows that
to rescue him he must escape. "The elephants," says Cooney.
"He'll get the elephants to help him out."

And, sure enough, there goes Tarzan exhorting the pachyderms
to get him out of his fix. They do so, bending the bars of the cage
so that he can flee. As Johnny Weissmuller swings, the plot comes
to its neat resolution, Cooney gathers up religious mementos and
telegrams from friends and fans and stashes them in a bag with his
fight gear.

Now Valle, who is sixty-two years old and has silver-gray hair,
begins pumping his fighter up: "You got people that love you. You
gotta make sure that they love you even more after this fight...You
gotta get through this guy to get to the championship. He needs
room to fight. Don't give him room. Alive. Alive. Be alive all the
time. Okay, let's go down and do our job."

Dressing Room No. 8 at Convention hall has a window overlooking the boardwalk. From there, Cooney can see the ocean, the
trams, the billboard with the Solarcaine ad.

A TV man with a portable camera and his lighting assistants
set up, advising the fighter that they will need a test shot in half a
minute.

Cooney rises from his seat, turning his back to the camera, and
pulls down his trunks, asking: "How's that for your shot?"—a sly
smile showing. Later, he jokes, "Let me know when it's for real. I
might wanna comb my mustache."

An hour before the fight, Valle is pacing the room. Each time he passes Cooney, he slaps his fighter's arms and legs, a kind of moving massage. Then he creaks into a chorus of "Gerry Boy."

After that, things quiet. Why not? Cooney's number one rating, his undefeated (22-0) record, his future are at stake. All that—and the burden. A few minutes before 3, Gerry and his people huddle. The fighter intones: "Our Father who art in heaven...."

Then it is the short walk down a corridor and into the arena, where the crowd is chanting: "Cooo-neee, Cooo-neee."

Four rounds later, Young's face is covered with blood from the pummeling Cooney has given him. The fight is over. Gerald Anthony Paul Cooney throws his arms up toward the rafters and jumps off the canvas for joy. The people whose hope he is respond: "Cooo-neee, Cooo-neee!"

GERRY COONEY AND THE STORY (1986)

On a wintry morning in Lancaster, Pennsylvania, Gerry Cooney is running up Lincoln Highway East. Traffic whooshes by, as Cooney—in a dark blue training suit and weighted blue fingerless gloves—strides past Pizza Hut and Hardee's, on by Murray's Men's Wear and the House of Shanghai.

He takes a right onto Oak View Road, a residential street of small houses with tidy front lawns, and pounds on. Old Philadelphia Pike has Rutt's Antiques and The First Deaf Mennonite Church, and soon Cooney is moving past cows grazing in a field and a billboard for Dutch Wonderland Family Fun Park.

For Cooney, the sights may be new, but the road work remains a familiar part of the prefight regimen. This time around, though, the skeptics insist that for all his work, Gerald Anthony Paul Cooney just may be, in a figurative sense, running in circles.

For when Cooney first checked into the American Host Farm Resort in Lancaster back in November, he did so to get in shape for a fight he anticipated having by March or April against the International Boxing Federation heavyweight champion, Michael Spinks.

But last week, as word leaked of Home Box Office's proposal to unify the heavyweight title through a series of bouts to be co-promoted by Don King and Butch Lewis—the first expected to be a rematch between Spinks and Larry Holmes—Cooney suddenly seemed the odd man out.

If Spinks does fight Holmes, it will leave Cooney once again groping to find his way back into a sport in which he once was a commanding figure. Ever since Cooney lost to Holmes, his only defeat in twenty-eight bouts, he has had more false starts than a jittery sprinter as he tried to get his career in motion again.

If it wasn't the psychological effect of the defeat that kept him away from the prize ring, then there were injuries and postponed fights and eventually, after a short-lived, two-bout comeback in late 1984, a retirement that was announced last July.

Back out of retirement after Spinks beat Holmes, Cooney was viewed by some as a blight on the sport. The prospect of his getting a title shot without having to fight real contenders to earn the chance galled his detractors, who saw his re-emergence as opportunism that made capital of his being a white man in a predominantly black sport. Cooney's critics regard him as a short-cut artist who has consistently refused to risk himself against stiff opposition, with the conspicuous exception of Holmes.

Yet somehow Cooney persists as boxing's special case, a fighter who intrigues, annoys and puzzles.

Gerry Cooney has a joke.

It is late afternoon in the games arcade of the Host Farm Resort. The bleeps and burbles of Pac-man and pinball machines go silent as the room is converted to a gym. A heavy bag is hung on a short length of chain in the low-ceilinged, fluorescent-lit room, and a speed bag is brought out, too.

Cooney appears. "I dreamt I swallowed a 30-pound marshmallow," he says. A few beats, then: "When I woke up, my pillow was gone."

He looks over his shoulder and, with an impish smile, engages a visitor's gaze until he gets the smiling response he wants.

That charmer's insistent eye holds a clue to the needs and character of Cooney, who more than most fighters wants—and apparently requires—the smiles and affirmation of others. "I, for one, like to catch people's expressions," he says. "To see them laugh and smile."

Through a career in which he has earned a reported $13 million in purses, he has made a point of kibitzing with fans and signing autographs for them until writer's cramp set in. He did it not as a reflex of celebrity but as part of an apparently deeply felt need to make contact. "I'm a real person," Cooney says. "I have real feelings. I have real thoughts. It's a quality people like about me. I wouldn't give it up for anything."

In his eagerness to please, Cooney, now twenty-nine years old, has occasionally gone to extremes. Earlier in his career, after scoring two straight one-round knockouts on Home Box Office telecasts, Cooney apologized on the air for the condensed entertainment, and then later apologized again to an executive of the pay-cable service for, so to speak, spoiling the show.

That is typical of Cooney, who is quite ingenuous in his concern for making an impression. Toward the end of a long day recently with a reporter who sought to keep his objective distance, Cooney—while driving his cream-colored Cadillac—took his eyes off the road and turned to say: "I can't tell whether you like me or not."

The loss to Holmes in 1982 sent Gerry Cooney into a deep depression, a period during which he stopped boxing.

The loss, and the reason it happened, led to a version of the event—hereafter, The Story—that Cooney told then and has not stopped telling since. The Story is by now a set piece, the same words and rhythms appearing, and in his incessant recounting, Cooney reveals just how deeply, despite denials, that night still cuts him.

The Story: "If I lost and he was the better man, I could have dealt with it. But I was buffaloed about going the distance. I didn't fight my fight. The distance. The distance. They put that in my head, the press."

The pain over his loss to Holmes was exacerbated when it became clear that Holmes was not about to give him a rematch. On one occasion, his manager, Dennis Rappaport, got a phone call from a friend of Cooney, who told him that Gentleman Gerry was planning to drive to Holmes's hometown of Easton, Pennsylvania, and challenge Holmes to a street fight.

"That's how personal the thing was," said Rappaport. "He wanted to do it so Larry would 'know' who the better man was. What headed it off? My screaming and yelling. Pleading: 'Gerry, you're a professional. You can't do it.'"

While The Story might explain, at least to Cooney's satisfaction, the reversal in the prize ring, it could not, and did not, prop him up for days and nights beyond boxing. In life after Larry, Cooney found his world had shifted, there were cracks now along the seams.

Newspapers that had treated him kindly began to malign him for his inactivity. Acquaintances to whom he had lent money—he earned a sum estimated at between $8.5 and $10 million for fighting Holmes—chose not to make good on the payback, leaving Cooney feeling betrayed. He was booed when introduced at fights. And even the comedians in the Long Island clubs in which he hung out made jokes at his expense.

"People used him," says Richie Minervini, a longtime friend. "He'd go out some place. A Penthouse Pet would jump in his lap. Boom—a photo, and all of a sudden in the newspapers, 'Gerry Cooney with Penthouse Pet so-and-so.' He was a sweet kid who had a nice happy attitude. But then they busted his bubble. And he felt hurt."

The fighter's mother, Eileen, saw her son become disillusioned. "Back when Gerry was fighting in the Golden Gloves," she says, "he used to love to see his name in the papers. And he used to think about turning pro and how great it'd be to be famous and make a lot of money. Now he wishes he was back being a Golden Glover again. In the Golden Gloves, everybody would rally around him, and really like him. He was happy-go-lucky."

Anger, not usually a part of Cooney's make-up, began to surface, particularly when he had a little to drink. He developed a strange habit, while hanging around the clubs in Long Island, of casually backhanding comedians below the belt as he talked to them, a perverse response, it seemed, to the criticism he had received in the press for punches of his that had landed low on Holmes.

"I swear," says John Mulrooney, a comedian, "I almost threw up when he hit me. I walked to the men's room, hunched over, like I'd dropped contact lenses. Came back. He's still laughing. Told him, 'You idiot.'"

Some nights, Cooney got up from his seat in the clubs and, wresting the microphone from a comedian, would tell a few jokes before lapsing into The Story, which invariably became an apology for his loss to Holmes.

They were not happy times, even at home, where Cooney—devoted to his family—saw his relationship with his brothers, Thomas, thirty-two years old, Michael, thirty-one, and Stevie, twenty-seven, cool. By Cooney's account, his brothers (the fighter also has two sisters, Eileen, twenty-four and Maddy, nineteen) found themselves constantly assailed by friends and strangers alike with questions about Gerry Gerry Gerry, and felt their own identities slipping away.

His home life became more difficult when one of the brothers developed an addictive dependency that required hospitalization and Cooney's constant attention. The fighter says it ate away at him, and added to his own difficulties in reviving his boxing career—enough to make him consult a psychologist. "It takes a strong person to admit he's got problems," he says. "Things are bugging you, you've got to get it out. Life is supposed to be peaches and cream, but it doesn't turn out that way. I sometimes found things confusing, and sometimes didn't understand how things can be so difficult."

Among the sensitive subjects discussed was a difficult relationship he had with his father, who had been a disciplinarian. Cooney is frequently depicted as a young man who fought more to please his father than himself, and probably there is a kernel of truth to that. When Cooney took up boxing as a teenager, it was his father who drove him. Tony Cooney monitored his son's road work, often rising at 6 A.M. and running with him to make sure the mileage was covered. Evenings, he insisted on early curfew, a stricture Cooney would circumvent by waiting until his father was asleep and then leaving.

"A lot of times," says Cooney, "he made it difficult. My mother was there, and she had so much love that it made up for it. I took the good from my father, and threw away the bad. I'd like to leave it vague. I don't want to hurt my mom—she loved my dad."

A few years back, Minervini, working a comedy club in Fort Lauderdale, got time off to go with Cooney to a fight in Miami. After the match ended, the comedian decided to try to get back to Fort Lauderdale in time to do his act. "I drove like a banshee," says Minervini. "And Gerry: 'You had the night off. Why are you doing this?' He couldn't understand. I told him I loved what I did for a living. And he said, 'Geez, man. Boxing's not like that. The best part about boxing is the five minutes after the fight.'"

MICHAEL SPINKS THE FRUGAL (1986)

In 1976, after he and his brother Leon won gold medals in boxing at the Montreal Olympics, Michael Spinks declined to turn professional.

What kept him from taking the step was his fear that he might end, as many fighters before him had, with none of the spoils of his labors.

"That bothered me more than anything," said Michael Spinks. "I couldn't stand to see another person living comfortably by jerking me out of my money. Treating me like a horse or cow. It was too vicious."

Saturday night in Las Vegas, Spinks—the first light heavyweight to beat a heavyweight champion—will defend his International Boxing Federation crown against the man he took it from last September, Larry Holmes. For fighting Holmes, Spinks will earn between $3.5 million and $4 million, according to the bout's co-promoter, Butch Lewis. By the calculations of Lewis, who has been Spinks's promoter for most of the fighter's career, that payday will bring Spinks's total fight earnings to between $9 million and $10 million.

So far at least, Spinks appears to have eluded the fiscal ruin he feared. Last June, in his ninth year as a wage-earning boxer, Spinks and his five-year-old daughter Michelle moved into a six-bedroom house on a five-acre estate in Greenville, Delaware. The house has a swimming pool in the backyard, and Spinks pulls into his driveway in a gray 1984 Mercedes.

But these material assets are not the measure of the security the fighter has gained, according to Lewis, who has worked more closely with Spinks than promoters customarily do with their fighters. "If Michael retired before his fight," Lewis said of the

Holmes bout, "he could live on his pension funds. If he never touched any of his principal for the rest of his life, he would have around $106,000 a year. He could live off that interest, and the money would be compounding.

"Michael has pension funds built on C.D.'s, Fannie Maes, zero-coupon Treasury bonds. In terms of pension, we've taken as much as the Government allows."

Many other fighters have been less farsighted with their money. But Spinks, who grew up in the hard and violent setting of the Pruitt-Igoe housing project in St. Louis and was raised on the family's welfare checks, appears to be a different story.

Lewis claimed the fighter is cautious about his finances, to the point of nearly comic frugality. "If he lends somebody a five or ten, he'll remember it," said Lewis. "This guy never forgets." Lewis cited Spinks' 1983 bout against Dwight Braxton—now known as Dwight Muhammad Qawi—to unify the lightheavyweight title. Spinks, Lewis said, could not overlook a loan he had made to Braxton in the days when Braxton worked for him as a sparring partner. Though a couple of years had passed since the money had been advanced, Spinks referred to it in a news conference before the bout, when he told Braxton, "One of the reasons I'm going to beat you is you didn't pay back the $145."

The picture of Michael as a fiscal conservative contrasts sharply with that of his free-spending brother, Leon, who upset Muhammad Ali for the heavyweight championship in February 1978 but was never up to the demands and pressures of holding the sport's most celebrated title. Success consumed Leon, as well as the millions of dollars he earned in purses.

"Money?" said Leon as he trained last month for a title bout against Qawi, the World Boxing Association junior heavyweight champion. "You have it and then you don't have it. You learn from your mistakes."

Leon's mistakes have come back to haunt him. By last month, he had been evicted from his $125,000 home in Detroit for failing to keep up the mortgage payments; his possessions had been auctioned off after he missed payment on a storage fee, and he was being pursued by the Internal Revenue Service.

"Leon earned over $5 million during his career," said Marvin Haupt, the fighter's present co-manager, "but he never had access to all of it."

The current I.R.S. claim, Haupt said, is for back taxes of $128,000, a payment Spinks thought had been made for him. In the days before the Qawi fight, Leon reportedly filed for bankruptcy to ward off potential claims of creditors on the $70,000 purse he was to receive for fighting Qawi. It turned out to be hard money, as Qawi taunted Spinks while he punched him, seemingly at will, until the one-sided contest was stopped in the sixth round.

Although Michael remains close to his brother and rues the troubles Leon has seen, he is more detached about them these days than he was in the past. As Michael sees it, the troubles started when Leon grew tired of the very active role that Lewis played in his career while Butch was a vice-president at Top Rank Inc., Leon's promoter.

Leon cut Lewis loose and sought counsel elsewhere, despite Michael's warnings.

The switch in allegiance from Lewis to the Detroit lawyers Edward Bell and Lester Hudson came soon after Spinks beat Ali for the title. "Everything went haywire after that," said Michael. "Leon let people turn him against the people who had helped him. I tried to pull his coattails and tell him: 'These people are not for you. They'll take you for a ride. They're ripping you off. You got to let them go. Or you'll wind up with no money.'"

Michael claimed that back in those days his brother would tell him, "Family and business don't mix." Michael said Leon's Detroit attorneys "were trying to turn him against me."

Michael became so convinced that Leon's ways were wrong-headed that one day he kicked Leon in the shins. "He said to me, 'Michael, you kick me again, I'm gonna knock you on your butt,'" Michael said. "I told him, 'Whatever it takes not to let those people put their names on your checks.'"

For his part, Bell said that his firm had no role in turning brother against brother. "That never happened," he said. He dismissed the charges that the blame for Leon's financial comedown can be put on anybody other than the fighter. "The Light Brigade and all the king's men couldn't stop Leon from spending," Bell said. "We put money in a trust fund for him. In excess of $1 million. In the National Bank of Detroit. *He* took the money out. It was there for a little while. But it was his money. And when he got ready to take the money out, he could. And did."

Whatever the truth, the tangled past of Leon seems to have shaded Michael's reaction to his business. "What Leon went through," said Lewis, "was like a rush through the Twilight Zone. Being so close to it, Michael's reaction was: 'You mean, this is what I have to look forward to? If that's it, I don't want it.' He had questions about whether he wanted to continue fighting. He wasn't in love with boxing after the Olympics and he still isn't. Michael Spinks doesn't like to fight. It's just his profession."

Michael Spinks came to that profession when he couldn't make do with life after the Olympics. Following his gold medal triumph, he found work as a maintenance man on a midnight shift at a St. Louis chemical plant. "One day," said Spinks, "I'd empty ash trays. The next day I was cleaning out latrines."

Caught napping on the job one night, Spinks was scolded by a supervisor, in language that troubled the fighter. "He cursed me out and talked as if I was trying to be a privileged character," Spinks said. "And told me, 'You ain't nobody.' I told him I deserved punishment, but he didn't have to talk to me like a dog. He talked to me so bad I broke down and cried. That day I decided I'd leave...Everything was pushing me to turning pro. I saw the signs. Breathing chemicals every day, I figured I'd die quicker here than in the ring. Told myself, 'Take your chances, brother.' When that man cursed me out, that was my cue."

In 1977, his first year as a pro, Michael Spinks won all six of his fights. And on the February night that Leon captured the heavyweight title in 1978, Michael earned a decision over Tom Bethea for his seventh straight victory.

But after beating Bethea, Michael put his career on hold while he tried to help straighten out Leon, who was having trouble coping with the complexities of holding the heavyweight title. The layoff lasted until that December, when he knocked out Eddie Phillips in four rounds.

A knee injury cost him another eleven months in 1979. He fought only once that year, knocking out Marc Hans in one round in November. By the following year, though, he was beating contenders like Murray Sutherland and Yaqui Lopez. In July 1981, he won the W.B.A. light heavyweight title with a fifteen-round decision over Eddie Mustafa Muhammad, setting up a rare lightheavyweight superfight against Braxton. He unified the crown by beating Braxton in March of 1983.

There was a moment that night, before Spinks went out to fight, when his trainer, Eddie Futch, worried whether Spinks would be able to perform. It occurred when Spinks's sister-in-law, Sibby, suddenly appeared in the dressing room, holding in her arms Michelle, then a baby. The mother of the child, Spinks's common-law wife, Sandra Massey, had been killed weeks before in an auto accident.

"I remember," said Futch, "his sister handed the child to Michael, he turned his back to me and started to cry. It brought back the memory of that tragedy.

"I thought, 'This is the worst thing that could happen. I'll never be able to get him back to where he should be!'"

But Spinks managed. He held the title until last year. Then came the chance to fight Holmes. The fighter laughed as he recalled Lewis advising him from his car phone of the opportunity and shouting: "You can beat him, Slim! You can beat him!"

Said Spinks: "I told him, 'You want me to, I'll fight him, I'll fight the big guy. What the hell.'"

Even now, as heavyweight champion, Spinks seems as skeptical about the fight game as he was before he turned pro. Apart from his bitterness over Leon's chaotic career, there is a sense of disappointment conveyed about the lack of recognition he has gotten despite a 28-0 record and a historical defeat of Holmes.

That lack of acclamation can be attributed to the public's perception of Holmes as a fading champion and to the cautious approach Spinks used in fighting him. In September 1985, when he won the International Boxing Federation title from Holmes, Spinks concentrated on making himself an elusive target and counterpunching enough to eke out the decision.

While the tactics got results, they did not necessarily endear Spinks to devotees of heavyweights, who tend to favor fighters who punch their foes to the horizontal while seeming to have smoke curling from their ears.

By that definition, Spinks is no crowd-pleaser. The closest he has come was when he fought pedestrian opponents—lightheavyweights such as Mustapha Wasajja and Oscar Rivadeneyra and the Norwegian heavyweight, Steffen Tangstad. In such bouts, Spinks would size up his man and then finish him, usually with the lightning-strike right hand that he refers to as The Spinks Jinx.

But in his more important, spotlighted matches, against big punchers like Braxton and Holmes, Spinks was not the stalking slugger. Rather, he was a survivalist, mixing strangely syncopated feints and retreats with often off-balance volleys of punches.

In those bouts, Spinks was the boxing equivalent of a junkball pitcher, patching together a little of this and a little of that to confound the other man. Lurching and twisting and sometimes actually running from punches, Spinks made his case for winning ugly.

"People don't understand what he's doing," said Futch. "They think he's lucky he beat this guy or that guy. They think like that because Michael Spinks is not physically imposing, he doesn't have a charismatic appearance, he doesn't have a ballet style...real smooth. What he is, is a great competitor. He's always looking for a way to win. If one thing doesn't work, he'll try something else."

Even other fighters, Futch has discovered, underestimate Spinks.

"They'll say, 'He can't do this, he can't do that,'" said Futch. "Or, 'He can't jab. He's awkward, off-balance.' But they find out it's a lot different when you're in the ring with him than when you're looking at Michael from outside the ring."

Spinks adds to that impression of ring inadequacy with a habit of sounding perplexed, even overwhelmed, by the very prospect of fighting his opponents. Let Spinks discuss a foe—be it a softy like Tangstad or a slugger like Cooney—and his sentences fill up with

despairing exclamations, frequently followed by a befuddled wag or
two of the head.

In fact, though, that tack of giving the opponent more credit
than he may deserve is part of Spinks's pre-fight preparation.

"I don't need to feel invincible," Spinks said. "My approach
works for me. I couldn't handle it any other way."

As the fight nears, the opponent may still be formidable to
him, but Spinks is soft-pedaling the urgency of the bout. "Just
another workout," he will tell himself. "Just another workout...but
it's a serious workout."

While Spinks is not, as Lewis puts it, "braggadocious"—the
fighter avoids making predictions about his bouts and does not
belittle his opponents—Spinks bristles at any suggestion that he
operates by chance in the ring.

When, for instance, a reporter passed on the assessment of
Holmes' trainer, Richie Giachetti, that Spinks was so unconven-
tional that from a purist's perspective he did things all wrong,
Spinks was offended.

"That lowdown saddle tramp," said Spinks. "What does he
know about right or wrong? Has Richie Giachetti boxed before? He
don't know what he's talking about. My style is unique. I do what
works for me. And that's it. Who wants to develop a style that
everybody can figure you?"

When he beat Holmes, there was no call from the White House to
congratulate him. No hue and cry from Madison Avenue for him to
do commercials. Spinks has not become a cross-over fighter—a
figure whose appeal goes beyond the hard-core devotees of boxing
to the marginal fans who elevate a fighter into a closed-circuit
attraction and eventually into a candidate for a picture on a box of
Wheaties.

Certainly his long residence in the lightheavyweight division, a
weight class lacking in exciting contenders, was no advantage to
Spinks' becoming a marquee name. Then, in the spotlight in the
bouts he did have, against Braxton and Holmes, he was more the
artful dodger than the devastating puncher he had been against less
distinguished foes. No big fight has defined Spinks, as the Joe

Frazier bouts did Ali, as the Thomas Hearns fight did Marvelous Marvin Hagler.

Though Spinks is a decent and straightforward individual who has shown the discipline and toughmindedness to succeed as a pro, he has proved a bit resistible as a superstar. For whatever reasons, nine years after he started, he has yet to ascend to that elite status. He will say that it is all right with him, but in words that send other signals:

"...If they never call my name, that's O.K. As long as they don't bother me.

"...I'm not looking for nothing. No recognition, or anything. The hell with all that.

"...No commercials? It doesn't bother me. I'm a professional fighter. I'm going to do it till I can't do it any more."

Michael Spinks' anonymity diminished when he TKO'd Gerry Cooney in June 1987. That victory led to a $13.5 million payday against Mike Tyson a year later. Tyson knocked out Spinks in 91 seconds, and later that year Spinks retired from boxing. In 1992, rumors of a Spinks comeback surfaced, but so far Spinks has confined his boxing to gym workouts.

BUSTER DOUGLAS: On Top and Loving It (1990)

Up on the top floor of a hotel suite in downtown Duluth, Minnesota, a bottle of champagne is chilling in an ice-filled bucket. The bucket stands on a table by a window that affords a scenic view of Lake Superior. Two delicate glasses—approximating champagne flutes—complete this still life of preferential treatment.

The recipients of the v.i.p. setup are Mr. and Mrs. James (Buster) Douglas of Columbus, Ohio. The last time *he* came to Duluth, two years earlier, he came alone, staying in a motel that was just down the street from a strip joint in which Douglas acknowledged he spent more than a few hours.

Then he was just another fighter with a shaky career. In May 1987, he had squandered his only shot at the heavyweight crown, running down after outboxing his opponent, Tony Tucker, through eight rounds. Tucker took advantage of Douglas' fatigue and stopped him in the tenth round to win the vacant International Boxing Federation crown.

When Douglas turned up in Duluth in February 1988 to fight Percell Davis, he felt low-down and adrift. But in Duluth he was treated with unexpected kindness and respect by the people there, as if he was somebody. Though he earned only $2,500 for stopping Davis in ten rounds, he was touched by the friendliness shown him. "It was a very inspirational moment," he would say later.

Last Wednesday, James Douglas went back to Duluth as the heavyweight champion of the world. He went back to say thanks to Duluth for being so good to him at a time when he needed that emotional lift, a need that no longer exists. For two and a half weeks after his tenth-round knockout of Mike Tyson on February 10, Douglas has enjoyed the world of sudden celebrity: a hometown parade, unending print and television exposure, his own 900 number that fans could phone (at $2 for the first minute) to hear the champion discourse.

What a time it was for Douglas; the future was bright with prospects. He had a conditional two-fight agreement worth $60 million with Steve Wynn's Mirage Hotel and Casino in Las Vegas, Nevada. His subsidiary ventures already included the 900 number and a T-shirt and apparel deal and were expected to expand once the fighter's manager, John Johnson, found the time to sort through other offers. Movie producers said they wanted the champion for cameo appearances, and so did television stars like Bill Cosby. Douglas seemed delighted by the acclaim and the opportunities, even imagining himself playing rogue characters in television soap operas. "I think I'd be a good villain," he said.

In real life, though, he was a hero: America's heavyweight. In contrast to the sometimes sullen and often remote Tyson, Douglas appeared accessible, a regular sort of guy. People admired him for what he had overcome and for the fact that he possessed the self-effacing nature of an old-fashioned 1950's hero.

The visit to Duluth was a departure from the glittery stops on the big-time celebrity wheel and appeared to have come about not just because of Douglas's gratitude, but also because of the instincts of Johnson, his manager. Johnson grew up in the coal-mining town of Red Jacket, West Virginia, population 200, and his origin left him with deep feelings for the so-called little people of this world.

The day in Duluth turned out to be nonstop with appearances that required the champion to give interviews, pose for photos and sign enough autographs to cause writer's cramp. But Douglas—a deadpan sort with a dry sense of humor—was nonplussed about the grueling business even when he was summoned from dinner in a Chinese restaurant to do still more interviews.

When he returned to the table twenty minutes later, and sat next to his wife, Bertha, he was still in a good mood as he dug into his special order of salad, New York strip steak and side order of lasagna.

"Bertha tells me she's an excellent cook," a dinner guest from Duluth said.

"You can't go wrong boiling hotdogs," said Douglas.

When Bertha cocked her head and looked at him, he let a sly smile play at the corners of his mouth. She smiled back.

From the restaurant, it was on to the Duluth Entertainment Convention Center, where a crowd of 2,000 people stood and cheered the champion's entrance, made to a tape-recorded song, "Win It All," which was sung by Johnson's daughter, Mary.

On stage, Johnson clapped his hands in rhythm and swayed on the heels of his rattlesnake-skin boots, inviting the crowd to join him. It did. Flashbulbs popped. Television cameras focused. Youngsters crowded the stage. A deep-throated chant of "Hoo! Hoo! Hoo! Hoo! Hoo!" resonated.

Dressed in a brown sweater, jeans and ostrich-skin boots, Douglas was introduced and then answered questions from the audience. About his mother, Lula, who died in January, and was, he later insisted, the inspiration for his victory over Tyson, he said, "She's looking down on me now, and she's getting a kick out of this."

And what about his appearance as a wrestling referee? Did he really punch the villainous Randy (Macho Man) Savage? "It's what you saw on TV," said Douglas, tongue in cheek.

A day later, aboard a private jet belonging to Wynn, Douglas was headed for Kansas City, Missouri. That's the home turf of Peyton Sher, a promoter who served as an adviser to Johnson and believed in Douglas's destiny when few fight men did. The stop there was in recognition of Sher.

A podium was set up in the lobby of the Allis Plaza Hotel, and from there the mayors of Kansas City, Missouri, and Kansas City, Kansas, paid tribute to Douglas. Once again he responded to questions from reporters and the public gathered there.

He spoke about his changed life: "It's a pretty hectic pace. I've been pretty busy. But I'm not complaining. My objective was winning the heavyweight title. I never thought this far along. Now I see: all this comes with the title. I appreciate it."

Later that day, back up in the air and headed for Las Vegas aboard Wynn's jet, he spoke of specific changes he envisioned, like the dream house he hopes to live in soon. It will be built, he said, by his bodyguard, Rodney Rogers, a general contractor back in Columbus who played football and basketball with him at Linden McKinley High School there.

"A five-bedroom home that'll have a horseshoe-shaped driveway," said Douglas, "so when Robin Leach shows up he can stand there and say"—in a deft impression of that nasalized British accent of the host of television's "Lifestyles of the Rich and Famous"—"Here we are at the home of James Buster Douglas, the heavyweight champion."

"It'll look nice on TV, that driveway," Douglas said.

Douglas continued his impersonation: "Aye'm Robin Leach, poolside at the James (Buster) Douglas house, where the champion and his missus are having cock-tails. For a night on the town, it's off in Steve Wynn's jet to the fabulous Mirage in Las Vegas."

If Douglas appears to be having a good time as heavyweight champion, it should be no surprise. It took him long years, and myriad left turns, to end up in the position he finds himself today.

For three years, at colleges in Kansas, Ohio and Pennsylvania, the twenty-nine-year-old Douglas said he was a scholarship basketball player. But by 1981 Douglas, a 6-foot-5-inch power forward, was academically ineligible—and looking for a change.

He went back home to Columbus and turned pro under his father, Bill, a former professional boxer who trained and managed him.

The record books list Douglas's debut as a third-round knockout of Dan Banks on May 30, 1981, in Columbus. In fact, Banks was the nom de guerre used by Dan O'Malley, a local salesman who had trained as an amateur under Bill Douglas.

James Douglas said the fight does not belong on his record of 30-4-1 (20 knockouts): "It really was an exhibition," he said. "O'Malley wore headgear and 16-ounce gloves."

Whatever. Douglas was 5-0 when he met David Bey that November in Pittsburgh. The bout would be the first of many unsettling nights in the ring.

"I was ready to fight," Douglas said. "I was strong. I shook out the night before, hitting the hand pads. Boom! Boom! Boom! Strong. That morning, I picked up a girl friend at the Pittsburgh bus station."

According to Douglas, love bloomed in the afternoon, leaving him enervated that night.

"That was it," he said. "All my strength was gone."

Bey knocked him out in two rounds.

Whether Douglas's hyperactive hormones were the cause of his defeat is subject to conjecture, but the incident reflects the casual regard Douglas had for his business. After Bey beat him, Douglas was back to fighting in obscure boxing towns like Canton, Ohio, and Johnstown, Pennsylvania, running his record to 11-1 by April 1982.

But the purses he earned were not nearly enough for him to be a full-time fighter. It was while working for Columbus' parks department at six to seven dollars an hour that a rider mower he was driving overturned, injuring Douglas and hospitalizing him for six weeks with a badly injured Achilles' tendon and a chipped bone in his left leg.

He was out of boxing for five and a half months, and when he did return he was, at 251 pounds, twenty-six pounds heavier than he had been before the accident.

In his first fight back, on October 13, 1982, he fought a draw against Steffen Tangstad in Chicago. Then Douglas reeled off five straight knockouts, which earned him a signing bonus of $7,500 from promoter Russell Peltz for a six-month promotional deal, renewable at Peltz's discretion. In the last bout of Douglas' initial option period, in December 1983, Douglas fought Mike (The Giant) White in Atlantic City.

Douglas said that when his father discovered he was 241 pounds a day before the fight, he ordered him to sweat enough weight to get down to the 230 range that Peltz favored. Douglas weighed in at 234 1/4 for the match, but said the radical weight reduction cost him.

Douglas, well ahead on points, said that when White hit him in the ninth round, "I wanted to move my legs, but they were gone."

Peltz declined to renew the option after White stopped Douglas at 2 minutes 57 seconds of the ninth round.

It was after that fight that Douglas replaced his father with Johnson as manager. At first, Bill Douglas declined to stay on as trainer, but when his son won a decision against Tex Cobb in November 1984 he turned up for James' next fight, a first-round knockout over Dion Simpson in an ESPN tournament in March 1985.

Douglas's next bout in the tournament came that May against Jesse Ferguson. But this time, Douglas said, when Johnson insisted Bill Douglas not work his corner, it left the fighter mentally blank: "I just was not there." Ferguson won a decision.

At a point where Douglas's career appeared hopelessly grounded, he managed to turn things around. In 1986 he scored victories over Greg Page, Dave Jaco and Dee Collier, and found himself offered a $200,000 shot at the heavyweight title that the International Boxing Federation title had stripped from Michael Spinks.

At the time that Douglas was awaiting his largest purse—to fight Tony Tucker on May 30, 1987 for that I.B.F. title—he was working for a Columbus carpet company, getting $5.10 an hour to measure and cut rugs and to deliver them. He needed the money in anticipation of his marriage to Bertha that July. She was bringing in a second salary working for the state of Ohio. He figured that with a victory over Tucker the scuffling for a living wage would cease.

Against Tucker, Douglas appeared to be on his way to a win when, as had happened before, he suddenly came undone. Tucker stopped a weary Douglas in the tenth round.

"Everybody was pulling at me, pulling at me, pulling at me," said Douglas, referring to bickering between Johnson and his father. "I walked into my title fight, and I didn't feel like a fighter. It was like I was walking through a dream. Mentally I was not there."

It was not easy resurrecting him this time.

Johnson had to persuade a friend to put up money to promote Douglas against Donnie Long that November in Columbus, Douglas' first bout since the defeat by Tucker.

Douglas knocked out Long in two rounds, but the promotion lost $3,000. As Johnson recalled: "That was a lot to us then, and we paid it back. We gave him his money back. Nobody in Columbus cared about us. It was like we had the plague."

With strong victories in 1988 over Percell Davis, Wimpy Halstead, and Mike Williams, Douglas moved up the heavyweight rankings and his name began to be mentioned as a prospective opponent for Tyson.

But by July 1989, when he was scheduled to face a Tyson sparring partner, Oliver McCall, on the undercard of Tyson-Carl Williams, Douglas once again was on the verge of getting untracked.

"My wife and I were having difficulties," said Douglas. "I wanted to back out of the fight. Because I wasn't ready. My head was not with it. I couldn't understand why things weren't going right with my career. Something was always blocking my focus. Keeping me from having total concentration."

A day before the fight, in his hotel room in Atlantic City, Douglas sat down with friends and began praying.

"We were just having a real good time expressing our emotions," said Douglas. "They left to eat. I lay down. Spirits moved through me. Like cool air, cleansing my soul. It was very touching."

While he would struggle through the fight against McCall Douglas said the religious awakening made him a new man.

"Jesus Christ was not in my life like he should have been," Douglas said. "I believed in God, but I didn't have total acceptance."

The troubles in his life would linger. Last September the couple separated. "She had to get away to think about things, and I had to think about things," said Douglas. "But I also had to continue on with my career. It was the biggest opportunity of my life."

While he prepared for that opportunity, against Tyson, he remained in contact with her, even through the separation. "We communicated," said Douglas. "We were in touch with each other. We just weren't in touch mentally."

On Tuesday, the separation ended and the Douglases got back together again, a reconciliation that nobody would have taken note of two months ago. The world was not anticipating Buster Douglas, heavyweight champion.

Consider this: the day after Douglas beat Tyson, when the W.B.A. decided to advise Johnson that it expected Douglas to fight Evander Holyfield rather than Tyson next, a hitch developed.

A W.B.A. official phoned a boxing reporter and, after apologizing for waking him at 8:15 A.M., asked: "Would you happen to have John Johnson's phone number?"

Aboard the DC-9 bound for Las Vegas, the hostess told the heavyweight champion that the late-afternoon meal was barbecue.

"I'm making it myself," she said. "Can you smell it?"

Without missing a beat, Douglas told her, "I thought it was the gasoline fumes."

The hostess turned to Bertha and asked, "Do you mind if I hit him?" James Douglas smiled that slow sly smile of his, a champion enjoying his reign.

In October 1990, in his first title defense, an overweight Douglas was kayoed by Evander Holyfield in three rounds. Douglas considered returning to the ring but apparently decided fishing at his vacation home in Florida was more to his liking. He has not fought since Holyfield knocked him out. When a reporter once asked about his being perceived as a fighter who had taken the money and run, Douglas bristled: "This is the writer's perspective: he took the money and ran. Look, everything I've got I earned. I didn't start with a luxury contract. When I started out, I lived in my father's basement. I went from the basement to where I am now. I went on my own blood and sweat. The public hasn't said nothing about take the money and run. That's the writers, and they don't know anything about the game. Half of them are wussies."

HOLYFIELD IS THE REAL DEAL (1991)

It's not as though he is the North American Boxing Federation champion. Or the ESPN champion. Or Stroh's Beer champion. Evander Holyfield is the undisputed heavyweight champion of the world, the standard bearer of boxing's three major governing bodies.

Remember what that used to mean? Once upon a time the heavyweight champion was thought of as a combination of Hercules and Albert Schweitzer, a hulk with a heart.

At 6 feet 2 1/2 inches and 208 pounds, Holyfield not only has the sort of contoured build that makes the average man envious, but also in an era when fighters wear sequined robes and routinely talk trash, carries himself with dignity outside the ring.

As he prepares for the first defense of his title, against George Foreman on Friday in Atlantic City, Holyfield is undefeated in twenty-five fights, twenty-one of which he has won by knockout, and would seem to be just the sort to be accorded the respect a heavyweight champion used to get.

Yet a few weeks ago, as he sweated through his third workout of the day—a weight-training session at a gym in a Houston mall— a stranger stepped up to him and said: "I like you, Holyfield, but Tyson is going to kill you."

The unsolicited opinion followed the victory Mike Tyson scored, with the intervention of referee Richard Steele, over Donovan (Razor) Ruddock last month. For days afterward, Holyfield kept hearing the same harsh assessment of his chances against Tyson from people who knew him barely or not at all.

"It happens to me all the time—still," said Holyfield. "I don't get mad. It's a matter of opinion." Maybe so, but it's clear that Tyson is always being thrown up in his face, to diminish his glory. And as the twenty-eight-year-old Holyfield tells it, it's not just the

241

sniping of so-called boxing experts that is troublesome. Not long ago, as he drove his black Mercedes Benz convertible along an expressway in his hometown of Atlanta, he noticed in his rearview mirror that he was being pursued by another motorist.

"He followed me a long way—two, three miles," said Holyfield. "When I exited the expressway, so did he. Finally, he pulls alongside of me at a red light and, with his girlfriend sitting next to him, calls out, 'Holyfield!' I smile. He says, 'Tyson is going to kick your butt.' It stunned me, because the guy was weaving in and out of traffic until he got himself in position to say that.

"But that sort of thing happens a lot. Even at football games I go to in Atlanta or Houston. There's always somebody in the crowd going to say something. Tyson's going to do this or that to you. Or, 'Let me tell you, I'm a Tyson fan.'"

It is not only in recent times that Holyfield's path has criss-crossed with Tyson's. The connection between the two fighters goes back to 1984, when both were amateurs—long shots to make the United States Olympic team—and friends.

"Tyson worked hard in the gym," said Holyfield. "He did everything a tad faster than anybody else. It was amazing, he being so big. He could hit the heavy bag like a 106-pounder. He had so much rhythm in the game of boxing. Outside the ring, he didn't have that much rhythm. In Colorado Springs, where we trained, he went to play basketball and did not play terribly well. There were a lot of things there he didn't fit in.

"Sometimes, he was like a little kid trapped in a man's body. He was the type that loved to have fun. He'd joke about how fast he could swallow a beer. He loved to hug you and embrace you. He was glad to be around somebody. But soon as he'd get into a situation he didn't understand, he'd become mad."

Holyfield said he and Tyson got along well back then, a friendship forged in their both being outside the inner circle of esteemed American amateur fighters. But in spite of their closeness, Holyfield recalled, a confrontation did occur.

"We were in Texas, training for the Olympics," Holyfield said. "I'd made the team; Tyson was an alternate. We were shooting pool. He lost to a fellow named Bennie Heard, and I had the next game. Well, he had an attitude. He wanted to take the pool cue from me. I had seen him take the cue from others. Tyson says to me, 'I'm playing.' I told him, 'You ain't taking this stick from me.' He became mad and started pacing. I'd noticed that when he's pacing, it means he's mad. I told him, 'Look here, Tyson. You ain't taking this stick. You might as well stop being mad.'

"He looked at me. All of a sudden, he starts laughing. Fact of the matter is, he didn't want to be that way, but he was used to having it that way. When he was mad, there were not too many people that would talk back to him."

In later years, Tyson would win the heavyweight championship as Holyfield went to the top of the cruiserweight division.

"We had no problems back then," Holyfield. "We got along just fine. When I started moving toward heavyweight, you could see some distance setting in. We might be at a party in Los Angeles and on the mike, the man would say, 'The two baddest heavyweights in the world—keep 'em apart.' But I'd always go over and say, 'How you doing?'

"In general, I've always been nice to him and try to cut him as much respect as possible. I understand where he came from and what kind of world you can be trapped in. A lot of people used him to be in the world they wanted to be in. A lot of people tell me now, 'You're the heavyweight champion—you can do anything you want to.' I know that's wrong and don't want those people around me."

So it goes with this champion whose career, like Roger Maris' sixty-one home run season, seems to come with asterisks.

"If you go back through my life, it's always been something," said Holyfield. "'Holyfield's too small.' 'Holyfield's too nice to be a winner.' 'Tyson'll whup him.' This or that, always something."

When he knocked out James (Buster) Douglas in three rounds last October to win the heavyweight title, critics ignored the savvy feint he used to bait Douglas' missed uppercut and the crackling knockout blow with which he countered it. Never mind the nifty pyrotechnics. What they dwelled on was a Douglas so porcine as to be a punch line in comedy routines and a mitigating factor in Holyfield's triumph.

Holyfield has become so accustomed to reservations about his legitimacy that when his hometown of Atlanta wanted to celebrate his heavyweight title, the fighter had an eerie thought: what if they gave a parade and nobody came.

"I didn't want to be embarrassed," said Holyfield. "See, I was disappointed with the reaction there when I won the cruiserweight title."

In July 1986, in only his twelfth professional match, Holyfield won a decision over the World Boxing Association champion, Dwight Muhammad Qawi, in a fifteen-round bout so grueling that Holyfield had to be hospitalized afterward.

"In Atlanta," recalled Holyfield, "it was like, 'Cruiserweight title? No big deal.'"

The heavyweight title, it turned out, counted for a bit more in Atlanta, much to Holyfield's relief.

"Everybody came out," Holyfield said of the parade that eventually took place. "It was great because they gave it on a work day, a Thursday, and it wasn't really a beautiful day. I rode with my mother in an open limo through downtown Atlanta. So many people were there, and we ended up at City Hall."

That was an antidote, for sure, to the more immediate reaction he had when he beat Douglas. He remembers the joy of well-wishers who flocked to his dressing room afterward, and the strangely empty feeling he had.

"Everybody's gone," said Holyfield. "You're in the room by yourself, thinking. 'Where's my happiness?' Sure, I made a lot a money, but money isn't happiness."

Holyfield earned more than $8 million for fighting Douglas.

In the weeks that followed, he vacationed in Jamaica and Aruba where, in reflecting on his victory over Douglas, he began to experience the pleasure absent the night it happened.

"You sit and relax and think about what you've done," said Holyfield. "When I was in the midst of it, I wasn't having fun. But on the beach, that's when the joy comes back in."

As champion, he made a cameo appearance on a television situation comedy, "Fresh Prince of Bel Air," and signed endorsement deals with Coca-Cola and Burger King. But he also experienced the darker side of his newly gained celebrity.

His divorce from his wife, Paulette, which is pending, became more public, particularly in and around Fairburn, Georgia. That's where Holyfield's six-bedroom house on 104 acres adjoins the four-bedroom house on three acres occupied by his wife and four children: Evander Jr., six; Ashley, five; Ebonne, three; and Ewin, nine months. But that was only part of it.

"People, if you're not doing something for them, you're going to be a bad guy," said Holyfield. "You realize you can't please everybody. If you're signing autographs and you've got to leave: 'Hey, why can't you sign mine?' People ask for donations to build a building, to buy a car. 'I heard you help people. I need help.' People don't realize I can't help everybody."

His sudden hair loss was, he suspects, a result of the pressure of being champion, and he took some encouragement from the fact that his nemesis, Tyson, underwent the same problem soon after winning the title.

Those who know him well say that more than most boxers, Holyfield is sensitive. When Showtime, which had been Holyfield's pay cable network of choice in leaner days, was forced into a bidding war with Home Box Office-TVKO for pay-per-view rights to the Foreman bout, Holyfield got involved in the negotiations because of the loyalty he felt to Jay Larkin, a Showtime executive.

"HBO had made an offer significantly richer than ours, and I figured that was the end of it," Larkin said. "But then I hear, 'Evander wants to talk to you.' Evander called and told me he was going to raise the price for HBO to pay. He says to me, 'If I get that money, I'll have to take the deal. If it's ten cents short, I'm staying with Showtime. Showtime is my family.' We had an understanding that if Showtime came within a certain percentage of HBO's best bid, he would stay with us.

"The next day was the day before Thanksgiving, and Evander got me by phone in Nantucket, Massachusetts, to tell me HBO didn't bat an eye at his price. I told him: 'Whoever you're fighting, we'll be cheering for you. Don't worry. It's not going to change how I feel about you as a friend.'"

Holyfield is guaranteed $20 million for fighting Foreman, who is guaranteed $12.5 million. But in a way the champion is in a no-win situation against a forty-two-year-old man who makes jokes about his eating binges.

While Foreman's happy-go-lucky fat man is a caricature created by big George himself to hype the fight, a residual effect is to undermine how the public is bound to perceive any victory by Holyfield. Is it farfetched to imagine the morning after Holyfield beats Foreman—if he does—hearing the by-now familiar line, "Yeah, but what would he do against Tyson?"

But that is for the future. For now, he does what he must: multiworkout training sessions that often leave him stooped over, eyes closed with fatigue, and grimacing in pain.

On a day not long ago, Holyfield had a morning gym workout that included six rounds of sparring. Then in mid-afternoon, Tim Hallmark, his fitness specialist, put him through a cardiovascular session in which he leaped sideways over coffin-shaped boxes—first on two legs and then from one leg to the other—and then slipped into a harness in which he threw punches while strapped to a resistance machine called a Vertimax.

That was followed by several minutes in a device called the Reaction Machine, which has an overhead boom that Hallmark can send hurtling at the fighter, thereby encouraging him to move his head and shoulders as he punches.

In the early evening, Holyfield's weight-training work consisted of hefting barbells and dumbbells, and straining against conventional resistance machines.

Few fighters are willing to endure the industrial-strength training Holyfield does, and sometimes he himself wonders, in pain and exhaustion, is it worth it? A hint of the energy expended comes through a remarkable aside Holyfield related while talking about his Caribbean holiday. Although it was a time of nearly total relaxation and indulgence, Holyfield lost weight, he said, because he was eating "just three meals a day."

"When I'm in training, I eat six meals a day," said Holyfield. "They're like fuel to me."

What does he eat? According to Holyfield, a typical six squares goes like this:

Breakfast—grits, four eggs, toast, a protein drink.

First Lunch—two turkey sandwiches and a protein shake.

Second Lunch (about 2 P.M.)—two baked potatoes and distilled water.

Late-Afternoon Snack—two turkey sandwiches, Carboforce (a 400-calorie carbohydrate drink) and a glass of distilled water.

First Dinner: chicken breast, beans, corn bread, collard greens, a protein drink or distilled water.

Second Dinner (after final workout): repeat of first dinner.

Of his dining preferences, Holyfield said: "I eat lots of beans. black-eyed peas, butter beans, pinto or lima beans. When my brothers eat with me, it gets them crazy. I tell them, 'You be with me, this is what you eat.' I also like collard greens, cabbage, spaghetti, baked chicken and rice."

When in training, Holyfield tends to lay off the desserts, he said. "When I'm not in training I eat a dessert everyday," he said. "I like peach cobbler and, my favorite, banana pudding."

Work. Hard work. that is the recurring motif in Holyfield's account of his rise in the boxing business. Unlike many other fighters, he does not appear to stoke his psyche with hatred of the other man. Douglas? He actually felt sorry for him ("the first time I ever felt sorry for an opponent") before their fight at the weigh-in that exposed how little work the champion had done. Foreman?

"He's real down to earth, a nice guy," said Holyfield. "But I'm not taking anything for granted: his age, size, nothing. I respect him a lot. I know George Foreman will use all his energy to try to take me out. And I'm ready."

Ready, through hard work. On one of those grueling triple workout days, there was a moment between aerobic sets when the champion stood, hands on hips, drawing deep breaths and thinking. Finally, without prompting, he said about his regimen, "It's hard but it's right."

He thought about that a moment and decided to amend the notion.

"It's hard," he said, "but it's fair."

GEORGE FOREMAN: Body and Soul (1991)

Typically, a fighter trains on the heavy bag in the same manner he attacks a live body. He will step here, step there and throw punches that mimic the arsenal he deploys in an actual fight—jabs succeeded by hooks and straight right hands.

Then there is George Edward Foreman, who was once the heavyweight champion of the world and hopes to be again. On a day not long ago in the Houston youth center named after him, Foreman stood before the heavy bag, pummeling it in a way no other fighter does.

As timer lights glowed green, yellow and finally red over a three-minute interval, Foreman, in white T-shirt and black-patterned sweat pants, threw nothing but the left—metronomic jab after jab. Then for the next three minutes he methodically hit the leather-covered bag with only his right hand. As he worked one hand and then the other over six three-minute rounds, seeking to perfect his punches through repetition, it was like watching a hulking automaton at work. Robby the Robot goes to the fights.

A strange sight it made: the big man poker-faced and deliberate as he thumped away at the bag, untroubled, as ever, by the orthodoxies of others. From the day in March 1987, when he ended a ten-year absence from the ring by winning the first of what would be twenty-four straight comeback fights, Foreman has been stone-indifferent to conventional wisdom, holding unswervingly to his own precepts about what was best for him.

That dogged reliance is what distinguishes the amiable, middle-aged Foreman from the often surly and insecure twenty-four-year-old he was when he won the heavyweight title in January 1973 by knocking out Joe Frazier in two rounds in Kingston, Jamaica. Foreman's conquest was so convincing a show of power

248

that the experts, acclaiming him to be invincible, heralded it as the start of a boxing era. But the notion went up in smoke less than two years later when Muhammad Ali, using an energy-sapping, psyche-twisting tactic he called "rope-a-dope," took the title from Foreman by knocking him out in eight rounds in a legendary fight in Zaire.

Foreman blamed the loss—and the only other professional defeat he has suffered, to Jimmy Young in March 1977—on dehydration, which he says was caused by a misguided policy of water deprivation his handlers insisted on in the days leading to a fight.

That he drinks water by the gallon these days is Foreman's belated reaction to past oversights, as is his painstaking work on the heavy bag. Back in the 1970's, Foreman says, it was not unusual for him—feared fighter though he was—to be stricken with self-doubt as he climbed into the ring.

"The man would be making the introductions," Foreman recalls, "and I'd be thinking: 'You shoulda worked on this. You shoulda worked on that.' Now I work on every single thing. The bell rings—I'm ready this time around."

That there is a this-time-around for Foreman is remarkable, given that he is forty-two years old and as big as a Winnebago— hardly the profile of a world-class heavyweight contender. In fact, with his shaven head and man-mountain bulk, Foreman would seem a more likely candidate for the garish world of wrestling behemoths.

What makes his return to boxing's center stage even more improbable is that for the ten years Foreman was away from the sport he paid no mind to it, read no columns on it and watched no bouts either in person or on television. Instead, this one-time street hood occupied himself with the work of God, becoming a self-ordained evangelical preacher and, eventually, the pastor of the Church of The Lord Jesus Christ, a block or two from his youth center in the Aldine section of northeast Houston. Who could have possibly imagined that this overweight do-gooder—presiding over church services Wednesday, Saturday and twice on Sunday and counseling neighborhood kids the rest of his working hours—

would ever again entertain the idea of a heavyweight championship?

And yet, come April 19 at the Atlantic City Convention Center, George Foreman—6 foot 4, roughly 250 pounds and a fighter whose plodding movements sportswriters likened to Dr. Frankenstein's monster when he started his comeback four years ago—will climb into the ring and try to wrest the title from the reigning champion, a sculptured twenty-eight-year-old athlete named Evander Holyfield. Even if Foreman loses he may still have the last laugh.

For the bout against Holyfield is big business. The Trump Plaza Hotel and Casino, which bought the live-site rights, has scaled the gate at $12 million—21,200 seats at prices ranging from $100 to $1,000. But the bulk of the revenues to be generated by "The Battle of the Ages," as Holyfield-Foreman is billed, will come from the pay-per-view telecast of TVKO, a new entity of Time Warner Sports.

About 16 million homes in this country are now equipped to receive pay-per-view programming. TVKO's price for Holyfield-Foreman is $35.95, of which about $18 will bounce back to the promotion. Shelly Finkel, a Holyfield adviser, predicts that TVKO will draw about 10 percent of its potential audience—1.6 million homes. "If that were to happen, it would mean $28 million in pay-per-view monies to the promotion," Finkel says. "That would top the previous best pay-per-view figures." With other ancillary revenues, Finkel calculates that Holyfield-Foreman will likely gross about $75 million, making it the most lucrative fight promotion in boxing history, surpassing the $70 million earned by the Mike Tyson-Michael Spinks title bout in 1988.

For the fighters, financial success is already assured. Holyfield (25-0, 21 knockouts) is guaranteed $20 million, and Foreman (69-2, 65 knockouts) $12.5 million. But the fancy figures have not quelled the recurring skepticism over whether Foreman has really earned the right to this title shot.

Start with the girth. During his absence from the ring, Foreman's weight ballooned to 315 pounds. For his first comeback fight, against Steve Zouski, Foreman was a blubbery 267 pounds—

49 1/2 pounds more than he weighed the night he won the title in 1973. In succeeding fights, he would pare down to a low of 235 pounds for Dwight Muhammad Qawi, whom he stopped in March 1988. Soon after, though, Foreman decided that the svelte look was not the real George; since then, he has fought, unapologetically, as the king-size model.

"At 250 pounds, everything I wanted was there," says Foreman. "To get to the 220's, I would have felt like the George Foreman from years ago, and I didn't want that feeling."

Even in his youth, Foreman was no Nijinsky. Straight forward he came, swinging fists with the subtlety of a wrecking ball. *Baboom* and the fight was over. But with his new outsized dimensions, Foreman's menace has sometimes been adulterated. At times during his comeback he looked ponderous to the point of comedy, though he still hit with punishing force. In his twenty-four straight comeback victories, Foreman has scored twenty-three knockouts.

But just who were the vanquished? To Foreman's detractors, they were patsies—blatant setups to build an eye-catching record and rouse public interest in just the sort of multimillion-dollar extravaganza that the Holyfield match represents. "George has compared himself to Nolan Ryan, the Rangers pitcher, another over-forty athlete," said Dan Goossen, a Los Angeles-based fight manager and promoter. "But it's not comparable, because Nolan Ryan is striking out top professionals, whereas George is fighting the equivalent of Double-A competition."

At the point he fought Foreman, Zouski had won only two of his previous eleven fights. Many others Foreman fought were either diminished names—like Qawi, Bert Cooper and J.B. Williamson—or, in the boxing vernacular, "shmear cases," opponents managers routinely line up to pad their fighters' records.

A number of Foreman's victims—Zouski, Dave Jaco, Mark Young, Mike Jameson—had been previously abused by Tyson on his way up the rankings. But the difference is that Tyson eventually fought enough contenders to merit championship recognition. Having beaten only one ranked fighter, a Brazilian named Adilson Rodrigues, Foreman is still viewed by some as a flimflam man and, worse, an accident waiting to happen. Goossen recalls a conversation with a Las Vegas casino executive, who told him: "I don't want that fat slob to fight at my place. If he has a heart attack, we'd never live it down."

Foreman has refused to be agitated by criticism. Instead, he employs the self-deprecation defense, making jokes at his own expense. Let a snide hint drop that his opposition was underwhelming and Foreman will say: "You know, there are some who claim I don't fight a guy unless he's on a respirator. That's a lie. He has to be at least eight days off the respirator."

With similar self-parody, Foreman has undercut the perception that he is grossly out of condition, triumphantly waving turkey legs in his meaty hands or blithely devouring packets of M&M's during the course of television interviews. The comedy is fairly obvious, but the high spiritedness with which Foreman delivers it has established him as that rarity in boxing: a lovable figure.

Still, to the many doubters, Foreman's ham-bone antics are just part of the larger sell job to make him an object of public curiosity—never mind whether the guy can fight.

Well, the gospel according to George is that the skeptics can go straight to an infernal place.

"There's an old saying, 'Faith is the substance of things hoped for and the evidence of things unseen,'" Foreman says. "I'm going to beat Holyfield. In me, he's going to meet a guy who's been torn apart and embarrassed, but a guy who's going to hit him with something he's never been hit with in his life. I visualize it— knockout, two rounds. I see Holyfield stumbling from a certain shot, and dat, dat, dat's all folks."

The differences between the Foreman who strutted through the glory years of the 1970's and the Foreman of today go well beyond the way he addresses the heavy bag. Foreman now is a man open to a world of tender feelings and concern for others.

Little of that mattered to the old Foreman, a sullen and distant fellow who, by his own account, flaunted his wealth and made a mess of his personal life. "I'd offend anybody," he says. "I did a specially bad job on females. I remember as a kid, I made a pact with a friend. We'd seen our fathers hit our mothers, and we agreed we'd never fight with women. Then, one night with my first wife, Adrienne—I was champion of the world then—I got into an argument. I had her on the floor and was hitting her when I got just a flash about that pact. I got up off the floor and called an attorney to get me a divorce. It was like punishing myself for breaking the pact.

"With strangers I wasn't all that nice either. People would ask for autographs and I'd get nasty: 'Don't you see I'm eating?' Sometimes I'd hire guys to make sure people didn't get in my face."

As Foreman tracks it, his transformation came after his last loss, to Young in San Juan, Puerto Rico, in 1977. Exhausted and delirious in his post-fight dressing room, Foreman says, he encountered death and God in one apocalyptic experience.

"I couldn't see anything," Foreman remembers. "It was like being hopelessly lost at sea. I thought: 'This is it. I'm dead.' There was a horrible smell and a feeling of loneliness. Then it was like a giant hand pulled me out—I wasn't scared any more. I had collapsed onto the floor, with people all around me, my brothers Roy and Robert, my trainer Gil Clancy. They picked me off the floor. 'It's O.K.,' I told them. 'I'm dying. But tell everybody I'm dying for God.'"

Foreman began recounting the tale of his epiphany to congregations, mostly in Houston. "I never intended to leave boxing," he says. "I just became consumed with telling my story. People would say, 'Great, great, good'—it made me feel normal, and I just never got back to training."

The first time he took his ministry to the streets was late in 1977, in Shreveport, Louisiana, "I was with a church youngster named Dexter, who was around sixteen years old, and he suggested we try it. I watched him do it first. Then I tried. Nothing. People walked by me like I was stupid. I said to Dexter, 'Man, they're not listening.' He said, 'Tell them who you are.' So I said: 'I'm George Foreman, the former heavyweight champion of the world. Praise the Lord.' A few people stopped. Then came five, six, eight, ten more people."

As word of his religious work spread, Foreman became a sought-after speaker, invited to address congregations all over the world. Meanwhile, in the midst of his changing values, he decided to streamline his life. He sold houses in Houston and Beverly Hills, his ranch in Livermore, California and reduced his flotilla of fancy cars.

"And in 1977 I just stopped watching TV," says Foreman. "I wanted to think, and people would come into my house and turn the TV on, so I couldn't. So I said, 'I'll fix this.' I had a house with six bedrooms. All the bedrooms had TV. The toilet had TV. The sauna had TV. So did the dining room and living room. Eight, nine, ten TV's that I gave away or sold. I didn't have time for TV because I wanted to talk. TV pushed in on my mouth."

Annuities from a boxing career in which he'd earned from $12 million to $15 million enabled Foreman to pursue his calling without serious financial concern. He lived comfortably in a five-bedroom house in the Houston suburb of Humble, making occasional visits to his 200-acre ranch in Marshall, Texas.

The abrupt metamorphosis proved unsettling at first to those close to him, like his younger brother Roy. "To me, it was difficult to believe," Roy says, "because the George I grew up with was tough and hard. You didn't expect him to be saying, 'Love somebody no matter what happens.'"

Foreman himself says that when he made his decision to be a preacher, "at first it embarrassed me. Where I came from, the kid with the Bible was a momma's boy, a coward hiding behind a book."

But Foreman overcame those feelings and immersed himself in church life. One day, he met a woman who was anxious about her son's erratic behavior and asked Foreman to speak to the boy. Foreman suggested she bring her son to the church. But weeks later, when the youth failed to show, Foreman learned that he had been imprisoned for a gas-station stickup. The news was so disheartening that Foreman began to question whether his life had become too insulated in the church. Says Roy: "That's when he told me, 'I've got to do something. Somebody helped me, and now it's time for me to help others.'"

The two brothers bought and fixed up a building in Aldine, an integrated working-class neighborhood of modest bungalows, many set on cinder blocks. Then they applied for and obtained nonprofit status for the George Foreman Youth and Community Center, which opened its doors in 1984. For the next few years, Foreman's life was given over to tending to the souls of his parishioners and to the futures of the youngsters who turned up at the center. On occasion, he would climb into the ring to spar with the larger boys.

To subsidize that life, Foreman began to collect fees for his outside speaking engagements. But while addressing a church congregation in 1986, he found himself growing uneasy with the local clergyman's hard sell on his behalf as the collection basket passed from hand to hand. "I know how to make money," Foreman thought to himself.

And at that moment, he says, at the age of thirty-seven, he decided he would devote himself once again to becoming heavyweight champion.

But was it really that simple? It is no secret that Foreman has long been haunted by his upset loss to Ali and his subsequent failure to land a rematch. The sour ending to his career no doubt diminished the many good memories. In any case, when Foreman told his wife, Joan, that he wanted to make a comeback, she was concerned not only about his welfare but about the impact on their marriage, Foreman's fifth. She had seen the scrapbooks from her husband's boxing past and worried that the pictures of *that* Foreman, in the company of a variety of alluring women, might be replicated.

Foreman assured Joan and his daughter (the oldest of his nine children, including four sons named George) that they needn't worry: the only excitement he was looking for was inside the ring, where he knew how to take care of himself.

Originally, Foreman was to have begun his comeback in France, far from the hard-eyed scrutiny of the American news media. But when complications developed abroad, Foreman began fighting here. He fought often—roughly one bout every six weeks—in boxing outposts like Springfield, Missouri, Orlando, Florida, Phoenix and Rochester. Frequently he took a percentage of the gate rather than the hefty guarantees big names usually demand. "Puddle-hopping" he called his grass-roots approach, the notion being that he would build slowly toward his objective—a shot at the title.

"I knew it'd take fights over a long period of time to do it right," Foreman says. "I'd seen others like Muhammad Ali and Joe Frazier fail in their comebacks because they were looking for overnight success. I treated myself like a young man, a prospect."

Because he had isolated himself from a decade's developments in boxing, he was obliged to rent a TV and a VCR to watch tapes of potential opponents. That led in 1988 to his bringing back television to his home and that, in turn, led to culture shock.

"We got cable TV and it blew my mind," Foreman says. "Back in the 70's, there were only three stations. Now you could turn to stations...click, click, click...all night long. Seven in the morning, we'd still be click-click-clickin' with that remote. I'd say, 'Man, we got to get some sleep.'"

Eventually, Foreman fought his way back onto that TV screen. In contrast to the fatigue-inducing tightness he exhibited in his early years, he impressed boxing insiders with the relaxed way he fought. But not until his fight fourteen months ago against the still-hard-hitting Gerry Cooney—when Foreman withstood heavy punches in the first round before ending it minutes later with a spectacular two-punch combination—did the big man sense he was beginning to be taken seriously.

"Here's how I knew," says Foreman. "Next door to me lived a young fella—I'd seen him grow from a little baby to 6 foot 1. And when I come back home to Humble from beating Cooney, he stopped the car, jumped out and said to me, 'Good fight, man.' He had never mentioned boxing before that. That made me know: 'You're there.'"

Houston's fifth ward was where George Foreman grew up. It was a dead-end place for most of those who lived there, a ghetto offering large doses of misery and violence.

The fifth of seven children, he dropped out of school in the 10th grade and spent his days drinking excessively, committing crimes with nothing more than his terrifying physicality. "He carried no weapon," Roy says. "He was the weapon."

Of the epic tales of his street-fighting prowess, Foreman concedes he is unsure which are true and which aren't. So often was he under the influence of cheap wine that his memory of events from those days remains shaky: "I do remember one time when a guy pulled a knife on me and shouted, 'I got you now, you dirty low-down so and so!' And his wife is hollering for him to stick me. I was so shocked I turned and ran. Found out that the night before I'd tried to rob him and he'd gotten away. I'd been so drunk I just didn't remember."

It was some time later, as he lay on the muddy earth beneath a neighbor's house, hiding from the police, that he decided to change his life. In August 1965, he left Houston to join the Job Corps in Grants Pass, Oregon. The shift of scenery, however, did not alter his nature. At Grants Pass and at his next Job Corps assignment, in Pleasanton, California, he was constantly in trouble.

Charles (Doc) Broadus, a former Air Force sergeant who ran the gym at the Pleasanton complex, was watching television one night when he got a call about a melee in the dorms: "Somebody said, 'there's a young man here trying to beat up everybody.' I go over there and find this sixteen-year-old kid, George Foreman, had taken the door off the hinges, beat up on a kid and thrown him out the window."

Broadus, who is 5 foot 5 (and a martial arts expert), walked over to Foreman and said, "Why don't you pick on somebody your own size?"

"That stopped him," Broadus recalls. "He looked at me sort of odd. I told him: 'Come on, big fella. Let's walk and talk.'"

Job Corps counselors were so incensed by Foreman's behavior that they wanted to lock him up in a nearby state prison. But Broadus dissuaded them, and then got Foreman thinking about a way out. "He told me, 'You big enough and ugly enough to be a fighter,'" Foreman says. "'Get on down to the gym.'"

Broadus kept after Foreman, especially after some embarrassing moments in his first ring encounters, and eventually coaxed the young fighter into an amateur career that rapidly took off. In only his twenty-sixth fight, Foreman won a gold medal at the 1968 Olympic Games in Mexico City. And then, by waving a small American flag after his victory, became the overnight darling of Middle America. Earlier in the Games, a pair of black American sprinters, John Carlos and Tommie Smith, had raised black-gloved fists during the playing of the national anthem to express their outrage at the treatment of blacks in the United States.

If Foreman's flag-waving ingratiated him with the American mainstream, the good will quickly dissipated once he turned professional in June 1969. When the fighter's handlers warned him of the ulterior motives of people who were approaching him, Foreman grew suspicious and even ornery as he withdrew more and more from the world.

"I was a product of what people told me," he says. "Then, all of a sudden, you look into the mirror and you start to like yourself. 'Hey,' you say, 'I'm just going to be George.' Evidently, when I decided to become George, it turned out to be a nice, round-faced good guy."

That contrast between Foreman's past and present is what makes his story so intriguing. There is a twinkle now to this man—and a natural ease with being just plain George—that he did not have the first time around. There is also a quirkiness. When his latest child, George 5th, was born in January, Foreman was prepared with a name for a girl, Judy George. She would have joined her older sisters, Georgetta and Freeda George.

In the 1970's, Foreman would hole up in his hotel room before a big fight, working himself up into a high-angst sweat. But last April, just days before his bout with Mike Jameson in Lake Tahoe, a far-from-stressed Foreman was in evidence.

"George called my room and said he'd like to ride around the lake," says Bruce Trampler, a matchmaker. "So I acted as a kind of tour guide. We got in the van, and George is funny about driving. He's petrified by excessive speed. So I made a point to go as slowly as possible. He says to me, 'I like the way you drive.' Anyway, I drove out to different scenic places—waterfalls and woods—and he was like a little kid enjoying it all.

"He says, 'Where else can we go?' I told him about the Ponderosa ranch from the TV show 'Bonanza.' It's a tourist attraction now. We went and looked at the cabin, the stables. He ate those monstrous Hossburgers.

"And wherever we went, people came up to him, and he took time with every single person. He didn't brush anyone. He signed autographs, always with the big smile. It was never, 'Get 'em away from me.'"

Some who knew the fighter in the 80's admit to having difficulty trying to reconcile that Foreman with the easy-going man of today. Mort Sharnik, a sportswriter then, had occasion to interview Foreman once on a television show not long after he became champion. "There was a report that he'd sold the ancillary rights to all future fights for just $250,000—a ridiculously low sum—and when I asked him about it, all I could get was 'hmmm' and 'ugggh,'" Sharnik says. "It was the longest three-minute interview I ever did."

Not long ago, the two men spoke at length about the war in the Persian Gulf. Sharnik, now a publicist for Foreman, heard the fighter quote the Bible to make the point that perhaps war is in the natural order of things. "I can tell you in 1970 George wasn't talking to me about the nature of man and there being a season to sow and a season to reap," Sharnik says. "It was well after midnight when we got through talking, and my assignment from that conversation was to get George copies of *War and Peace* and Arthur Schlesinger's *The Age of Roosevelt: The Coming of the New Deal*."

That Foreman has evolved far beyond the mug he was is part of his appeal. But it would be a mistake to think that this expansive George exists only in a vacuum outside the ring. The truth is that the same mother wit that has amused and beguiled so many is probably what's gotten him this far as a fighter.

While boxing handlers will often disingenuously flatter a fighter by saying he is his own boss, it would be no hype to say that of Foreman. He has no manager, and the advisers he relies on, including his key man, Ron Weathers, operate solely at his instruction. Whether staging his comeback at his own puddle-hopping pace or calling Weathers at 2 in the morning to critique a deal, Foreman has shown a decisiveness that now makes him, some think, a better fighter.

"Before, he was not at all self-assured," says Gil Clancy, his former trainer. "He was afraid of accepting challenges. It's why he'd get so tired during a fight. He was so tight that it drained him. He was tight and reluctant to let punches go. Now things just flow."

Sometimes what flows raises the purist's brow. The day after belaboring the heavy bag, Foreman slipped into the gym next door to his youth center and played ninety minutes of three-on-three basketball, positioning himself as close to the hoop as his wide body and a moratorium on the three-second rule would allow.

Foreman's sparring sessions are not just unconventional, they border on the bizarre. Some of his sparring partners are not professional boxers at all, merely personal friends taking time away from their regular jobs—an accountant, a salesman, a pipe fitter.

At one recent session, the accountant, a slim man easily one hundred pounds lighter than Foreman, moved like a jittery rabbit, ignoring the hecklers while forcing big George to try to corner him. When Foreman caught up, he threw only soft underhanded blows, hitting the accountant gently on the buttocks and hipbones. Next came the salesman, a 230-pound former tackle from Auburn. He rushed Foreman like a dog attacking a bear, throwing wild untutored punches that Foreman calmly parried. The pipe fitter's style was more routine. But like the others, when his turn came, he bolted into the ring so as to give Foreman no rest break.

What manner of world-class fighter trains like this?

"In this game," Foreman replies, "there are predator and prey. I am predator. I seek and destroy. You can't rehearse for that."

Foreman claims to be unimpressed by the high-tech conditioning program that Evander Holyfield uses to whip himself into states of anatomical perfection. A big edge in fitness is regarded as crucial to the champion's battle plan: avoid Foreman early, when he is likely to be most dangerous, and erode his strength later with a furious pace that will finally make him act his age.

For his part, Foreman has taken note of Holyfield's team of specialists—a body-building champion for strength, a ballet teacher for flexibility, an aerobics instructor for endurance—and joked that his own strength coach is his wife.

"She's always trying to figure out what kind of chains she's going to put on the refrigerator at home," he says. "Ones that I can't break."

Foreman lost a unanimous decision to Holyfield, but was applauded for his spirited performance. In 1992, he continued to be active as a fighter—victories over Alex Stewart and Pierre Coetzer—and as an entertainment figure, doing commercials, commentary on boxing telecasts and a pilot for a situation comedy.

HOLMES AT HOME (1987)

On a Wednesday night earlier this month, at the Larry Holmes Commodore Inn on United States Route 22 in Phillipsburg, New Jersey, friends and relatives of the proprietor gathered in a ballroom there to throw him a surprise birthday party.

Holmes, who turned thirty-eight years old, had come straight from his workout at the Larry Holmes Training Center in nearby Easton, Pennsylvania, his hometown, thinking he was about to deliver an anti-drug speech to a local youth group.

When the former heavyweight champion, dressed in a black Stetson, black satin jacket and denims, stepped through the dimly lit ballroom doorway, he heard the cry of "Surprise!" and stood there momentarily transfixed, trying to cover a sheepish smile with his hand.

While the motel at which the approximately 150 invited guests had gathered is part of Holmes' expanding business portfolio, the crowd—which included Holmes' wife, Diane, and his four children, Misty, nineteen; Lisa, eighteen; Kandy, seven; and Larry Jr., five—had come to honor not the young entrepreneur Holmes but the old fighter of the same name.

At each table, there was a single pink rose held in the grip of an Everlast boxing glove. The large birthday cake on a table at the rear of the room had a pair of boxing gloves sculpted from frosting. Then there was the T-shirt that Diane Holmes gave her husband, who goodnaturedly sorted through a series of wrapped containers to get to it.

There would be other gifts that night—framed photos, oversized birthday cards, a bottle of champagne that Holmes kiddingly offered to his youngest child—all of which he seemed to enjoy as much as the chance he got to sing doo-wop music with The

262

Manhattans, a group hired specially for the occasion. But it was the white T-shirt with the red block letters that appeared to please him most. For what Holmes read when he held up the shirt to examine it was:

"Mike Tyson: 32-1."

The "32-1" referred to the record that Holmes' partisans expect Tyson, the undisputed heavyweight champion, to have after Holmes meets him on January 22, at the Convention Center in Atlantic City.

Tyson, of course, is twenty-one years old and Holmes nearly twice that. In fact, last August Holmes became a grandfather when Misty gave birth to 6-pound-7-ounce Jeffrey Allen Dorsey Jr.

If age is more than enough of an encumbrance against a fighter like Tyson—thirty-eight is ancient in boxing—Holmes will also have to contend with a layoff that dates back to April 1986, when he lost a disputed decision to Michael Spinks and retired from the ring with a 48-2 record.

Yet at the party in Phillipsburg, Holmes didn't sound like a man who believed he would be laboring under a handicap on January 22. Never mind that Tyson has knocked out twenty-eight of his thirty-two opponents, that in his consuming aggression he has become a sort of Robo Slugger, a heavyweight unrelenting in his need to damage, or that Tyson habitually turns the prefight boasts of opponents into reassessments with virtually the first punch.

None of that seemed to faze Holmes, who told friends and family in Phillipsburg that Tyson didn't scare him one bit.

"This guy," said Holmes, "is made for me."

When he quit boxing, Larry Holmes did not go away gently.

In a postfight interview on HBO, Holmes, who felt victimized by the decision awarded to Spinks, said, "The judges, referees and promoters can kiss me where the sun don't shine."

Since the remarks came only seven months after he had disparaged Rocky Marciano following the loss of his championship to Spinks, they dealt a serious blow to Holmes's public image.

The long-respected champion was suddenly viewed as an embittered soul who lacked the good sense to take his leave with a modicum of dignity.

But to hear it from Holmes, the backlash rolled straight over his broad shoulders, leaving the president and chief executive officer of Larry Holmes Enterprises quite intact.

"After that loss to Spinks," said Holmes, "people thought I'd go hide. Or I'd get a gun and blow my brains out. But the Monday morning after the fight, I was back in Easton, seeing where I was going to invest the $1 million they paid me."

Since then, Holmes tended to his businesses in and around Easton: a disco called Round 1; a restaurant and lounge named John Henry's after his father; the motel on Route 22; the training and recreation center, and his investments. He began promoting boxing matches and broke ground on a five-story office building on 3.2 acres on Larry Holmes Drive in Easton.

"I sit in Easton," Holmes said, "and take care of our little business. People shake my hand. I'm a happy guy doing it."

Maybe so. But was business success simply a buffer against his ring disappointments? It sometimes seemed so. This past June, for instance, during the week preceding the Spinks-Gerry Cooney fight, Holmes appeared in the showroom of an Atlantic City casino, co-featured with another former heavyweight champion, Joe Frazier, and performed a medley of songs. The lyrics from one were particularly memorable:

I trained real hard to do the job,
Then beat the man and I got robbed.
Yeah, won that fight.
(Pause)
Everybody knows I beat Spinks,
That's O.K.
Politics stink.

The singer delivered the lines as though he believed them.

In June, Holmes was, to all appearances, holding to his retirement. There had been attempts to lure him back into the ring, against Cooney, against Tyson, even against Tyrell Biggs. But nothing came of the offers.

While Holmes worked out from time to time, and even joined the Easton Y.M.C.A. so he could do laps—nineteen to the mile—on the overhanging oval track, it was not until he sat at ringside with his trainer, Richie Giachetti, at Tyson's August 1 bout against Tony Tucker that the former champion got serious about being back in boxing.

"He turned to me during Tyson-Tucker," said Giachetti, "and said, 'Richie, I can knock this guy out.'"

Last month, Holmes signed for a reported $3.1 million to fight Tyson. According to the promoter, Don King, the negotiations began with Holmes giving him the grand tour of his business holdings.

"Then," said King, "he pulls out a $50,000 interest check and says: 'See this, Don? I ain't fighting for the money.'"

Why then, at his age, is Holmes coming back?

The answer to that question may lie in the contradictory nature of Holmes. Here is a man who can be engaging and antagonistic by turns—one moment joking, the next fuming; here professing indifference to the opinions of others, there currying their kind words.

"Did you ever meet a fighter like me?" he asked a reporter. "Tell me what impresses you about me."

And moments later: "What don't you like about me?"

In the world according to Holmes, there is a strong adversarial sense—people refusing him his due, detractors who won't recognize him for what he has accomplished.

"How do you feel about yourself?" he asked. "Do you like yourself?

"Do I have the same right to feel good about myself? How come when I say I love me, someone puts me down? How come when I say I'm greater than Rocky Marciano, I should apologize?"

And in practically the next breath, he does apologize, for saying in September 1985 that Marciano couldn't carry his jock.

"It was a poor choice of words at the time. But it was too late. I said it. They didn't let me take it back."

On the afternoon of his surprise party, Holmes worked out for about forty-five minutes—mostly shadowboxing and aerobic movement—and then, in private dressing quarters, did sit-ups to tighten his somewhat thickening waistline. After he weighed himself (232 pounds, only about ten pounds more than he weighed for his last two fights, with Spinks in April 1986 and September 1985), he began to speak.

It started with his stream-of-conscious projection of a Tyson-Holmes bout:

"He'll be throwing forty-five to fifty punches a round—forty-eight blocked, two will graze me but look like they landed. And I'll be jabbing, thirty to thirty-five punches a round. Landing. All of a sudden a right hand out of nowhere. Bam bam! Uh, oh. I changed up."

Then the Holmes monologue took a turn, as the fighter recalled the various men who had worked with him, in one capacity or another, and gone on to enjoy success elsewhere. Why their success? he asked, rhetorically. The answer, in Holmes' own singsong crooning words: "Be-cause of Lar-ry Holmes."

One after another he traced the greening of these people in their life-after-Larry—trainers and therapists who, as Holmes saw it, would never have made it but for the start he gave them. Soon he was asking Giachetti and the others in the room why these men had prospered.

Grinning and laughing, they took the cue and chanted along with him the singsong answer.

"Be-cause of Lar-ry Holmes."

Later in the night after the surprise party had ended, Holmes wandered into the bar of his motel.

Spying Giachetti, he asked, "Do you love me, Richie?"

The same question for a reporter.

And looking to a handful of drinkers along the bar, one more time: "Do you-all love me?"

At the bar, there was a half-hearted murmured assent, enough apparently to send the former heavyweight champion of the world out the door and into the night, for the moment at least, a happy man.

Larry Holmes was knocked out by Mike Tyson in January 1988. A little more than three years later, he came out of retirement again—a second comeback he launched by knocking out Tim (Doc) Anderson in April 1991. His comeback culminated in another title shot, this time against Evander Holyfield. Holmes made a respectable showing in losing a unanimous decision in June 1992.

BOWE ON THE GO (1992)

A tricky business this being heavyweight champion. Coco, who is furry and has probably never heard of the Marquess of Queensbury, offers an object lesson.

On Tuesday of Week No. 1 in the reign of Riddick Bowe, Coco was taken by Bowe to be groomed. By Wednesday, Coco, a two-year-old gray chow, had yet to make it back to the Bowe household on Lourdes Drive in Fort Washington, Maryland.

The pooch was stranded.

"I couldn't get her," Bowe said Wednesday, "because it got so hectic. One thing after another. Phone didn't stop ringing. But you know what? Evander warned me."

That's Evander Holyfield, the former champion, to whom Bowe spoke the day after he beat him in the ring at the Thomas and Mack Center in Las Vegas.

On that Saturday morning, November 15, Bowe was lounging in his suite on the twenty-sixth floor at the Mirage, sore all over from the match and thinking about the very determined man who had battled him for twelve spirited rounds.

Bowe tried but couldn't raise Holyfield on the phone, but when Holyfield eventually returned his call, Bowe was touched ("A very sincere individual; most guys you beat wouldn't call you," he said), then edified.

"He told me, that being champion is practically a full-time job, and that I'm not going to have a lot a time to myself," Bowe said.

Holyfield's words resounded in Bowe's first week as the holder of boxing's most prestigious title. While his aides wore red sweatshirts with the words Bowe Transition Team on them—a humorous reference to the Presidential changeover going on just down the beltway at 1600 Pennsylvania Avenue—Riddick Lamont Bowe was experiencing the changes first hand.

"Evander told me," said Bowe, "hard as you make your money, people will try to take it away. He told me, 'Be careful.'"

That conversation was Saturday. Bowe got home Sunday night, and by Monday, he was shaping up as boxing's version of a lottery winner.

"Yeah, a lot of cousins came out of the woodwork," Bowe, a native of Brooklyn, said. "Tell me how much they love me. They act like they're real concerned and interested, and by the way, they sure could use money to get a car. I told them 'A year ago, you were riding the subway. Don't start no bad habits.'

"One guy, a friend from Brooklyn, he asked me for $100,000, so he could buy a house. Said he'd pay it back. I told him no. He says, 'All the times I come to see you fight.' I told him: 'I didn't know you were coming to be paid. If I'd known, I'd have told you to stay home.' And it ain't like he paid to get in. Told him, 'I got you free tickets, man.'

"You know something, I don't think people realize the struggle it is, what a fighter puts in. The sacrifices he's had to make."

For the twenty-five-year-old Bowe—who was raised in the Brownsville and Bedford Stuyvesant areas of Brooklyn—the pleasures of being winner and new champion will probably far exceed the reasons for keeping his guard up.

On Wednesday, for instance, he drove his burgundy BMW—the one with BOWE on its license plate—into Washington to meet his manager, Rock Newman.

Newman had a surprise for him—a silver metal case inside of which was the first of the three championship belts due to the fighter. This one was from the International Boxing Federation, and Bowe was like a kid under the Christmas tree, touching and caressing the silver, bejeweled belt. A fighter friend of his, Gerard Jones, threw the smiling champion a high-five.

"This is where it's supposed to be, this is where it's gonna be, this is where it's gonna stay," Bowe said as Jones helped him slip the belt around his waist.

The sight of Bowe standing triumphant along a residential street slowed traffic. A beer truck rumbled by and the driver beeped and waved. A cab driver pulled over to the curb just to gawk.

"Where them other belts, Newman?" the champion teased his manager.

An hour later, back in Fort Washington, he was still wearing the belt as he showed a visitor pencil sketches of the various rooms he envisioned for the $1.3 million dream house he expects to break ground for in March.

The master bedroom, forty feet by forty, comes with a sunken sitting room that Bowe remembers from the film "Scarface," starring Al Pacino.

The bathroom—with a bidet and two commodes ("My wife Judy always complains I leave the toilet seat up,") he said was inspired by the posh bathroom he had had at the Mirage.

There are plenty of other touches—a quarter-mile track in the backyard so he can do road work without being bothered for autographs; a twenty-five seat screening room and an arcade-style game room. With the purse from his title match expected to settle in at around eight million, and expectations of a bigger paydays, Bowe has the means now to think big.

Later Wednesday, he rode out to the three-acre site for the new home. It was about a mile from Lourdes Drive, and Bowe was still wearing his I.B.F. belt when he got there. When the builder finally arrived, Bowe asked if an architect had ruled the sketches doable.

Told they were, Bowe began conjuring up his next modification.

"Could we change the name of the street?" he asked with a smile. "Make it Riddick Bowe Drive? Or Riddick Bowe Boulevard? Hey Newman, what do you think of Riddick Bowe Cul de Sac?"

The Bowe smile is a muted one, befitting his easy-going humor. While his words sometimes carry barbs, the champion's delivery is a lot softer. It's like George Gobel meets Leo Gorcey, and Gobel wins.

Over the next twenty-four hours, Bowe's wit was on display. Riding to a screening of "Malcolm X" he joked about his first glance of his tall wife, Judy, back in Brooklyn when he was a teenager.

"I saw her and thought, 'There's a yellow Sasquatch comin' out of that house,'" said Bowe, as Judy and others in the limousine laughed.

The next day, at a rally to honor him at a shopping mall in Oxon Hill, Maryland, he took on a noisy but good-natured youth who had been shouting up to him. "You-all be quiet, fat boy, or we're gonna get it on," the champion said. "Don't be lookin' behind you. I'm talkin' to you."

The rally was the starting point of a parade that took him into Washington, to a ceremony at Union Temple Baptist Church. It was there that Bowe took note of Dr. Arnold Woodrow McKnight of the District of Columbia Boxing and Wrestling Commission.

"That's a lot of name," Bowe said. "I don't know what his mama was thinking about."

The heavyweight champion was having a good time. Beginnings are always easy.

PART FOUR: THE SMALLER MEN

There is no Harvard Business School curriculum for success in the fight game. Boxing resists neat thinking. Yet somehow fighters keep finding their way to the top.

NINO BENVENUTI: Boxing, Italian Style (1967)

It looked more like *la dolce vita* than the training camp of the world's middleweight champion. In the mornings, the pride of Trieste, Italy—champion Nino Benvenuti—was playing golf even while the dew was on the grass. It was not a particularly athletic diversion: Nino did not walk between shots, he rode. Heavyweight Dante Cane, a stablemate, chauffeured him in a three-wheeled cart.

In the late-summer afternoon, Benvenuti lounged at poolside in racer's swimtrunks, while trainer Libero Golinelli shooed away anybody foolish enough to stand between Benvenuti and the sun. Nino would lie back, Golinelli would swag tanning oil onto his legs. Sometimes the fighter rose and swam a lap or two. For exercise, he jogged once around the pool to keep from getting chilly.

Then he returned to his chaise lounge.

"Road work, the ring, punching bag, et cetera," said Benvenuti, "taken in too big a dose they'll poison any organism."

"Swimming is good for his spirit," said Golinelli.

It was enough to make the hard-nosed veterans of the Jacobs Beach era swallow their all-day stogies.

Appearances aside, everything was not strictly fun-and-games in Benvenuti's camp at the Villaggio Italia here in Haines Falls, New York. In short bursts of hard work that he did not relish, Nino was getting ready for his Thursday night title rematch with Emile Griffith at Shea Stadium. "This time it's twice as important to be prepared," he said. "People expect more." Golinelli, a partisan colonel in World War II who resembles actor Charles Bronson, was making sure that Benvenuti's deeds matched his words.

At dawn, Benvenuti—in ski cap and sweat suit—swigged a concoction of fruit juices, egg white, cognac, and sugar, and jogged six to nine miles over Catskill Mountain roads. Nino did not fake it. He couldn't if he wanted to: Golinelli ran right behind him.

Later in the day, there were rhythm exercises. Nino walked in circles around the basement gymnasium, Golinelli chanted instructions—as if reciting mass. To his orders, the fighter bent, flexed, ran, jumped—all with a dancer's supple grace. From a standing position, Benvenuti then went through a series of isometric and deep-breathing exercises. Golinelli intoned and waved his hands theatrically, like Leonard Bernstein. Benvenuti huffed and puffed and was renewed in strength.

After the exercises, Golinelli threw medicine balls at Benvenuti. The first medicine ball was standard-sized and Nino kept catching it against his stomach. When the trainer used a medicine ball the size of a cantaloupe, Nino bounced it off his stomach back into Golinelli's hand. Then came the rubber balls. Some of the balls were striped, some a solid red. Golinelli stood fifteen feet away and began pitching them at Nino. Benvenuti punched the striped balls and ducked the red ones. None of them hit him. Before the workout was finished, Nino also banged at an electronic punching bag that recorded the frequency and velocity of his punches, sparred with three other fighters in the same ring ("It makes him concentrate," said Golinelli) and hummed snatches of music.

It was boxing Italian style and, if American purists found it somewhat disconcerting, Golinelli didn't mind. He knows what is best for Nino. "I place great emphasis on mental attitude," he said. "Thirty years ago, fighters were less complicated. Now you have to make training more appealing for them. Nino is a particularly cerebral boy. He needs enthusiasm; his spirit must be inspired." Said Benvenuti, "I trust Golinelli completely." If boxing purists never cared about the psyche of a fighter before Nino fought Griffith, they do now. Golinelli's methods have a Felliniesque madness, but nobody can argue with the results.

Benvenuti's record is 72-1, but not until Golinelli took over as his trainer some three years ago did he become a fighter of championship caliber. "At that time," said Golinelli, "Nino was a one-handed fighter. (Most of his knockouts had been scored with left hooks.) The left side of his body was much stronger than the right. I gave him a lot of exercises to build up his right side, to give him more stamina. We used weights up to forty pounds, then isometrics."

The Italian progressed under Golinelli. He won the European middleweight title by knocking out Spain's Luis Folledo in six rounds in October 1965, only a few months after he'd knocked out Sandro Mazzinghi for the World Boxing Association junior middleweight title. He successfully defended his European title twice with knockouts over Jupp Elze and Pascal DiBenedetto.

His only loss was to Ki-Kim-Soo in Seoul, Korea, in June 1966, and that was a bout clouded by strange events. In the thirteenth round, Nino cornered the Korean and was punching him groggy when the ring ropes mysteriously gave way. A ten-minute halt was called while the ropes were fixed. When the bell finally sounded for the fourteenth round Ki-Kim-Soo rushed out and began punching Benvenuti, as the Italian sat on his stool, a towel around his head. The decision was predictably bad: The Korean won.

Despite his record, Nino was not highly regarded in the boxing world before he fought Griffith...not even in Italy. The trouble on his home soil was with the boxing writers. "The press gave Nino a hard time when he first turned pro," said Bruno Amaduzzi, his manager. "They did not think he was putting out in every fight. It wasn't so. Nino just didn't have the stamina until Golinelli came to work. Nino felt that everybody was against him. It made him defensive. He'd debate with the press. Most fighters are punch drunk. Nino is different. He likes to talk. If they asked stupid questions, he'd give them ironic answers." It was not an approach calculated to make Benvenuti a national hero. Before he left Trieste for the States last spring to fight Griffith for the title, Benvenuti complained to a friend: 'If I had lived in another country, I would be a national glory. But people in Italy still snub me."

The fact is that the snub was not simply geographic. People everywhere could not take Benvenuti for real. The American press tended to regard Nino's record with suspicion. In part, Benvenuti was guilty by association. European fighters in the past—with a few notable exceptions (Marcel Cerdan, Randy Turpin, Ingemar

Johansson)—have not fared well against Americans. What made Benvenuti even more suspect was that he had rarely fought outside Italy, only occasionally against name fighters.

Benvenuti changed all that with his victory over Griffith in April 1967. He beat him with such skill that he quieted all critics. That night at Madison Square Garden, he fought from the classic stand-up posture, and he fought with his hands carried low—like Muhammad Ali. Whatever way he fought, he baffled Griffith. "Griffith," said fight publicist John F. X. Condon, "likes to stick his head on a guy's chest and belt the hell out of his body. Benvenuti didn't allow him to fight his fight." Added manager Amaduzzi: "Nino knows the art of defense very well. He was jabbing and moving from side to side. He didn't give him any target."

The fight made him, at last, a hero. In Italy, he was received by Pope Paul VI and the Lord Mayor of Rome, and had a biography published. Everywhere he went, he was a celebrity. Benvenuti took his new status with mixed feelings. "Now I have an official personality," he said. "My life is no longer private....I can never make a move without people crowding around me." Even the Italian press warmed up to Nino, but it no longer mattered to him. "Nino doesn't care what they think now," said Amaduzzi. "All his fights will be in America now. That's where the money is."

When he returned to New York on board the Italian Line's Raffaello a few weeks ago, a large crowd was waiting. Even before he stepped down the gangplank and onto Pier 90 on Manhattan's West Side, fans of Nino were chanting: *Nee-no, Nee-no.* When a hired limousine tried to leave with the twenty-nine-year-old Italian, Nino's fans pounded happily on the hood of the vehicle and physically restrained it. Said Condon, "The public has fallen in love with Nino."

It was true. Benvenuti receives hundreds of fan letters each week from all over the world. Little girls send him religious medals, older women send him propositions, even though he is married. He has fans on all levels. When tickets went on sale for the Griffith rematch, actor Rex Harrison immediately bought two of them.

It is all indicative of Benvenuti's style. He is—as Amaduzzi said—different from other fighters. For one thing, he does not look like other fighters. He is ruggedly handsome, he wears his razor-cut hair long, his sideburns deep. ("I pay $2 in Italy for haircuts and tip as much. Barbers are underpaid.") Nor does he train like other fighters. He goes through Golinelli's unique regimen, then sips wine with his meals. "The alcohol content in three ounces of wine," said Nino, didactically, "is minimal. When wine is good, it's part of the meal. It helps the digestion."

In still another way, he is a rarity among boxers: Nino has culture. In Italy, Benvenuti is called *Intellettuale*, an image that he pooh-poohed at Villagio Italia recently. "I don't pretend to be an intellectual," he said. "I'm just interested in knowing about everything. I read some books, and everybody thinks I am an intellectual." For the first Griffith fight, Benvenuti brought with him books by Voltaire and Hemingway. For this fight, Nino read books by Steinbeck (*Tortilla Flat* and *Of Mice and Men*) and Guaraeschi (*Mondo Piccolo*).

Nino's interests extended to art, too. When he was in his home town of Trieste, he showed off an art collection that included a limited edition of Toulouse-Lautrec lithographs. He also had an original pencil sketch by Picasso given to him by an admirer after he won the title. It was enough to get Benvenuti excited about retaining his title. "If I win again," said Nino, "he'll give me another Picasso."

Not that Benvenuti needed to be given anything. Unlike the average pug, Nino has kept his money and made it grow. He has already accumulated an insurance company, a piece of an aluminum factory, $250,000 in stock, a nine-room villa, and four cars—a Maserati, a Lancia, a Flavia, and a Fiat. For winning the championship last April he got roughly $30,000, and this time he stands to earn at least $150,000.

And yet, though he has become a great man in Italy and though he is wealthy by any standard, he has chosen a monk's life. When he is in Italy, he spends ten months of the year living in a sparse dormitory-type arrangement with a few other fighters and his trainer, which may help explain why he is such an impish free spirit. He has to maintain his sanity somehow.

"It is a big sacrifice for me, especially now with my family," he said. "But this is my dream. It is what I love. Most fighters fight from misery; for me it is sport. Now that I am fighting for the championship, I fight for my friends, my family, myself."

For a man who professes to box for the sport of it, Benvenuti can be awfully businesslike in the ring. In the first Griffith fight, when Emile's head kept bobbing up against Nino's face, the Italian responded by poking Griffith's eye with the thumb of his glove.

Benvenuti needed no prod to dislike Griffith. It developed naturally. At the official signing before the first fight, Griffith—miffed at an alleged affront to him by Benvenuti—cursed in Italian and even threw a punch at him. Said Nino: "Griffith's not very intelligent, not even as a fighter. I don't know anything about him as a person and I don't care to know him socially."

The one thing that worries Golinelli is the overhead right that Griffith likes to shoot from a crouch. In the first fight, that punch knocked down Benvenuti. It was about the only bad moment he had with Griffith that night. But Nino isn't worried. To Griffith's prediction that he would regain the title by a knockout, Nino could only laugh. "Bravo," he said, clapping his hands, "but I hope he still remembers what he got from me last time."

If he doesn't, Nino intends to give him a professional reminder.

Benvenuti, a two-time world middleweight champion, fought from 1961-1971, and finished with a record of 82-7-1.

HECTOR CAMACHO: Boxing's Bad Boy (1989)

In 1986, in Washington D.C., Hector Camacho broke protocol at a World Boxing Council black-tie dinner honoring Ray Leonard.

As fellow boxers such as Michael Spinks, Trevor Berbick, Azumah Nelson and Marvis Frazier arrived in formal wear, Camacho, the W.B.C. lightweight champion, appeared at the predinner introductions as his showtime persona: Macho Man.

He strutted across the stage wearing an unbuttoned silver-and-black sequined shirt with a matching scarf, tight black pants and silver boots. There was a gold pendant hanging across his bare chest with the word "MACHO" on it, and an earring twinkling in his left ear lobe.

When the spotlight hit him, he smiled, waved and took the applause that followed with the ease of a born performer—and just a hint of comic mischief in his eyes.

But to hear it from Camacho, this "Macho" side of him is as distinct from just plain Hector as Clark Kent is from The Man of Steel. Macho Man, he says, is the logical extension of the slick prizefighter, the crowd-pleaser who insists on your attention and knows he'll get it.

"Hector is not as bad as Macho Man," he says. "Macho Man is the performer, the boxer. Hector is the humble nice guy who lends money out on the streets of Spanish Harlem."

As Macho Man, he drives (and occasionally demolishes) deluxe autos at raceway speeds, turns up in *Playgirl* magazine as a centerfold, admits he has smoked a little *chiba* (marijuana) and is—as he matter-of-factly tells you—smart, handsome, humble and one awesome prizefighter.

Yet Camacho has had his share of doubts and fears, and on occasion has exposed them. The most vivid instance came January

19, 1985, when he knocked out Louie Burke in five rounds on CBS. The bout took place after Camacho's self-imposed eight-month absence from the ring, a period in which his life seemed to be unraveling. In a postfight interview that day, Camacho cried on the shoulder of the CBS announcer Tim Ryan, saying: "I hope everybody keeps supporting me. Just be my friends. I need friends."

Camacho's life as Hector/Macho has been in constant turmoil in recent years. In part, the trouble stems from a childlike nature. The rest has to do with Camacho's keen sense that his talents are short-term goods.

"One day," he says, "the light goes dead and people forget you."

With that thought fixed firmly in mind, Hector has sent his alter ego out into the spotlighted world to make a lifetime's wages before the glow is gone.

The problem is that Macho Man has his limits as a business sophisticate. Because of that, he has sometimes gotten in his own way, as he ran from promoter to promoter, from manager to manager, seeking his fortune.

The confusion started in the summer of 1984 when Camacho, then the W.B.C. super-featherweight champion, relinquished his title.

In part he did it because of the difficulty he was having making the 130-pound weight limit for the division, and in part because he felt his promoter, Don King, was underpaying him. Because King's promotional options applied to Camacho only while he was super-featherweight champion, the fighter decided to go after the light-weight title, figuring he would lose King and gain purses more suited to Macho's grandeur.

But a fight scheduled for Las Cruces, New Mexico, fell through because, Camacho says, the promoter there reneged on the $500,000 to be paid him. Then Camacho began arguing with his longtime manager, Billy Giles.

Giles contends that when Camacho won the title, he changed radically. "When he took my money, it was O.K.," Giles says, recalling that he constantly gave the fighter money early in his career. 'Then when he started making money, he didn't want to pay me. He was trying to beat me out of my money."

Camacho agrees that money was a problem, but insists that Giles was at fault. The parting was bitter. Giles was quoted as saying: "Camacho's career is over. He's drowning in drugs. He'll never make it back." Camacho felt betrayed and depressed. Mort Sharnik, the CBS boxing consultant, got a phone call from him during this period and heard Camacho ask out of a CBS fight while sobbing that his world was coming apart.

"So depressed," Camacho says. "I'd take the car to the airport, take my dob kit, $2,000, a credit card. I'd look at the arrivals-departure board and pick a place. Hawaii. I slept a whole week there without going swimming. I'd sleep, eat. I was always tired. Come home for two days. Go to Detroit...."

When he was finally ready to box again, he consulted promoters, managers and attorneys to find the right person to guide him. Eventually, he began working out under Jimmy Montoya, a trainer from Los Angeles, and he signed a new deal with King—$2 million for five fights. But once against the relationship between Camacho and King—each of whom professes to feel kindly toward the other—floundered over money.

When he won the lightweight title, Camacho thought there were big paydays ahead. But the television market for boxing went soft, and King said he was unable to get the $400,000 a fight their contract specified. With his own strict sense of what was owed him, Camacho turned down a $250,000 fight of King's against Sergio Zambrano of Mexico and instead took $50,000 to fight Freddie Roach in Sacramento, California in December 1985.

But by 1986, Camacho's career was stuck. Once, he had seemed the heir to Muhammad Ali and Leonard as boxing's biggest attraction. "I saw him as a crossover star who'd attract nonboxing fans," Sharnik says. "A handsome young man who could be the first Latin boxing star with universal appeal."

By early 1988, though, what Sharnik had, with King holding options on his next four title fights, was an impasse. Then Camacho remembered Marty Cohen.

Cohen, an eighty-eight-year-old former New Yorker now living in Miami Beach, made his fortune in coal mining. Years ago he managed fighters and promoted them, and he has kept his hand in boxing. He is a vice president of the W.B.C. and a member of its executive board.

A few years ago, he was the financial advisor to the heavyweight Michael Dokes, and Camacho heard that Cohen had invested well for Dokes.

And so Macho and Cohen became a team. Cohen, as his unpaid adviser, told him he had two rules: Say no, and tell the schemers to talk to Marty. What Macho apparently got was some order and a sort of father figure. (Camacho and four brothers and sisters were raised by their mother, Maria, after she and the fighter's father separated when Hector was three.)

"Marty Cohen is my guardian angel," Camacho says.

But in Camacho's world, angels turn out to be transient. After lackluster victories over Edwin Rosario, Cornelius Boza-Edwards and Reyes Cruz, Cohen was gone and once again Camacho was a body in motion, seeking to put the excitement back in his career.

It led to his signing for a match against former champion Ray Mancini in March 1989. Not long after Hector Camacho was giving a visitor a tour of his Clewiston, Florida home.

On the living room wall hung a photo of Elvis Presley as well as a guitar-shaped clock with Presley's likeness on it.

Camacho pointed to Elvis-the-clock and allowed that Presley was a hero of his.

"For his sexiness and natural ability," Camacho explained. "All the girls loved him, all the guys hated him."

Because that sounds suspiciously like what Camacho has promulgated as the prevailing view about himself, the visitor was prompted to remark: "So you're Elvis?"

With his boyish—and somewhat abrupt—laugh, Camacho said, "Yeah."

The Camacho-as-king equations would suffer a small setback in his fight against Mancini. While Camacho won a twelve-round split decision from Mancini, and with it the junior welterweight title of the newly created World Boxing Organization, he failed to revive memories of vintage Camacho, as he promised to in the days leading up to the Mancini bout.

The Camacho who fought Mancini showed flashes of the speed and cunning that he had back in 1982-83, when he fought regularly and, with spectacular effect, on network television. But that Camacho may be, like Elvis, nothing but a fond memory now.

Although he nailed the lunging, wild-swinging Mancini early and often with smart counter punches and the occasional left-hand lead, he failed to rouse the emotions because of the caution with which he worked, particularly in the later rounds when he appeared to tire.

It may be that the twenty-six-year-old Camacho can no longer sustain a fight the way he used to; or that his ego won't allow him to risk danger that can be outwitted or outwaited. Whatever. Camacho's hit-and-hold tactics grated on the crowd at the Lawlor Events Center—a partisan Mancini bunch that booed Camacho throughout the bout.

In contrast to Mancini, who literally ran from his corner at the start of rounds to do battle, and threw punches without letup (and often without landing), Camacho's caution was so calculating and extreme that it raised questions about his readiness for combats against the big-money opponents—Julio Cesar Chavez, Meldrick Taylor, Marlon Starling—to which, he forecast, the fight against Mancini would lead.

And while he may no longer satisfy those fans who want chills-and-thrills fights, Camacho still has the ability to provoke them. He is a presence—the closest thing his sport has to an old-fashioned villain. His Macho Man character, the Camacho of outrageous sequined loin-cloth trunks, of street wit and staged strut is, like the bad guys of wrestling, an enticement to the ticket buyer.

As Camacho put it at two o'clock in the morning at an impromptu party in an empty lounge at Bally's Casino Resort in Reno, "I'm the bad boy of boxing."

He raised his glass of Dom Perignon to the notion and laughed.

In February 1991, Camacho appeared to have lost his W.B.O. junior welterweight title to Greg Haugen, who was given a split-decision thanks to a twelfth-round point deduction from

Camacho's score by Carlos Padilla. A few days later, a reporter who'd spent a night watching a boxing card at the Forum in Inglewood, California, saw Camacho strut before the anti-Macho Man crowd there. Then, shortly after the bout, Camacho was standing with a friend on a street corner near the Forum when the same reporter pulled up to a stoplight in a car. Camacho saw the reporter and smiled, and then acknowledged the realities of his comedown. "No champ, no limo." But it turned out otherwise. Post-fight tests revealed traces of marijuana in Haugen's system. The W.B.O. vacated the title and mandated a rematch that Camacho won in May 1991. Possession of the title did not curb Camacho's appetite for the antic. Later in the year Florida police stopped Camacho because he was tooling down the highway in his Ferrari with his girlfriend, Amy Torres, astride him. On July 4, 1992, the couple had a son that was, as Camacho calls it, the product of that vehicular "wild thing."

BOBY CZYZ: White, Bright and Polite (1986)

When Bobby Czyz first appeared on television screens in the early 1980's he was depicted as a boxing Galahad: a good-looking, clean-cut kid who graduated sixth in a class of 335 students at Lakeland Regional High School in Wanaque, New Jersey, and just the sort of boxer that middle America could take to heart.

"Matinee idol" was the catchphrase that Lou Duva, the fighter's manager, and Duva's son, Dan, who frequently promoted Czyz's fights, used to fix him in a world ever conscious of image. "White, bright and polite" were the assets Czyz said he had going for him back then.

Beyond possessing the kind of personality that generates favorable television ratings—Czyz appeared four times on NBC in those days—he could fight, too. As a middleweight, he won his first twenty bouts (fifteen by knockout), including a major victory over Robbie Sims, the half-brother of Marvelous Marvin Hagler. The Czyz-Sims fight had a 12.4 rating, the highest daytime boxing rating that the network had gotten until then. "It looked like nothing could go wrong," said Czyz.

Things went wrong. On November 20, 1982, Czyz's world began to come undone. He lost that night for the first and only time of his professional career, a ten-round decision to Mustafa Hamsho. Had he won, Czyz would have been in line for a title shot against Hagler.

After the loss, Czyz's appeal as a television attraction declined and he entered a troubled period. The suicide of his father, Robert Sr., in June 1983, compounded the tailspin. In July 1984, Czyz was arrested in New Jersey after a dispute at the home of his fiancee's mother. He eventually pleaded guilty to a charge of burglary and was placed on four year's probation and ordered to pay a $3,500 fine. He also was ordered to obtain psychiatric help.

In the ring, he was fighting as a super middleweight and then as a light heavyweight. He did not lose after the Hamsho bout, but most of his victories came far from the boxing limelight.

Recently, though, Czyz came back to public notice when it was announced that he would fight Slobodon Kacar of Yugoslavia, the International Boxing Federation lightheavyweight champion, for the title in Las Vegas, Nevada on September 6. For the twenty-four-year-old Czyz, whose record is now 28-1 with nineteen knockouts, the way back has been a sobering experience.

The loss to Hamsho, according to Lou Duva, was brought on by Czyz's insistence on fighting his opponent from a southpaw stance rather than from his natural right-handed side. Czyz disputed that, saying that while he did have certain moves planned as a left-hander, an injury to his right hand during the bout forced him to compensate with more left-handed tactics than he had intended to use.

The real problem, said Czyz, was the trouble he was having making the 160-pound middleweight limit. "They were giving me water pills so I'd make the weight," he said. "Then after the weigh-in, I'd rehydrate. But there was a strength loss. The pills were debilitating. By the fifth or sixth round, I was tired against Mustafa. I never fought at 160 again."

That sort of charge and countercharge marked the gap between manager and fighter, but their most serious differences concerned money. "Bobby and his father were forever arguing over money with the Duvas," said Ferdie Pacheco, the boxing analyst for NBC. "It's a repetitive story in boxing. You bring someone along. Then the father insinuates himself in the situation and says: 'I'm the boss. I make the decisions.'"

Czyz said that Pacheco's is a "partially fair assessment."

"But let's face it," Czyz said. "My father wanted a fair shake for me. An injury and I could be out of business. If not him, then who should be concerned?"

Czyz's biggest purse under the Duvas was the $175,000 he and Lou Duva agree was paid him to fight Hamsho. After the Hamsho bout, though, Czyz and Duva rarely saw eye to eye on money, and the boxer was particularly concerned that when Duva, the manager, did business with his son, the promoter, it cost Czyz. "He was one of the best matchmakers, if not the best," Czyz said of his former manager. "And he could build you and make you a star. But he refused to pay."

Lou Duva and Czyz split in 1984. Duva claimed that while Czyz fought under him, the boxer made about $500,000 in purses, a figure Czyz said is too high. "We were marketing Bobby Czyz, and getting the good exposure for him," said Duva. "So when he talks about not enough money and collusion, he's crazy."

Pacheco said Czyz canceled two NBC fights, and became persona non grata at the network as a result. He sees the loss to Hamsho as a blow to Czyz's self-esteem from which Czyz did not quickly recover. "Then there was the great tragedy, his father's suicide," said Pacheco. "And rather than taking up the pieces, he was looking for excuses. Like Gerry Cooney after the loss to Larry Holmes."

Czyz reminisces about his complex relationship with his father.

"There's home movie footage of me at four years old," said the fighter, "throwing punches in front of the camera."

By the time Bobby was six, the elder Czyz had him working out in the basement and in an improvised backyard ring at their East Orange, New Jersey, home.

Originally, the objective was to instill in the boy the kind of discipline the father felt he himself had lacked as a youngster.

"My father was brought up on the street—his dad died when he was a child—and he got into a lot of trouble," said Bobby. "Stolen-car type stuff. Gang fights. He ended up doing time at a juvenile penal institution in New Jersey when he was fifteen, sixteen years old."

In an effort to insure that his three sons (Bobby was the oldest) would not repeat his mistakes, Czyz was a strict father. "I had to get straight A's in school or..." said Bobby. "I was taught how to respect elders, and how to behave. There was a right way, a wrong way and his way. I learned his way quite well."

With his father watching, Bobby learned his boxing lessons as he grew up. According to the fighter, his father (who had wanted to box when he was young) was "obsessed with perfection." Once, on learning that the fifteen-year-old Bobby had broken his leg in a gym class before an important amateur bout, the father overreacted.

"He was so upset that he punched me in the mouth," said Bobby.

In spite of such moments, the fighter said he loved and respected his father. But when Bobby later established a national reputation as a boxer, the elder Czyz apparently felt his paternal grip was loosening. There were arguments between father and son that reflected the difficulties in the changing relationship.

After one such argument, in June 1983, Bobby attempted to apologize for his harsh words but his father refused even to acknowledge him. "He was sitting in an easy chair and it was is if I wasn't there," said Bobby. "I can't remember him blinking or focusing on me once in thirty minutes. Finally, I just went to bed, figuring he'd be cooled down in the morning."

In the morning, Robert Czyz Sr. was found dead of a self-inflicted gunshot wound.

Czyz knocked out Kacar to win the IBF light heavyweight title in 1986. In 1991, following a short-lived retirement, Czyz stepped up in class and won the W.B.A. cruiserwieght title from Robert Daniels.

SUGAR RAY (1979)

The moon is dimming in the early-morning sky over Landover, Maryland, as two men appear at the top of a hilly street called Belle Haven.

One wears a rust-colored knit mask that covers his face except for slits where the eyes and mouth are supposed to be. The other has on a blue watch cap that is pulled back on his head, revealing a high-cheekboned dolorous face.

At the bottom of the hill is George Palmer Highway. On the corner is a shoe store designated as the place where they are to meet a pair of strangers—one with a note pad, the other with a camera—whom they find sitting on the hood of a rented car.

"Who you waiting for?" the one in the knit mask asks.

Told it's Sugar Ray they want, he rolls the mask up his face and smiles, an agreeable 100-kilowatt smile that has become as much Ray Leonard's trademark as the deft footwork and blurring combinations of punches that constitute his wage-earning skills.

At 5:52 A.M. on this cool spring day, there is good reason to be cheered at the thought of being Ray Charles Leonard. For as he and the other man, his fighter-brother Roger, cross George Palmer Highway on the start of a three-mile jaunt through Prince Georges County, Leonard is professional boxing's newest hero, an undefeated welterweight (147-pound limit), with high standing in the boxing rankings and in television's Nielsen ratings as well. The twenty-three-year-old Leonard has fought on all three major networks and Home Box Office, and has become a unique commodity, a contender whose box-office appeal exceeds that of most of the current champions. Already, the former gold medalist at the 1976 Montreal Olympics is being groomed as the man to fill the void created by the apparent retirement of Muhammad Ali. As the fight

291

game's newest hero, Leonard has rapidly progressed through the pro ranks—maneuvered by sharp boxing and business minds. With a 22-0 record, he is on the verge of a title shot, an opportunity he puts on the line this afternoon when he fights Tony Chiaverini, a rugged southpaw, on ABC-TV.

Leonard's appeal is based, in part, on a boxing style evocative of past crowd pleasers like Kid Gavilan and Ray Robinson (a.k.a. Sugar Ray) and Ali himself—fighters so smooth, so photogenic as to bring an element of art to a brutal sport. But there is more to the success of Leonard than his flash in the prizefight ring and the skein of victories—several over ranking fighters—that it has produced. Quite simply, Leonard, by the variable magic of personality, has become a hero, the reasons for which go beyond the euphonious name, the smile and the style.

"What everybody gets with Ray," says Eddie Hrica, a matchmaker from the Baltimore-Washington, D.C. area, "is the all-American boy. He loves Mom, apple pie, the American flag. His kind has been gone for a while. But Ray is bringing it back."

Warming to his subject, Hrica says, "There's a boy named Bobby Haburchak—maybe twelve, thirteen years old—who's a great fan of Ray's and comes to his fights in a wheelchair because he suffers from cerebral palsy. Well, Ray always makes it a point to spend time with him at each fight. One night, Ray gave the boy the set of gloves he fought with and autographed them. Bobby's mother wrote me. I've got the letter I think. Yes. Here. 'Dear Mr. Hrica. Thank you doesn't seem sufficient. If you could have seen how happy all of you made my boy. He is still riding high.'

"And the thing with Ray is he doesn't do things like this for show. One time Ray made money for a TV commercial and ended up donating it to the Palmer Park [Maryland] Recreation Center, where he learned boxing. Donated it so they could buy equipment. And it never got in the newspapers or anything.

"That's typical. With the money Ray's earned [in excess of $2 million to date], he's become the provider for his whole family. He could have said this is *all mine*. But instead he's taken over the role as the head of the family. I've never met anyone who did not like him or feel he was genuine."

In a business where the working stiffs utter slanders about one another as routinely as hello/goodbye, boxing men tend to sound out of character when speaking of Ray Leonard, resorting to the kind of nice-Nelly idioms more familiar to a church supper than the manly art. And yet such is Leonard's reputation that the truth compels these ready encomiums. In an era of athletes spoiled rotten by inflated salaries and given to outrageous egotism, Leonard is an anachronism: He is nice. A Joe Palooka. A straight shooter.

That he looks the part does not hurt either. Leonard is clean-cut and smooth-featured. And though he is by nature a private person, not covetous of the spotlight, he takes on a glow when he is before the public. The smile, the soft speech—reasoned and mostly grammatical—convey an essential decency.

Heroic in deed, Leonard is cut from ordinary dimensions. At 5 feet 9 1/2 inches, 147 pounds, he is not constructed with the brute force "V" torso of many fighters but along sleeker, merely mortal lines. After an epoch of the larger-than-life Ali, this is a swing back the other way.

The gym is in Capital Heights, Maryland, a white frame building set atop a sloping lawn. The sign says Oakcrest Community Center. Sugar Ray Leonard trains here. The place is a disappointment to those seeking the colorful seediness associated with the fight game. Oakcrest is a long, low-ceilinged room, clean and well-lighted. No debris clutters the floor. A sign reads: *Our gym is your gym. While you are using it, keep it C-L-E-A-N. [signed] Jake.*

"Jake" is David Jacobs, a balding sunny man whose portly figure belies the fact that he fought professionally as a feather-weight nearly thirty years ago. Jacobs trained Leonard as an amateur in Palmer Park and has stayed on in that role since Leonard turned pro.

Moving through Oakcrest—he is boxing director there—Jacobs has the clear-eyed serene manner of a man at peace with the world. Something of his role as a deacon in the Pentecostal Holiness Church in Washington, D.C. is reflected in the signs that proliferate among the fight posters at Oakcrest: "Any man that believes in God is a winner." and, "Do unto others as you would have them do unto you."

On the afternoon of Leonard's early hour roadwork, Jacobs is on his knees in the gym's green canvas ring, sparring with five-year-old Ray Charles Leonard Jr., who is frequently referred to as "The Little Sugar Man." A few weeks earlier, Sugar Ray's son had put on boxing mitts and tried them out by belaboring the ring posts, an experience he found so satisfying that he has insisted on regular workouts ever since.

On this day, Sugar Ray Sr. is seated outside the ring in street clothes as Jacobs circles on his knees, encouraging the boy ("There you go. Yessssirrr. Good shot.") to assault a padded red glove that the trainer wears. "Miss the glove and hit Jake one time," a ringsider jokes.

As Ray Jr. rests between rounds, an observer tries to trick him, shouting "Tiiime," the gym equivalent of a bell. The boy looks straight ahead, not budging. When Jacobs cries "Tiiime," he moves out smartly from his corner, his sharp-witted response provoking laughter.

Later, Leonard himself works out. He shadowboxes, hits heavy and speed bags, all in five-minute timed rounds. The session is conducted in a not overly martial atmosphere. Family and friends stop by and kibitz; laughter is not considered out of place. Even Roger Leonard, a prelim fighter who must box in his brother's considerable shadow, is able to joke about his lack of fame.

Jacobs: Roger, where's your black robe at?

Roger: I don't know. One of my many fans stole it.

Jacobs and others stagger around the gym in amusement. The laughter subsides: soon the workout is over. Jacobs peels the gauze wrapping from Ray's hands, telling him: "Gotta take care of them million-dollar hands."

"Two million, Jake," says Leonard, smiling. "Inflation."

In August 1976, when Ray Leonard returned to Palmer Park from the Olympics, his visions did not include the lofty finances of big-time boxing. After he won the gold medal, he told the press: "This is my last fight. My decision is final. My journey is ended. My dream fulfilled."

Back home, he planned to enroll in college and to enjoy the spoils of Olympics glory: his picture on the Wheaties box, subsidiary income rolling in. The reality fell short of that. Way short.

Days after his return to Palmer Park, *The Washington Star* ran a story under a bold-faced headline that read: "SUGAR RAY'S PATERNITY SUIT." The "suit" came about after Juanita Wilkinson, the mother of Ray Jr., applied for public assistance. At the time, Leonard (who never denied paternity) was in Montreal. As the *Star*'s ombudsman, George Beveridge, later wrote: "First impressions are important. And standing alone, [that headline] could well have suggested to readers that the question of Leonard's paternity might itself be at issue. It wasn't—the 'suit' to affirm legal paternity was, as the story said, a part of the mechanism required in Maryland to determine an applicant's eligibility for public assistance."

Things were to grow worse. Leonard's sudden celebrity brought out the schemers and scam men, with offers and ideas supposedly to enhance Ray's fiscal position. But when it got down to the gritty particulars, Leonard's end of things somehow was always on hold.

The irony was that Ray was running himself ragged, driving long distances to speak to school-age audiences for free. At the same time, he was finding that his Olympic celebrity was yesterday's news. Accompanying his insurance salesman friend Janks Morton, thirty-nine, on his daily rounds, Leonard was often met by blank stares when he was introduced to prospective policyholders.

Though he had declared he was through fighting, people tried to change Leonard's mind. He and Morton went to New York in late September 1976 as guests of fight promoter Don King at the Ali-Ken Norton championship fight and came back with an offer to turn pro. Other offers followed. By now, Morton, a college football player who had himself tried but failed to make it professionally with the Cleveland Browns, moved to get Leonard's life in order. He brought Ray to Michael G. Trainer, a Silver Spring, Maryland, attorney, to sort out the complications that had arisen after Leonard's success at Montreal.

Working for several months without a fee, Trainer hired a publicist to sift through requests for personal appearances. And he himself screened offers involving commercial possibilities, circumspectly asking all callers to put their proposals in writing, a request that killed off most of the deadbeats.

Leonard's life simplified, but he now was having second thought about boxing. Before the Olympics, his mother had suffered a minor heart affliction. And now his father required hospitalization for a lingering serious illness. "I saw," says Leonard, "that the family was not moving." He also saw the obvious. Ray Charles Leonard was about to be Sugar Ray again.

There was one hitch, though. As an amateur, Leonard had chafed when professional fight managers referred to their charges as "my fighter" or "my boy"—the possessive pronoun had a demeaning sound to him. So while he wanted to turn pro, he did not want to be owned.

That obstacle was overcome after Trainer remembered that he had borrowed money from a bank to launch himself as a lawyer. He decided to put together a group of backers that would lend Sugar Ray the capital to get started and would receive in turn 8 percent interest on the loan.

As word of his idea got out, Trainer was so besieged with calls from interested parties he convened a public meeting. "What happened," he says, "was, I guess, predictable. A traveling salesman—he sold jewelry—said he'd put money up if Ray would go on the road and help him sell twice a week. A retail store owner wanted Ray to work the floor once a week. I told them to get out, adjourned the meeting and decided to ask only friends and clients for the money."

Trainer got twenty-four people to kick in $21,000, and then incorporated the fighter as Sugar Ray Leonard Inc. "I issued all the stock to Ray," he says, "and signed him to a personal services contract with the corporation."

The wheels were in motion. Jacobs signed as Leonard's trainer. Morton became assistant trainer and adviser. Trainer agreed to continue handling business matters. Only one thing was lacking: expertise in the pro boxing business. "The only way I could see

Ray being sidetracked," says Trainer, "was if we got snookered. We needed someone who knew the business inside and out. We wanted every edge we could have."

Enter Angelo Dundee.

Angelo Dundee is a small, wiry, fifty-six-year-old, most noted for being the trainer of Muhammad Ali.

Angelo is an old-school boxing man. In 1948, he quit his job as an inspector of naval aircraft in Philadelphia and moved to New York, living and sleeping in the Capital Hotel office of his brother Chris, then a fight manager. The hotel was catty-corner from the old Madison Square Garden on Eighth Avenue (between 49th and 50th Streets) and was a few blocks from Stillman's Gym.

At Stillman's—and in boxing arenas—Dundee was educated by a now vanishing breed of wily trainers. Angelo got an eyeful and in time became an expert at maneuvering a boxing career. A fighter of Angelo's is not apt to be snookered. Nor is he likely to be over-matched. Dundee has a wide-ranging knowledge of opponents. And what he doesn't know he can find out. Angelo is an easy-going man, who tells you, "Costs nothing to be nice." As a result of that congenial outlook, Dundee's friends in boxing are legion. In a pinch, he can phone anywhere in the country or to Latin America and get the lowdown on a prospective opponent.

The sentiment among boxing people is that Dundee has done his job well, that Leonard has grown as a fighter in a series of measured tests. *Slow-teach*, Dundee calls it. Others refer to it as *the thumbscrew principle*. By either label, it refers to the small and calculated risk an astute manager exposes his fighter to in each opponent, hoping his man has the "reach"—the ability to stretch his skills to meet the increasing challenges.

Dundee's approach has brought Leonard to worldclass status— he is ranked number three by the World Boxing Council and number two by the World Boxing Association. Frequently, though, Leonard has outrun Angelo's slow-teach pace. In March 1978, for instance, Dundee matched Leonard against Javier Muniz. Muniz had gone the distance in a ten-round bout against Roberto Duran, the hard-punching former lightweight champion, a certifiable indication, Dundee felt, of the staying power he wanted Leonard's next foe to have. Sugar Ray knocked Muniz out in two minutes and forty-five seconds of the first round.

Against most foes, Leonard has been simply too quick and too clever. "Ray's success," says Dundee, "is based on doing what he has to do to be champ. He never flubs on his roadwork or rest. He don't burn the candle. He's clean-living. Family-oriented. And he's a little like Muhammad—he's a student of boxing. You should see him studying boxing films. I think he's happiest when he's sitting in front of the TV with the Betamax and a bunch of cassettes of different fights."

For his pro debut in February 1977 against Luis (The Bull) Vega, CBS-TV paid Leonard $10,000. Sugar Ray added $30,000 more from his share of the $72,320 gate. By March he was in the enviable position of owning himself.

Trainer's approach with his incorporated fighter has been to maintain nearly complete control of Leonard's commercial potential, rather than relying on fight promoters to stimulate his revenues (and take the lion's share of the profits).

"O.K.," says Trainer. "Let's say you want to promote a Leonard fight. Forget TV. We get all the TV money, though we'll black out your market. As promoter, you'll work off the gate. But before we walk in, we get a guarantee [in a letter of credit]—and we'll also end up with a percentage of the gate—usually at least half of the net profits.

"I'll ask you to figure what it will take for you to make a buck. I might say, 'How much do you want to make?' If it's consistent with our own ideas I'll say, 'Go ahead and make the fight.'"

The margin of profits—Trainer claims promoters average $10,000 to $15,000 profits per bout—is considered too small for boxing's two major promoters, Bob Arum and Don King. And this suits Trainer fine. Part of his scenario is to keep Leonard free of the entanglements that Arum and King weave when they secure options to the services of both boxers signed to a title bout. Trainer insists that any deal for a future championship bout will exclude options on his fighter's service. "They may turn around," Trainer concedes, "and say, 'Well, you won't get the fight.' But I don't think so. Money has a way of taking care of things. And whoever promotes a Ray Leonard title fight would make a lot of money."

Leonard's drawing power appears to support Trainer's theory. In his very first pro fight, against Vega, Sugar Ray attracted 10,170 people to the Baltimore Civic Center, a boxing record for that arena. This past January he broke his own Capital Centre (Landover, Maryland) record when he TKO'd Johnny Gant before 19,743 fans. Six of Leonard's first ten bouts were in the Baltimore-D.C. area. Since then, he has fought regularly outside his home base—mostly for unknown promoters, some of whom are curious additions to boxing.

Dan Doyle is the thirty-year-old head coach of the basketball team at Trinity College in Hartford, Connecticut. While working on his doctoral thesis on sports administration, he began promoting athletic events in Hartford, Springfield, Massachusetts and Providence, Rhode Island. Eventually he approached Trainer and asked to promote a Leonard fight in Hartford: "I think Trainer was interested intellectually in what I was trying to do. But he was also pleased with the $12,000 guarantee I offered, back when not every boxing guy thought Sugar Ray was worth that kind of up-front money."

Doyle's Hartford event on June 10, 1977—it was Leonard's third pro fight—grossed $40,000, according to the promoter. Since then Doyle has staged Leonard bouts in Providence, Springfield, New Haven and Portland, Maine. The Portland bout—Sugar Ray won a ten-round decision from Bernardo Prada there on November 3, 1978—had a reported gate of nearly $54,000 and a state record crowd of 6,000 fans, more paid admissions than even Ali and Sonny Liston managed in their return title match in Lewiston, Maine, in 1965.

"Places like Portland," says Trainer, "are necessary. People in Detroit, Cleveland, other big cities, look at what Ray draws in Portland, and think: 'If he does that kind of business there, imagine what he can do for us.' It makes it an easier sell."

Trainer can afford to experiment with his markets because Leonard's purses are usually sweetened by television revenues. Television has been the key to Sugar Ray's growth as a fight attraction. At the outset of his career, he signed a six-bout nonexclusive agreement with ABC-TV for a reported $320,000. (A new five-bout nonexclusive agreement for an undisclosed amount was signed early this year.) Leonard's appearances on NBC-TV, CBS-TV and Home Box Office are also part of Trainer's idea of leaving his options open.

At present, the welterweight division has two champions—the W.B.A.'s Jose (Pipino) Cuevas and the W.B.C.'s Wilfredo Benitez. Cuevas is a brutally effective puncher whose blows have hospitalized foes. As former Madison Square Garden assistant matchmaker Bruce Trampler says: "Fight Cuevas? God bless you. This guy throws rocks." Leonard's title shot is more likely to be against Benitez.

Benitez, who is twenty-years-old, has grown beyond welterweight proportions. For his last title defense this past March against Harold Weston, Benitez was forced to lose fourteen pounds in five days to make the 147-pound limit. By next year he is expected to be fighting among the middleweights (160-pound limit). A bout against Leonard makes sense for Benitez's last hurrah as a welterweight. Sugar Ray is the only foe who can carry him to prime-time money.

Leonard now draws a six-figure annual salary as the sole employee of Sugar Ray Leonard Inc. In addition, a pension fund, maximally funded, has been set up. Other monies have been invested in real estate, such as apartment houses, and tax free bonds. "I'm a conservative individual," says Trainer. "I wear dark blue or gray suits. I don't own stock. Neither does Ray. I'm more careful with his money than mine. His pension plan is in bank certificates of deposit and Government securities. The money's going to be there."

Ray Charles Leonard was born May 17, 1956, in Wilmington, North Carolina, one of seven children. His father, Cicero, moved the family to Washington, D.C. when Ray was four. The Leonards struggled. As the fighter's mother, Getha, a warm effusive woman, recalls: "I worked at night as a nursing assistant at a convalescent center, and my husband worked in the produce market from 2

A.M. to 10 A.M., loading trucks. The children took care of themselves. "I wanted Ray to be a singer, I named him after [rhythm and blues singer] Ray Charles. As a boy, he was a little shy guy. I never had to go to school because of problems with him. Ray was good. He sang with two of my daughters in church, and people said he sounded like [rock'n'roll singer] Sam Cooke. He sang till he was fourteen-and-a-half. Then his older brother Roger turned him over to boxing. And like Ray used to tell me, 'Mamma, I put the singing into swinging.'"

By the time Ray turned to boxing, the family had moved to Palmer Park, a small beltway community. Even then, he was, as trainer Jacobs discovered, still a shy individual: "Very bashful. Like you'd explain something to him, he couldn't look at you. He'd look to the side or drop his head."

The shyness stemmed from a boyhood of poverty. "A feeling of inferiority," says Leonard, "from not having anything. There were never clothes to wear. Or money for things as simple as school field trips—like $1.25 to go to the Smithsonian. On days there were field trips, I wouldn't go to school. Even lunch money was a problem. In our family, there were always bills, always bills."

As a boxing beginner, Leonard took his lumps for a while. Getha Leonard recalls her son's coming home from the gym with black eyes and swollen lips: "I'd say, 'Hey, you wanna stop?' He'd say, 'No, Mama, I'm going on.' Each night that he'd come home like that I'd go in the room and cry."

In time, Leonard was the one handing out the lickings as an amateur boxer. By 1974, he'd caught promoter Hrica's eye. "Even at that date," says Hrica, "I thought he could beat the best pros we had around the area. Like Johnny Gant, who fought for the W.B.A. welterweight title. That's how good Ray was. I proposed his turning pro. But Dave Jacobs had other ideas. He told me, 'No, Eddie. This kid's going to win the Olympics.'"

The flash of Sugar Ray in the prizefight ring—right down to the prefight kisses he throws the crowd—is part of his boxing persona, a creation that, but for Leonard's graciousness, would verge on being secondhand Ali. Out of the ring, though, the strut disappears and the image changes. He becomes the classic case of the sports star as a good guy.

He is conscious of the image and says that it is based on respect: "If you give respect, you receive it." What worried him most about *The Washington Star* brouhaha was how it would affect his standing with young people. For many athletes, helping small fry is obligatory P.R. But Leonard's concern seems real enough. Without coaxing, boxing people cite the unpublicized visits to amateur gyms that Leonard makes to affirm the hopes of others.

The evidence is that though he is a pleasing presence in public he is not an eager one. "I consider myself," he says, "a loner. I have a couple of friends. But in my mind, I'm a loner."

Hrica: "Ray would like to be left alone. But he realizes that the limelight is part of the business. He indicated to me once that he used to like to go to dances. But now he can't go as Ray Leonard. Now he's Sugar Ray. Everyone wants to talk with him."

Dundee: "Ray enjoys little things. Sitting down, rapping with the guys he grew up with. Meeting the amateur fighters. Being with his family." (Leonard lives with his high-school sweetheart, Juanita Wilkinson—she wears his engagement ring; no wedding date has been set—and Ray Jr. in a two-bedroom apartment in Greenbelt, not far from the home he bought his parents in Landover.)

Trainer: "When we interviewed people for the job Angelo Dundee has, some of them wanted Ray to relocate in places like New York and Philadelphia. That was out of the question. Ray Leonard wants to stay here."

Jacobs: "He's a home boy. Four, five days away and he wants to come home."

Though others characterize Leonard with words like "decent," "level-headed," "mature," "sincere," he is not a caricature of the type, a Goody Two-shoes. He has what Steve Eisner, a fight promoter from Arizona, calls compuscture. "Compuscture," says Eisner, "is a word I used to hear in Detroit among fight people. They mistakenly combined composure and posture, as in, 'He lost his compuscture.' Or, 'That cat got real compuscture.' Somehow, though, I like the word better than the one it was trying to be, that is—'presence'"

Leonard has presence—and more. "Let me tell you a story," says Eisner. "I wear a pair of diamond-studded boxing gloves around my neck. They're worth a fortune. Fighters are impressed by diamonds. And a lot of them have asked me to get them a pair. But I never would break out the mold until Ray asked. He came on straight-up, said, 'I'd really like to own a pair of those gloves.' I felt comfortable saying I own a pair and he has the other. So sometime later, I had the designer make another pair. When I told Ray, he seemed really touched. And because I had remembered, he was almost in tears. His eyes were definitely watery."

Tucson, Arizona. It is Sugar Ray versus Daniel Gonzalez, a world-ranking boxer from Argentina. The afternoon of the bout, last March 24, mariachi musicians are serenading the patrons in the expensive seats of the Tucson Community Center. In the ring, a peewee bout finishes, followed by a local tradition—the tossing of coins and crumpled bills to the grade-school gladiators.

Away from the tumult, off a narrow corridor of the arena, Sugar Ray sits in room 135-1.

Meanwhile, promoter Eisner is wondering about Angelo Dundee. "Before he showed up in Tucson," says Eisner, "he sent me three pairs of Everlast gloves, one of which Ray Leonard was to use. Now he tells me he wants a different brand—Reyes, a Mexican glove. Everlast gloves have more padding around the knuckles. Reyes are more uniformly padded, which means they make more impact when they strike. I tell him, 'Hey, Angelo, Reyes are a puncher's gloves. Your guy's not a puncher.' Angelo says to me, 'You may be surprised, my friend.'"

"See, what happened," says Dundee, "is I walk into 134-1, Gonzalez's room. I notice there are a lot of guys in there. Lotta guys. Too many. Because of that, I notice Gonzalez hasn't been able to warm up properly. He's not sweating. And, my friend, that's a no-no."

Dundee returns to room 135-1, tells Leonard: "This guy is cold as ice, nail him."

Sugar Ray nails him in round one with a quick left-right combination that knocks Gonzalez down. He rises glassy-eyed and spits out his mouthpiece. He is in orbit. Leonard finishes him with a right-left-right combination two minutes and three seconds into the fight.

At ringside, some news photographers (who did not see the blows causing the first knockdown through their viewers) are suspicious about the results. In 135-1, though, there are no complaints, except from Getha Leonard. "They gave me five milligrams of tranquilizer," she says, "and it hasn't even taken hold." A few minutes later, her son, Ray Charles Leonard, wearing a training suit and richer by more than $200,000, walks out of the arena. He does not need a shower.

In April in Las Vegas, Leonard decisions Adolfo Viruet. A month later in Baton Rouge, he wins his twenty-second straight victory with another decision—this one over Marcos Geraldo.

By early summer, negotiations had begun for a year-end Benitez-Leonard title fight. For Sugar Ray, everything is still no sweat.

Leonard did fight Benitez for the W.B.C. welterweight title, in November 1979, and scored a fifteenth round knockout. He would go on to win the W.B.A. junior middleweight title by knocking out Ayub Kalule in nine rounds in June 1981, and then unify the welterweight division by knocking out Thomas Hearns in fourteen rounds that September. In 1982, Leonard declared he was retiring from boxing because of a medically-repaired detached retina.

THE FIGHT BEFORE THE FIGHT (1986)

"The best thing Marvin Hagler has going for him, his special quality, is that he's a proud champion. He's a rare breed. He loves his craft. He walks into the ring with the kind of vanity that a select few movie stars have. Not like some guys—certain heavyweights—who look like used cars."—Ray Leonard on the world middleweight champion, March 1986, one and a half months before Leonard declared he would come out of retirement if Hagler would agree to fight him.

Not long ago, in a dressing room one flight up at the Sugar Ray Leonard Boxing Center in Palmer Park, Maryland, images of Hagler fighting Roberto Duran flickered across a color television screen.

Ray Leonard, dressed in an olive-green military flight suit he had bought in a Los Angeles boutique, watched the video cassette replay of the November 1983 bout that Hagler had won, unimpressively, by decision.

Boxing gear was strewn across the floor. A sparring partner of Leonard was packing his gym bag to leave. Aides of the former champion came and went.

On the TV screen, Duran eluded a Hagler punch by deftly moving his head out of range.

"That's the key," said Leonard. "Making him miss."

"Every time Hagler loads up," said Dave Jacobs, Leonard's trainer, "Duran slips him. He's slipping beautifully."

"Isn't he!" agreed Leonard. Turning to a reporter, he said: "It's the movement that does it. Not a lot of it. Just enough."

And so it went on a brisk autumn afternoon in Palmer Park. Using a remote-control device, Leonard played and replayed the

305

images of Duran foiling Hagler through shrewd defensive feints, occasionally followed by counterpunches that landed cleanly.

On the screen, sometimes slowed, sometimes frozen for his scrutiny, was a Hagler who was not the regal pug that Leonard had described back in March but rather a fallible athlete, a Hagler edited to merely mortal dimensions. A Hagler as necessary for Ray Charles Leonard to conjure up as the quarry for the hunter.

For in his mind, the fight against Hagler, scheduled for April 6 in Las Vegas, had already begun.

Leonard's mind—and what it can muster for him—should not be discounted as he embarks on what many see as a fool's mission. That view of his return to the ring is a conventional one and has a certain amount of supporting data behind it with which a regular-thinking man can feel comfortable.

Who but a wildly deluded soul would think to jump back in the ring against the master fighter of the day when all he could claim for ring readiness was two fights in five years, and those against very ordinary foes?

In February 1982 he knocked out Bruce Finch in three rounds. In early May of that year, Leonard was operated on for a detached retina of his left eye that would prompt his retirement from boxing in November 1982.

While out of the ring he worked as a commentator on boxing telecasts for CBS-TV—often teamed with Gil Clancy—and for Home Box Office, and he attended to commitments from his commercial endorsements (Franklin Sporting Goods, Devon Stores and Carnation Hot Chocolate).

Then, in May 1984, Leonard came out of retirement to fight a journeyman named Kevin Howard.

"The night he announced he was coming back," said Alex Wallau, ABC-TV's boxing analyst, "I was with him, waiting for a limo to take him to a TV studio in Washington, D.C., for a half-time appearance on Monday Night Football. And he said to me, 'What do you think?'

"'I think you're crazy,' I told him. 'Obviously it's your decision. But the thing that interests me is the motivation—why you're doing it.' He told me that it was the discipline of boxing that he missed. I got the sense he was just drifting without boxing. I was impressed by that. I thought it was pretty thoughtful."

Against Howard, Leonard showed the ring rust. Howard knocked Leonard down in the fourth round before the former champion stopped him in the ninth. The performance was hardly vintage Leonard, and he was so disappointed that he announced afterward he was retiring again.

"In retrospect," said Mike Trainer, Leonard's attorney, "it probably was not the best time to be deciding anything. I'm not so sure he'd have felt the same if he waited."

Leonard returned to analyzing fights for HBO (his deal with CBS expired and was not renewed). Then, when Trainer became the manager in 1984 of a Canadian Olympic medalist, Shawn O'Sullivan, Leonard got increasingly involved in that fighter's development. He went from being a ringside observer to an unpaid cornerman of O'Sullivan, and even began sparring with the welterweight to give his advice a hands-on authority.

"To stay in the ring," said Trainer, "he found he had to get in shape. Running and going to the health spa, which was what he had been doing, were not enough to be in boxing shape. Remember: I never asked him to spar. He volunteered. But I thought it was great because I know he had had the itch about getting back in the ring. I figured with Shawn he'd get it out of his system. He'd get banged and that'd solve it."

It might have solved it had Hagler not still been active. With Hagler's fights routinely shown on HBO, Leonard, as commentator, was at ringside for them. Watching Hagler—whom he regarded as a special fighter—he would project Ray Leonard as the opponent. "I can whip the sucker," Leonard would tell HBO colleagues.

"Marvin," said Trainer, "was the only one Ray considered in his class. Down deep, Ray resented the fact that he had not fought him."

On the very afternoon that Leonard, now thirty years old, was reviewing the footage of the Hagler-Duran fight, he was already deep into prepaing for Hagler. Before he hunkered down in front of the TV screen, Leonard would work twelve rounds against alternating sparring partners, Robert (Boo Boo) Sawyer, a welterweight, and against Charles Ingram, a middleweight who turned pro last month. Twelve rounds of slick stick-and-move tactics that had Jacobs and Janks Morton, another of the fighter's corner men, murmuring, "All right, all right, beautiful."

Yet to the general public and even to many boxing men, Leonard's return seems not all right at all. For them, the former undisputed welterweight and World Boxing Association junior middleweight champion appears a victim of hubris, a fatal sort of pride. The earliest Las Vegas betting line, which made Leonard a 4-1 underdog, served to strengthen that perception, and Leonard's refusal to fight a tune-up bout ("Hagler is my tune-up," he said) has made few converts.

But the smug orthodoxy of his critics is precisely what fuels the fighter's sense of mission. "The reason I will win is because you don't think I can," he said at the news conference last month in New York where formal announcement of the fight was made.

In Palmer Park, as he watched Hagler, who is listed as thirty-two years old, box Duran on the TV screen, he added: "I know a lot of critics think what I'm doing is crazy and ludicrous. But they never had a pair of gloves on. They can't relate. For me to win is everything. That's what gives me additional strength.

Leonard's critics, seeking to account for his ambitious scheme, have wondered aloud whether he has come back to the fight game because his money ran short—Leonard has reportedly been guaranteed $11 million to fight Hagler—or because rampant egoism required him once again to have the adulation of a crowd.

According to Trainer, the fighter earned $40 million to $45 million during his career, up to $2 million of which came from endorsements and other subsidiary earnings.

"He could live off just the interest of his money, off what it earns every year," Trainer said, fixing that interest at "close" to seven figures annually. "It's based on bonds and real estate investments. It's a generous income."

Leonard lives in Potomac, Maryland, an affluent suburb of Washington, in a $1 million home that, in Trainer's phrase, "looks like a mini-castle," a reference to a turreted corner of the stone residence. Set on two and a half acres, Leonard's house has five bed-rooms, a wine cellar, a screening room and a swimming pool. In the driveway are a mini-fleet of his cars, including a red Ferrari, a black Rolls-Royce and a white BMW.

But when Leonard became one of several partners in Jameson's, a restaurant that opened late last year in Bethesda, Maryland it fueled speculation that his partnership in the restaurant had put him in fiscal jeopardy.

Trainer, who is also a partner in the restaurant, adamantly denied that Leonard was at risk. "He has no money invested," the attorney said. "If the place went belly up, Ray wouldn't lose a dime. He became a partner as a favor to me. All he has to do is eat there and sign autographs." Yet against the denials, skeptics persist in their belief that only the almighty dollar could nudge a fighter of Leonard's caliber back into the ring. At the news conference in New York, there was this exchange between the fighter and a sports columnist.

Q. Why are you doing it? Ego? Money?

A. All of the above. I need the money. And it's ego.

Q. Do you need money?

A. I'm broke.

Q. Is this a serious press conference?

A. Yes.

Q. Then you don't have money?

A. Except what's in a trust fund. But thanks for your concern.

For a man who is uncommonly gracious in public, who even adds a curlicued smiling face to the autographs he gives, such face-tiousness seemed out of character. But with Leonard, questions about his financial state—questions he declines to address in specifics—apparently touch a nerve when they bracket him with the stereotypical fighter obliged to return to the ring because of a cash shortage.

Nothing insults him more than to make him out to be a pug. Leonard has always regarded himself as a special case, and during a pro career that began in March 1977 has made a point of acting that way.

He avoided extreme promotional entanglements, made the lion's share of the live gates for which he fought and kept his own counsel. For instance, after he lost to Duran in June 1980, the only defeat on his 33-1 record (24 knockouts), Jacobs advised him to take a tune-up bout to restore his confidence. Leonard declined to do so; their differences on the matter reportedly led Jacobs to depart as Leonard's trainer.

But Leonard's instinct about what was right for him proved correct. Without a tune-up fight, he defeated Duran in a November 1980 rematch that became famous for the abrupt "no mas" exit Duran made in the eighth round.

Leonard rejects the word "comeback" for what he is doing. Mere fighters assay comebacks, and do so for easily deciphered reasons, like money. An artiste—the view he has of himself—takes on a "challenge" and does so to excite his soul.

"Hagler's the ultimate, the Olympics of my professional career," said Leonard, an allusion to the gold medal he won at the 1976 Montreal Olympics to cap his amateur career.

"I never left boxing," he said. "This is my job. This is what made me. Boxing has been beneficial to me and my family." He and his wife, Juanita, have two sons, Ray Jr., thirteen, and Jarrel, two. "Boxing opened doors. I love the sport. For me, fighting Hagler is like entertainers who stay in the business, the same principle."

As with most athletes, Leonard is not without a degree of vanity, a quality that he has ascribed, favorably, to Hagler. Leonard's vanity tends toward an easygoing and sometimes self-mocking quality. Back in May, when his fight with Hagler was but an invitation, Leonard said that if the bout did not happen, no problem. With the gym work he had been doing he would look good in his designer jeans.

The athlete's vanity obliged him during his "retirement" to keep in shape by running several times a week and, eventually, by working out in a boxing gym. It led him to feel more restless every time, in his HBO job, he covered a Hagler fight.

In March, after Hagler's difficult bout against John (The Beast) Mugabi, Leonard heard Hagler hint at retirement and, realizing

time was running short for the challenge, he set the Hagler-
Leonard match in motion by saying he wanted it.

Back in the upstairs dressing room in Palmer Park, the tape of
the Hagler-Duran bout rolled forward and back. On the screen, at
the bell ending a round, Duran shouldered Hagler contemptuously
and stalked back to his corner.

Leonard, a smile playing across his lips, tapped the side of his
head.

"You can't be intimidated," he said.

"That's right," said Jacobs. "And we're gonna do some things
to Marvin that's never been done before."

Ray Leonard listened, and then nodded. In a fighter's mind,
where hope lives and dies, he was easily persuaded.

MARVELOUS MARVIN HAGLER
Boxing's Angry Man (1987)

Marvelous Marvin Hagler is out of sorts.

Inside a ring set up in a 50-by-75 tent in Palm Springs, California, Hagler is miffed because his sparring partner, James Lucas, is showing too little of the shifty footwork and punching flurries that mark the style of Hagler's next opponent, Sugar Ray Leonard.

So Hagler does what he must: He whacks the laggardly Lucas a couple of heavy-handed blows on the head and, through his mouthpiece, growls, "Come on. Speed, speed. Come on."

For Hagler—a fearsome-looking, well-muscled, shaven-headed man—that is a relatively benign response compared with the white-heat rage he is capable of displaying when a fight is for real.

"Elemental" is the word to describe Hagler's mind-set when he is in the ring. "Destruct and destroy" are, in his words, the objective. That fighters build up a spirited dislike for their opposition in order to induce hostile intentions in themselves is, of course, not late-breaking news. But Hagler's enmity toward his opponents seems to be in a class by itself, so pure and incorruptible is his hatred.

An anecdote. In his earlier days, Hagler had admired the Panamanian fighter Roberto Duran, who, in his fiercely direct approach to boxing, embodied traits that Hagler himself coveted. In 1983, Hagler was to appear with Leonard on a Bob Hope television special, but Leonard canceled and Duran, who was training in the United States at the time, agreed to replace him.

That should have been an occasion for two formidable champions to become acquainted. But Duran, a former lightweight and welterweight titleholder preparing at the time to fight Davey

Moore for the World Boxing Association junior middleweight crown, made a fatal mistake. After meeting Hagler and observing that he was about as tall as the 5-foot, 9 1/2-inch Hagler, Duran said to his manager, Luis Spada, "I almost tall like Marvin. I fight him." When Hagler heard that, he treated Duran to the narrow-eyed squint he directs at opponents and, turning his back to him, would speak not a word more.

"You know how fighters two, three years after they fight become friends," says Bob Arum, Hagler's promoter. "Not Marvin. Believe me, Marvin Hagler still hates every one of his opponents. If [Vito] Antuofermo comes into the room, he won't talk to him. Duran? Forget it. [Mustafa] Hamsho, he can't stand. It's not for effect. With him, it carries over forever. If he sees Tommy Hearns, he won't go near Tommy. 'Get him out of my face. What the hell is he doing here?' 'Marvin, the fight's over.' 'The hell it's over.'"

For boxing's angry man, the next fight—his thirteenth title defense—will be the biggest of his career. On April 6, at Caesars Palace in Las Vegas, Hagler (62-2-2, 52 knockouts), the thirty-two-year-old reigning star of boxing, faces Ray Leonard (33-1, 24 knock-outs), the thirty-year-old former welterweight and W.B.A. junior middleweight champion who is returning to the ring after a three-year absence. Both rank among the great champions.

It is an engagement that promises to be as much of an "event" as the World Series, the Super Bowl, the Olympics, Bobby Riggs vs. Billie Jean King. When the 15,336 tickets for the twelve-round showdown between the two great champions were put on sale in November by Caesars, they sold out within a month.

Far from Vegas, the bout has captured a constituency broader than boxing matches have known in the past. According to Arum, who is promoting the fight, the interest that women, for instance, have shown in buying tickets to closed-circuit outlets has been far greater for this fight than for the myriad other matches he has promoted, including Muhammad Ali's.

In the United States and Canada, three million people are expected to watch the fight on closed circuit television. The diversity of the audience can be gauged just by looking at the closed-circuit sites in New York City. They range from the honky-tonk movie houses of West 42nd Street to the New York Athletic Club on Central Park South to the Palladium, the trendy nightspot on 14th Street.

When Hagler vs. Leonard was formally announced in November, Bob Arum predicted that the fight would gross $100 million. At the time, most boxing people thought Arum's figure was heavily inflated to boost box-office sales. Whatever. Hagler is guaranteed a reported $12 million and a percentage of the gross; Leonard gets a reported $11 million and a percentage of the closed-circuit revenues for the District of Columbia-Maryland area (he and his family live in Potomac, Maryland).

The appeal of Hagler vs. Leonard goes beyond the mere expertise of the fighters. With these men, there is the matter of two sharply contrasting personalities.

Hagler sees himself as a boxing outcast. A man with blue-collar beginnings, he looks askance at princely types who never soil their hands. He calls Leonard "Mr. Politician," "Mr. Middle Class," caustic labels by which he means to convey a Leonard whose populist manner—the easy smile, the gracious ease before strangers—is a hype, built on image-making rather than substance. "He is a phony," says Hagler. "He's been protected all his life. Besides, if he hadn't become a boxer, he could have done other things. Me? I had nowhere else to go."

Through much of Hagler's career, in fact, Leonard was a special case in boxing, a hero whose success seemed practically preordained. Not only that, but Leonard's progress through the ranks—largely on his own terms—seemed to mock Hagler's struggle. For instance, in June 1977, both men appeared on the same card in Hartford, each scoring a quick knockout. For his victory, Hagler earned $1,500 in what amounted to his thirty-sixthth fight as a professional. Leonard got $40,000 for the third fight of his career.

When the two men embarked on a twelve-city publicity tour shortly after the current match was announced, their behavior remained true to form. As they traveled from city to city, Leonard would praise Hagler for the great champion that he was—leaving Hagler's emotional tank on empty. "At least Hearns said he was going to knock my block off," Hagler would complain. Since the sweet talk didn't fit his program, Hagler—midway in the tour—altered its content. He left.

"Deep down I've been bothering him," Hagler now says. "Something about me is bothering him. He sees me all over, doing 'Punky Brewster' on TV, the commercials. That's me. I just keep doing what I do—winning and taking care of my family."

Apart from the pronounced differences in the two men's personal styles, the Hagler-Leonard match has a large element of mystery going for it. Can a fighter as formidable as Hagler be overcome by a man who has been away from his sport as long as Leonard has? Leonard's leap back into boxing—no tuneup bout for him—seems, at first blush, so improbable as to be doomed to failure. Yet, such is Sugar Ray Leonard's mystique that his challenge of a champion as powerful and resourceful as Hagler has become credible.

When the fight was announced, the bookmakers made Hagler the four-to-one favorite, but the odds have since dropped to five to two. What has probably tilted the odds is the often-contradictory pronouncements about the fighters' ring styles by laymen and boxing people alike.

Leonard's tactics are expected to be aimed at frustrating Hagler in the ring. "That's the key," says Leonard. "Hagler is very tight, very sensitive, very rigid. That's his mentality."

Hagler is not as nimble on his feet as Leonard, but he is a skilled boxer. Through most of his title defenses, he would box his opponents at long range and then, when the toll of punches had reduced them appreciably, move in for the kill. Against Duran in November 1983, though, he was criticized for being too conservative, especially since the fight went the fifteen-round distance. He took the criticism to heart. In the April 1985 fight against Thomas Hearns, Hagler launched a savage attack right from the outset. For that bout, he wore a cap with the word "WAR" on it; for the April 6 match, there is a "WAR II" cap. The feeling from Hagler's camp is that in the forthcoming match push will come to shove very quickly if Hagler has his way.

In a sport in which champions tend to acquire entourages and to lead lives so complicated that they become harmful to their careers, Hagler is an exception.

His prescribed regimen is to train hard, fight hard and then retreat into a zealously guarded private life in Hanover, Massachusetts. There, the fighter and his wife, Bertha, and their five children live in a-ten room house with an indoor swimming pool, a sauna and skylights.

The simplicity of his life extends to boxing as well. In 1970, as a sixteen-year-old amateur, Hagler walked into a gym in Brockton, Massachusetts, run by two brothers, Pat and Guerino (Goody) Petronelli, to become a fighter. He is still with the Petronellis. Pat and Goody co-manage Hagler, and Goody continues to train him. (The Petronellis were friends of Rocky Marciano, who lived in Brockton, and they have managed and trained other fighters, including Hagler's half brother, Robbie Sims, a ranked middleweight.)

When Hagler began with them, the Petronellis were small-town guys who ran a construction company by day and a boxing gym by night. During the day, Hagler worked for the Petronellis' company and was paid $3 an hour. "He needed money very bad," recalls Pat Petronelli. "So he'd only eat what he had to. He'd borrow 50 cents for a submarine sandwich, 25 cents for a soda—we'd deduct it on Fridays. He didn't spend unless he thought it was necessary."

At eighteen, Hagler capped his amateur career by winning the national Amateur Athletic Union tournament in the 165-pound class. He turned professional a week later. Once Hagler showed the promise of a world-class contender, the Petronellis were hard-pressed to maneuver him into the big time. There were occasions back then when Hagler worried that his career might wither on the vine. One night in the mid-1970's, concerned about the modest purses he was making and the reluctance of the contenders to fight him, he found himself knocking at Pat's door at 10 o'clock to tell him, "I don't want to die in no man's gym."

"What I was saying to Pat," says Hagler, "was that I didn't want to be sitting here in Brockton forever. I had read about how

old a man Jersey Joe Walcott was before they gave him a break."
(Walcott was thirty-seven years old when he knocked out Ezzard
Charles in July 1951 to win the heavyweight title.) "I wanted to get
out and see the world. A lot of people back then would tell me they
could move me better than the Petronellis. A lot of blacks would
say, 'Stick to your own. The whites will take your money and,
once you're done, drop you.' I told them all, 'Forget you.'"

These days it is not unheard of for a fighter to try for a world
title after a dozen or fewer professional bouts. By contrast, Hagler
waited a Godot-like wait for his break. When the chance finally
arrived—six and a half years and fifty matches after he turned professional—the moment was snatched from him.

The night he fought Vito Antuofermo for the middleweight
crown on November 30, 1979, the referee, Mills Lane, was sure
Hagler had won, a view most ringside newsmen shared. Just before
the decision was announced, Lane motioned to where the ringside
photographers were positioned and told Hagler to face in that direction when he, as referee, raised his hand in victory. But the judges
had a different opinion. They called the bout a draw, which, by
boxing's rules, left the champion, Antuofermo, still in possession
of his title.

When Hagler finally won the title ten months later, on
September 27, 1980, in London, it was not a moment he could
savor. His opponent was the British fighter Alan Minter, and the
match was stopped in the third round. The partisan crowd was so
angered by this that it barraged the ring with bottles and debris.
Hagler and the Petronellis were forced to flee the ring into a ladies'
room and, finally, their dressing rooms. They waited there two
hours before leaving the arena in a limousine whose windshield
had been bashed out by the angry mob.

All of this—the difficulties encountered on the way up and the
discord surrounding his success—appears to have shaped the champion he has become. "He is one of the few champions who became
better *after* he won the title," says Larry Merchant, an analyst on
Home Box Office's boxing telecasts. "Other fighters, as they make
the big money, slow down in their training methods, but Hagler

keeps pushing himself. It's a rare thing in sports, particularly in boxing."

Before there were boxing opponents to contend with, Marvin Hagler—who was nicknamed "Short Stuff," and occasionally called just "Stuff"—was obliged to stand up to the bullies of Newark, where he grew up.

"I hit you with a stick, brick and bottle—anything I could get my hands on," he recalls. "And kicked you when you were down. It was known as survival. My mother taught me, 'You better not come back crying.' She raised us up by herself, without a father. I still don't talk back to her."

Hagler's mother, Mae, admits she was a little strict with her oldest son ("Being Newark, you have to be," she says), but Hagler fell in behind her, a first sergeant keeping the rest of the brood— five girls and one other boy—in line.

"We used to share the same bedroom," says Hagler's half brother, Robbie Sims, who is twenty-six. "And every day he made sure I'd make my bed, clean my side of the room, put my shoes away, the dirty clothes in the dirty-clothes bag."

As a youngster, Hagler tacked to his wall a fight poster of Floyd Patterson, the heavyweight champion, that he had removed from a neighborhood telephone pole. "He said he was going to be just like him and buy me a home," says the fighter's mother. Sims remembers Hagler "always talking about 'making it,' about having his face on a poster."

It was not until the family moved to Brockton after the Newark riots of 1967 that Hagler got serious about boxing. Feeling that his family needed the extra income, he dropped out of high school and went to work in a tannery (later, he quit this job to work for the Petronellis). Evenings, he trained. "He couldn't get enough hours in the gym," says Pat Petronelli. "The first one in, last one out."

As an amateur, Hagler sparred one day against an established pro named Lloyd Duncan, who proceeded to work him over. Afterward, the Petronellis heard a clatter in the dressing room, and when Pat went to investigate, he found Hagler tearing the doors off their hinges.

"He was mad at himself for not performing better," says Petronelli. "I told him, 'Marvin, you're sparring with a main-event fighter.' But he wouldn't hear it. 'Nah, nah,' he says to me. 'I got to do better than that.'"

Through his boxing, Hagler kept close to his family. At night he showed Sims the moves he learned in the gym, and each morning he had his mother time his training runs. Even when he moved to an apartment across town from her, he would phone just before starting his roadwork ("I'm leaving now") and then again on his return ("I'm home") so she could time him.

But increasingly he came to rely on the Petronellis—a relationship that had developed slowly. "Because I grew up in New Jersey," says Hagler, "where there was a color barrier between black and white, and where everybody uses everybody, I protected myself by staying distant from people. But Pat and Goody didn't ask a lot of questions. They waited for me to tell about my life."

On Hagler's early fights as a pro—preliminary bouts for $300, $400, the Petronellis declined to take their 33 1/3 percent managers' share from his purse. Those were the days of budget-minded meals, of sleeping three to a hotel room (two beds and a cot), of being forced, for lack of willing opponents, to fight men who sometimes outweighed him by ten or fifteen pounds. Throughout these early years, he held on to his job at the Petronellis' construction company.

In 1976, when it became clear that Sam Silverman, then the fighter's promoter, could not induce the leading contenders to go to New England to fight Hagler, Hagler went to Philadelphia, which, in those days, turned out ranked middleweights the way Juilliard does concert pianists. There, for a $2,000 purse, Hagler lost for the first time in his career, to Bobby (Boogaloo) Watts, in a questionable decision. Two months later, weakened by a cold, Hagler returned to Philadelphia and lost again—this time to Willie (The Worm) Monroe.

Finally, in September 1976, Hagler beat a Philadelphia stalwart, Eugene (Cyclone) Hart. The following year, he defeated Monroe twice, knocking him out both times.

"For those Philadelphia fights," says Pat Petronelli, "We used to get paid in cash. A brown paper bag with cash inside. Marvin lived in Stoughton, Massachusetts, then. Had this apartment—two rooms upstairs, two rooms down. I'd go there a day later with the cash in the bag. Marvin would ask Bertha to go upstairs. I'd bring a six-pack of beer. We'd take out the money and count it on the table. We used to have more fun counting the money. Rows of 20's and 10's. We'd do it for hours and drink more beer."

Winning prize money, however, was not enough for Hagler. He wanted to be middleweight champion, but was thwarted in his ambition. He was even excluded from the made-for-television tournament that Don King organized in 1977 to produce United States boxing champions.

With their man apparently frozen out of a title fight, the Petronellis took what was for boxing an extreme measure. They wrote to Massachusetts politicians—Edward M. Kennedy, Thomas P. O'Neill Jr., Paul E. Tsongas—and to a Rhode Island Congressman, Edward P. Beard, and asked for their assistance. The politicians contacted the movers and shakers of boxing, Bob Arum among them, and threatened an investigation. Having been an Assistant United States Attorney during the Kennedy Administration, Arum was sensitive to Teddy Kennedy's involvement and, in 1979, guaranteed Hagler a title shot.

But even after he won the middleweight championship title, Hagler continued to feel snubbed. He earned his first million-dollar purse, against Mustafa Hamsho, in October 1981 but envied superstars like Ali and Leonard and Hearns, who did even better at the box office.

"There was always a whininess about Marvin in those days," says Arum. "He was a complainer. He complained about not getting 'big money' fights. People don't want to hear that from a guy who's just made a million bucks."

The breakthrough in Hagler's career finally came with Sugar Ray Leonard's retirement and Hagler's fight against Tommy

Hearns in 1985. The hellbent way in which he demolished Hearns in three rounds instantly upgraded his standing among fight fans and among the advertising wizards who decide which athletes get the commercials. The bout therefore brought not only money—Hagler reportedly made about $10 million—but the commercial endorsements and television cameo roles that Hagler had always wanted, equating them as he did with superstardom.

"For Hagler to feel happy," says Arum, "he had to feel happy within. He had to attain the prominence he felt was his due before the bitterness and hurt would go away. It didn't happen till he knocked out Hearns. In his own mind, with that fight he finally considered himself accepted. And it was after he defeated Hearns that his personality came out.

"He became more relaxed," Arum continues, "when he got commercial opportunities. Two years before, Diet Coke, the same company that is using him now, rejected him....There was a harshness there. The smile was not easy."

With Leonard back in business, one can see the smile turning down at its corners as past discontent again disturbs a champion's self-image. Leonard poses a threat to Hagler's standing in boxing—the historic place he will occupy years from now. That is no small matter to a man who has gone to a court of law to legitimize the "Marvelous" in front of his name.

In a sense, Hagler has much more to lose in this fight than his opponent does. Should Leonard fail, there is enough slack in his ambitious scheme to soften the blow. Leonard's is a dreamer's obsession. Hagler knows he hasn't the same margin. It is this dilemma that gives a constantly contradictory texture to a recent conversation with the champion.

He is seated in a grassy hotel courtyard in Palm Springs. "I've always felt that I've been growing as a fighter," he is saying. "Getting better and better with every fight. If this is my last fight, it'll be my best. All I learned in boxing will come out that night...."

Yet a moment later, scarcely missing a beat, he says, "The way I see the fight, I'm a little scared because Las Vegas is a gambling town. Vito—they gave him the decision. But I've kept the bitterness from that in my mind and in my thoughts...."

Time and again, he voices variations on that theme. He'll knock Leonard out. Then again, why put pressure on himself to flatten the guy? But if he doesn't score a kayo, will he get a fair shake should the fight go the distance?

Hagler acknowledges that with fighters fear is fuel, an essential part of the equation. "I make myself intense," he says. "I make myself nervous. I make myself think the guy can beat me. I tell myself, 'The only way he won't is, you got to work hard. You got to pay attention to your art.'"

Art. An odd word to hear when only moments before Hagler has been describing the survival code he adopted in the Newark ghetto in which he grew up: "Nobody takes nothing away from me; I'll get you sooner or later." *Art* becomes a strange word amid the braggadocio and insults that are more typically the stuff of a fighter's talk.

But, of course, the word is an open-sesame to Hagler, evoking the paradox of a brute's sport that, when executed by the very best, can and does soar to breathtaking heights. With Hagler, a listener senses in the word the ripples beyond it: one man's care and concern for a sport, and the pride he has developed in doing it well.

For Hagler, who has earned from $25 million to $30 million in purses, there are always forces "out there" that conspire against him. His ego remains as fragile as an artist's under siege.

"This one and that one that they keep thinking can beat me," he says. "Where do they find a guy like [Fulgencio] Obelmejias? Where do they find a guy like [John] Mugabi? Where do they find a guy like [Juan] Roldan? Where you find these people?"

He laughs at the thought of a kind of middleweight star search. "Looking high and low," he says. "Finally, Leonard: 'I got what it take. I know what it take. I can do it.' They been looking under rocks."

Hagler rises from a lawn chair and steps across the grass, pausing in front of a flat, circular concrete "stone." He lifts the stone at an angle, six inches off the ground, making a show of peeking beneath it. "Got to find somebody," he says. "Anybody under there?" He sets the stone down.

"They don't come up the rankings the way I did. They just beat a guy, any guy. And next thing you know, they throw him to me. And I just keep drilling 'em down. 'Next.' Tall ones. Big ones. Hard-punching ones. Fast-hands ones. Ones can cut you up. All these people with different techniques. But I always find the strategy and technique to beat them.

"Now they got me going against The Brain. Ray Leonard. Heh, heh, heh. Brain against brain. Art against art. The final test for Mr. Hagler."

Hagler lost his title to Ray Leonard by a split decision. Though he has talked of staging a comeback, Hagler has kept his distance from the boxing world and has yet to fight again. In recent years he has taken to a different stage, trying his hand at starring in Italian action films.

INDEX OF NAMES

325